Restructuring
Higher Education

Other titles recently published under the SRHE/Open University Press imprint.

Michael Allen: *The Goals of Universities*
William Birch: *The Challenge to Higher Education*
Colin Evans: *Language People*
Gunnar Handal and Per Lauvås: *Promoting Reflective Teaching*
Vivien Hodgson *et al.*: *Beyond Distance Teaching, Towards Open Learning*
Peter Linklater: *Education and the World of Work*
John Pratt and Suzanne Silverman: *Responding to Constraint*
Marjorie E. Reeves: *The Crisis in Higher Education*
John T. E. Richardson *et al.*: *Student Learning*
Derek Robbins: *The Rise of Independent Study*
Gordon Taylor *et al.*: *Literacy by Degrees*
Malcolm Tight: *Academic Freedom and Responsibility*
Alan Woodley *et al.*: *Choosing to Learn*

Restructuring Higher Education

Proceedings of the Annual
Conference 1987

Edited by Heather Eggins

The Society for Research into Higher Education
& Open University Press

Published by SRHE and
Open University Press
Open University Educational Enterprises Limited
12 Cofferidge Close
Stony Stratford
Milton Keynes MK11 1BY

and
242 Cherry Street
Philadelphia, PA 19106, USA

First Published 1988

British Library Cataloguing in Publication Data
Restructuring higher education: proceedings
   of the annual conference 1987.
   1. Great Britain. Higher education
   I. Eggins, Heather   II. Society for Research
into Higher Education. *Conference (23rd:*
1987)   III. Society for Research into
Higher Education
378.41

ISBN 0-335-09527-5

Library of Congress Cataloging-in-Publication Data
Restructuring higher education: proceedings of the annual conference
   1987 / edited by Heather Eggins.
      p.   cm.
   Includes index.
   1. Education, Higher – Great Britain – Congresses.   I. Eggins,
Heather.   II. Society for Research into Higher Education.
LA637.R48   1988
378.41 – dc 19   88-17790 CIP
ISBN 0-335-09527-5

Typeset by Rowland Phototypesetting Limited
Bury St Edmunds, Suffolk
Printed in Great Britain by
St Edmundsbury Press Ltd, Bury St Edmunds, Suffolk

To Sheila Richardson

Contents

Contributors

Sir Christopher Ball, Chairman of the Board, National Advisory Body, Metropolis House, 22 Percy Street, London W1P 9FF.

Derek Birley, Vice-Chancellor, University of Ulster, Cromore Road, Coleraine, Co. Londonderry, N. Ireland BT52 1SA.

Robert Jackson, MP, Parliamentary Under-Secretary of State for Higher Education, Department of Education and Science, Elizabeth House, York Road, London SE1 7PH.

Sir Peter Swinnerton-Dyer, Chairman, University Grants Committee, 14 Park Crescent, London W1N 4DH.

Rob Cuthbert, Staff Tutor, The Further Education Staff College, Blagdon, Bristol BS18 6RG.

Malcolm T. Deere, Education Adviser, TVEI Unit, Manpower Services Commission, 236 Gray's Inn Road, London WC1X 8HL.

Professor Anthony J. Pointon, Professor of Microwave Physics, Portsmouth Polytechnic, National Adviser, Association of Polytechnic Teachers, Coxton Chambers, 81 Albert Road, Southsea, Hampshire PO5 2SG.

Alan Crispin, Registrar, Council for National Academic Awards, 344 Gray's Inn Road, London WC1X 8BP.

Jeffrey Weeks, Assistant Registrar, Council for National Academic Awards, 344 Gray's Inn Road, London WC1X 8BP.

Professor John Sizer, Professor of Financial Management, Department of Management Studies, Loughborough University of Technology, Loughborough, Leicestershire LE11 3TU.

Professor Frank R. Hartley, Principal and Dean, The Royal Military College of Science (Cranfield), Shrivenham, Wiltshire SN6 8LA.

K. Srinivasan, Dundee College of Technology, Bell Street, Dundee DD1 1HG.

C. McCallum, Dundee College of Technology, Bell Street, Dundee DD1 1HG.

Keith Percy, Department of Extra-Mural Studies, University of Lancaster, Cartmel College, Lancaster LA1 4YL.

Edmund P. Clark, Education for Capability Fellow, The Royal Society of Arts, John Adam Street, London WC2N 6EZ.

Margaret Kinnell, Department of Library and Information Studies, Loughborough University of Technology, Loughborough, Leicestershire LE11 3TU.

Robin Middlehurst, University of Surrey, Guildford, Surrey GU2 5XH.

Professor John Elliott, Centre for Applied Research in Education, School of Education, University of East Anglia, Norwich NR4 7TJ.

Peter W. G. Wright, Faculty of Humanities and Social Sciences, Portsmouth Polytechnic, Nuffield Centre, St Michael's Road, Portsmouth PO1 2ED.

Acknowledgements

This book is the final fruition of much endeavour. It began with the SRHE Activities Committee, which decided on the topic of the conference, and, in particular, with Sheila Richardson, who was instrumental in bringing the conference to Birmingham but, sadly, died before she could see her work fulfilled. A heavy burden subsequently fell on the conference organising committee, chaired by Peter Knight, Director of Birmingham Polytechnic. Much work was put in by the many contributors to what became one of the SRHE's most successful annual conferences and especially by the presenters of papers that were later submitted for the *Proceedings*. To those whose papers we were unable to include, we offer our appreciation and apologies; all were of a high standard but it just was not possible to accept them all.

Every paper published in this book has been independently assessed. To those supporters of the SRHE who have given their time to this task we extend our thanks. Finally we thank those who gave their secretarial skills to help in the preparation of the text for publication.

List of Abbreviations

ABRC	Advisory Board for the Research Councils
ACAS	Arbitration Conciliation Advisory Service
AUT	Association of University Teachers
BTEC	Business and Technician Education Council
CNAA	Council for National Academic Awards
CDP	Committee of Directors of Polytechnics
CPVE	Certificate of Pre-Vocational Education
CVCP	Committee of Vice-Chancellors and Principals
DENI	Department of Education in Northern Ireland
DES	Department of Education and Science
GCSE	General Certificate of Secondary Education
GERBIL	Great Education Reform Bill
HMI	Her Majesty's Inspectors
ICAEW	The Institute of Chartered Accountants in England & Wales
ICAS	Institute of Chartered Accountants of Scotland
INSET	In-Service Training
LEA	Local Education Authority
MSC	Manpower Services Commission
NAB	National Advisory Board
NCVQ	National Council for Vocational Qualifications
PCFC	Polytechnics and Colleges Funding Council
PSHE	Public Sector Higher Education
SERC	Science and Engineering Research Council
SSRC	Social Science Research Council
THES	*The Times Higher Education Supplement*
TVEI	Technical and Vocational Education Initiative
UFC	Universities Funding Council
UGC	University Grants Committee

Preface

The conference on 'The Restructuring of Higher Education' was timely, coming
as it did with the introduction of the great Education Reform Bill into the House
of Commons. The publication of the *Proceedings* of that conference, despite a
certain lapse of time, is just as pertinent in that it indicates the constant flux of
thinking that impinges on directions taken by policy and policy-makers in
higher education.

To a marked extent, indeed, this book crystallises the positions of the leaders
who influence such policy at the time of their speeches in December 1987:
Robert Jackson, Minister for Higher Education, spokesman for the position of
the government; Sir Peter Swinnerton-Dyer, spokesman for the University
Grants Committee, soon to undergo a sea change into a rather different
University Funding Council; and Christopher Ball, Chairman of the Board of
the National Advisory Body, similarly about to be transmuted into the
Polytechnics and Colleges Funding Council. Derek Birley's keynote address as
Vice Chancellor of an institution of higher education merged across the binary
divide presents a case study of a possible model for the future. This book, then,
catches the movement of events at, one might say, the crest of the wave. Every
area of higher education is and will be affected by change. These papers serve to
give some indication of the thoroughness and insistence of the change in
direction. They do not attempt to offer a succinct drawing together of every
theme considered in the conference, but they do indicate just how radical are the
changes taking place in higher education in the late 1980s and how inescapable
are the implications.

The papers on restructuring the national system set a broad background
against which the articles relating to funding methods, particularly that of
funding research, point up an area of debate which will be of crucial importance
as we enter the 1990s.

The representative papers from the important theme of restructuring regional, local and institutional structures indicate areas which affect us all, at
one level or another. Indeed, more papers were offered on this subject than on
any other for the *Proceedings*; we are all becoming experts on merger, closure
and take-overs.

Another point of change is seen in the constant shift of professional and disciplinary boundaries, sometimes by stealth, sometimes by decisive action taken to meet a new demand. The paper included here which deals with accounting is one of a number of such studies drawn from disparate disciplines. This paper stands as one example of a widespread phenomenon.

Access to higher education continues to be of vital importance to the shape of the future. The drop in the birth-rate during the late 1960s and early 1970s had led to expectations of a consequent reduction in numbers entering higher education in the late 1980s and 1990s. This, in its turn, had initiated pressures from government to 'trim down' the system. Instead, there has been a small but significant improvement in the age participation rate, coupled with a growth in demand from mature students. The changing role of women in society is mirrored in their increased desire to enter higher education. A recent phenomenon is the marked nervousness of employers, who fear that they may soon be starved of the graduates they require. Their demands for the expansion of higher education together with those of the other groups are already having an effect on thinking about the future patterns of access. We could not publish all the work offered on the topic: what is here must stand as an indication of the great deal of thorough and imaginative thinking on this subject.

The marketing of higher education, related as it is to access, can be perceived as a newcomer to the central themes. We still have much to learn in the United Kingdom on how to approach this subject. The paper offered here gives some indication of the work that is now beginning. The 1990s may well see a mushrooming in sophisticated marketing techniques employed in the presentation of higher education.

The growing emphasis on the need to manage the whole process of higher education as efficiently and smoothly as possible has been partially set in train by such reports as that of Jarratt on the universities in 1985 and that of the National Advisory Body with its Good Management Practice report in 1987. The dialogue continues apace. The paper included here serves to highlight the need to address such problems.

No individual member of staff within our institutions can escape the effects of the present restructuring, whether it be in terms of his/her response to curriculum changes and to the shifts in teaching styles, or in his/her involvement in staff development, staff appraisal and the declared aim of establishing quality control. No part of the higher education sector can any longer choose to ignore such pressures. The article included here again serves to indicate the wealth of activity in these areas. Much more will be done in the ensuing years.

Perhaps one can claim that at the heart of our current debate on the restructuring of higher education lies a deep-felt and urgent reconsideration of the values that underlie our higher education. Perhaps the philosophical enquiry which searches for some definition of the values we wish to express in higher education is one of the healthiest manifestations of the present restless and constantly shifting debate. It is a matter of great credit to our leading policy-makers that they can be seen in their public pronouncements, as in these *Proceedings*, to be actively considering value along with quality, availability and efficiency.

We offer this volume to our readers not only as some record of the proceedings of the conference on 'The Restructuring of Higher Education' held in December 1987 but also as an indicator of a number of key subjects for discussion, agenda items, if you like, that will be with us well into the next decade.

Heather Eggins
London
March 1988

Part 1

The Keynote Speeches

1

Sir Christopher Ball

The theme of this conference is the restructuring of higher education. I congratulate the organisers on their choice of title, one that is at once bold, apt and timely. For with the advent of the Education Reform Bill it is now clear that we are witnessing nothing less than revolutionary changes in our national education; whatever one thinks of the proposals for school education (which it is not my business to comment on) a significant and distinctive part of this greater upheaval is the revolution in higher education. It seems a surprising and unusual revolution, inasmuch as it is stimulated and led by our legitimate government, which describes itself as conservative. But, like all revolutions, although it is rooted in deep social and economic changes, it is promoted by a few visionaries who believe they see a better future (and which of us does not hope that they are right?), it claims the authority of the people, and it seems to threaten a privileged class – us! (the established practitioners of traditional British higher education). What are we to do about it?

Keith Joseph's Green Paper of 1984, Kenneth Baker's White Paper (DES 1987), and the Education Reform Bill now before Parliament, together offer a most serious challenge to all of us who work in universities, polytechnics or colleges. At its simplest, the question is: should we resist the changes thrust upon us, and try to prevent them taking effect, or should we accept them, and try to make them work? Conventional wisdom among academics appears to favour the former: I want to argue for the latter. It is possible, I suggest, to believe that major changes are desirable – without questioning the value or quality of British higher education or the commitment of those who work in it. It is possible, for example, to think that in the present economic plight of our nation the highest priority must be given to wealth-creation – without doubting the value of the arts or the humanities. It is possible to seek improvements in the management of the institutions and sectors of higher education – without impugning the competence or integrity of those responsible for them.

Few human institutions are quite perfect: the good can always be made better. It is a pity, and a mistake, that higher education is so defensive in the face of the challenge of change. Those who are promoting it may sometimes be misguided: they are never malevolent. Moreover, I take it as axiomatic that in a democracy the government cannot be the enemy.

Those of us who believe that we should accept the changes forced upon us by the revolution in higher education and try to make them work, do not, of course, thereby disqualify ourselves from questioning or criticising certain aspects of what is proposed. For example, the government would be well advised to reread the report of the National Advisory Body's (NAB) Good Management Practice group (*Management for a Purpose*), to think again about the issue of academic freedom, and to reconsider the case for the integrated planning of higher education. I shall say more about these topics later. But, just as I have urged upon my friends and colleagues in higher education the axiom that in a democracy the government cannot be the enemy, so I would urge upon the government another (and equally important) axiom: that educational reform cannot be carried through effectively without the wholehearted co-operation of teachers.

There is no alternative to a consensus approach in education. Confrontation may have its occasional uses in startling complacency or stimulating change, but it must not become the regular method of educational management or government. For the educational process, the interaction between teacher and pupil, or student and lecturer, is at heart a private affair. What happens in the classroom or lecture room, or in a seminar or tutorial, is not accessible to management or government, and must be based on trust. That is why teaching is a profession. And so those who wish to promote change in education must do so not in opposition to, but in partnership with, the teaching profession.

The initial stimulus for the revolution in higher education which we are experiencing comes, I believe, not so much from the concern with wealth creation (real though that is), nor from the desire to control public funding and seek better value for money (though that too is important), but from the outcome of the access debate.

> The Government has reaffirmed that places should be available for all with the necessary qualities to benefit from higher education . . . it now invites all those with relevant responsibilities to consider carefully the steps necessary to secure increased participation by both young and older people, and to act accordingly (*The 1987 White Paper*, 'Meeting the Challenge' Cm 114, para 2.14).

That means us. How should we respond? (I take the question seriously: I don't want just to *talk* about wider access, I want to see it *happen*.)

The outcome of the 'access debate' – the decision to plan for increased participation – is a triumph of common sense, with some important consequences. I need not repeat here the persuasive social and economic arguments which have prevailed: they are well known and have often been deployed, nowhere more cogently (I think) than in NAB's 1984 report (*A Strategy for Higher Education in the late 1980s and Beyond*). The consequences are what concern us now. They will affect courses in higher education, as well as the management of and the resources for higher education. And they will lead over time to a substantial restructuring of the British higher education system.

The Robbins Report of 1963 led to a massive expansion of what was (and still is) an essentially élite system of higher education. Characterised by a relatively high threshold of entry (typically measured by A-level grades) and placing a high value on specialised research-related courses, the 'élite university model' is also expensive: residential costs, the student award system (which manages to be at one and the same time both costly and inadequate), and the research provision (which adds about 50 per cent to the University Grants Committee's funding of the teaching of students in universities), all combine to produce a model of higher education with relatively high unit costs which have to be met largely from public funds.

It was never likely that the Robbins model of 'élite universities' would succeed in providing the wider participation that we all seek and need. And within a few years of Robbins the Crosland White Paper of 1966 was bringing into being what we have come to know as 'public sector higher education' (PSHE), and must in future call the polytechnics and colleges sector. PSHE initially laboured under a number of disadvantages: it was of low status in comparison with the universities, and yet under the Council for National Academic Awards (CNAA) charter it was required to achieve equivalent standards. It was also the marginal sector and (as such) was used to accommodate awkward political and managerial problems (such as the reorganisation of the Initial Teacher Training colleges in the 1970s) and to serve as the header-tank for the main system of British higher education, expanding and contracting as need determined. It was a sector characterised by too many external constraints (as the Good Management Practice report emphasised), and which all too often seemed to be merely a pale imitation of the élite university model. But it provided the potential to develop a popular model of higher education which, with low unit costs, might complement (and contrast with) the élite model and at last offer a way forward towards the goal of wider participation.

During the 1980s PSHE has prospered, though it may not always have felt like that. We have developed a genuinely distinctive popular model of higher education, to set beside the élite research university model: it seeks to be readily responsive to the nation's changing needs, to be relatively inexpensive, and (above all) to offer wider access. It now constitutes more than 53 per cent of our higher education system. In December 1987 the Secretary of State publicly praised what I have termed the popular model and the

> major contribution [of the polytechnics and colleges] towards providing access to higher education for all who might benefit from it. The White Paper gives the highest priority to the need to secure increased participation in higher education by both young and older people. I am certain that the polytechnics and colleges will have a central role to play in achieving that objective in the years ahead.

He went on to give recognition to 'the achievements of the Polytechnics and Colleges Funding Council institutions in providing access to higher education of assured quality'; and stated that 'we are all united in our aim of providing wider access to a cost-effective and useful higher education'. Those words also express my own views and I readily endorse not only the tribute, but also the recognition that what was once the marginal sector now has a central role to play.

The popular model has prevailed. With a remarkable 20 per cent improvement in efficiency since 1981, and a 53 per cent (and increasing) share of the student market, the polytechnics and colleges are well placed to prosper in the years ahead. Corporate status and accreditation will remove some of the external constraints – without losing the advantages of external quality assurance – and will promote self-reliance and a further growth of confidence. The status, too, of the popular model is rising in our society. I predict that before the end of the century the polytechnics and major colleges will adopt the coveted title 'university' – and rightly so. They have earned it, but should not make the mistake of losing their real vocation or aping the élite research university model.

If this account of the growing marginalisation of the traditional university system is seen as mere inter-sectoral rivalry, you will have missed my point. Of course, we need both models – the élite university research model and the popular model of higher education – but we need to achieve the right balance between them. In the years to come I expect the popular model to grow to account for some two-thirds or even three-quarters of the British higher education system: and this will be achieved, I suspect, by the decision of a number of traditional universities to restructure themselves according to the 'popular model' I have described.

This is the major restructuring we shall have to face, and undertake, in response to the Secretary of State's aims (which I hope and believe we all share) of providing wider access to a cost-effective and useful higher education. But, we must also expect significant restructuring and reform in the courses, the management and the resourcing of higher education.

New students will require new courses – or the reform and adaptation of existing courses. We must expect and encourage a systematic and widespread review of degree and diploma courses on both sides of the binary line. We need to review entry requirements, the length, nature, assessment, mode of attendance, design and content of our courses. We need to address the marketing of, access and recruitment to, courses, and the provision for learning support. If it ever was so – which I doubt – it is certainly no longer appropriate to try to fit students to courses. We must learn to adapt our courses to fit the students' needs. The Secretary of State's phrase ('a useful higher education') is an interesting and challenging one, but we should not be afraid of it. It is for institutions and course-teams to interpret this idea, and give reality and value to it, in their regular task of reviewing and revising courses. As a young Oxford don, I used to think that course content (a body of knowledge) was all-important: I gradually came to believe that skills, especially the transferable personal skills, were equally important. I now wonder whether the development of motivation and aspiration isn't at the heart of education. We must all seek the best educational balance in our courses between knowledge, skills and aspiration. This is a task for the institutions – and it is urgent. I would advise any prospective student to enquire whether the course he or she is thinking of applying for has been fundamentally reviewed and significantly reformed within the last seven years (and if it has not, I would advise the student to apply elsewhere).

In trying to understand the managerial challenge faced by higher education I would advise you to cast away any prejudice and suspicion, and consider whether what is being urged upon us is not simply to be fully responsible and accountable for our affairs. The key to the government's intentions (I believe) is nothing sinister, but the worthy and proper insistence on the concepts of responsibility and accountability. At the system and sectoral levels, the two new funding councils, the Universities Funding Council (UFC) and the Polytechnics and Colleges Funding Council (PCFC), have been criticised, first, because they are two and not one; second, because they are to operate in an open way; third, because they are to replace grants with 'contracts'; fourth, because they are to have substantial lay (or non-academic) membership; and fifth, because their terms of reference do not include a duty to advise the government on the needs of higher education. I find those criticisms, on the whole, unimportant or unconvincing. NAB is open, has developed a method of funding that is identical with contracting in everything but name (I must give the Department of Education and Science credit for this contribution to our technical terminology), has substantial non-academic membership, and has terms of reference which omit a duty to advise the government on the needs of the sector. Openness works. NAB's funding methodology is stable, just, comprehensible and effective. Its lay members are as valuable and sensible as are the academics. And nothing has stopped it, or ever will, from giving firm advice to the government (publicly or privately, as appropriate) on the needs of the sector.

The criticism of the UFC (voiced mainly by colleagues in the universities) is largely misplaced and irrelevant. PSHE has been silent on this subject, and appears to see little seriously wrong with the plans for the PCFC. (Since it is being developed so obviously on the model of NAB, I am tempted to wonder why any change of funding body was necessary at all.) Nevertheless, I am inclined to advise the government to concede the point about the terms of reference of UFC and PCFC. If they make it their duty to advise on the needs of the sectors anyway, as I believe they will, it would be tidier (and politically expedient) to amend the Bill in this respect before it goes very much further.

It is, however, a pity that the government has not had the courage at this stage to unite the planning of higher education under one body. As I have said before, the strategic management of the whole of higher education needs attention. The Croham Report, together with NAB's Good Management Practice report, set out the options. I have been disappointed, but not surprised, at the resistance of the government to the idea that we need an 'overarching' intelligence or authority which could review the whole of British higher education (universities, polytechnics and colleges alike) and redirect it appropriately. Unless we can develop integrated planning across the sectors, nations and phases of education, we shall continue to stumble. This must be the responsibility of government. However, I believe that the two new bodies, similar in formation and open in operation, will soon grow together. Common sense will triumph in a few years and integrated planning will at long last be achieved.

For the institutions on either side of the fading binary line the key managerial issues are also responsibility and accountability. I can do no better than to recommend a most careful reading of NAB's Good Management Practice

report. It is entitled *Management for a Purpose* and insists on the central importance of the selection of definition of objectives, the idea that every institution
should have a mission statement. In my experience failure occurs for one of only
two reasons: *either* a lack of defined objectives (without definite objectives
success is impossible) *or* a failure of will, that is, inadequate commitment to the
ends in view. This is no small matter for higher education because morale
(which is low everywhere, and dangerously low in some universities) is a
function of a sense of purpose, not of the adequacy of resources. Managers in
institutions must remember that conditions are always adverse for good
management and the art is to manage in difficult circumstances, not just to
deplore them. The Minister has been accused of 'washing his hands' – be that as
it may, I agree with him in believing that we should indulge less in the wringing
of hands, and spend more time effectively seizing the initiative and determining
our own future. After O-level there is no one to blame but oneself. If higher
education is in a mess, *we* must take the blame, and shoulder the responsibility of
putting things right. Do not ask what the government or the funding councils
are going to do about it: ask yourself what you are going to do. Each of us must
define for ourselves our responsibility *for what* (objective), *to whom* (accountability) and *by when* (delivery). I believe that higher education will benefit
greatly if the leadership within institutions can regain the initiative from those
who determine and distribute resources.

As for resources, they are, as always, in short supply – and we must expect,
and learn to live with, some reordering in their delivery. I think the government
hopes to achieve a partial shift from state funding to the individual or the
employer. This will obviously be difficult, but I do not believe it is totally
impossible. Robert Jackson's review of the student award system, if carried
through boldly and effectively, will be the most important example of the
restructuring of the resourcing of higher education in 1988. We must also expect
a shift from the single provider (UFC or PCFC) towards a system with multiple
providers – of which the Manpower Services Commission enterprise initiative is
merely the first example. In the system of multiple provision I foresee, we will all
have to learn to seek funds from a variety of sources, private as well as public.

Moreover, we have little hope of achieving the increased participation that is
sought until we identify and start to fill the marginal capacity in the system. We
shall not (I believe) be able to afford to do this at average cost, as far as the
contribution from public funding is concerned. This has led me to the idea of
marginal funding for marginal capacity. Probably the best approach to this
would be through the conscious use of the fee mechanism as an instrument of
policy. I hope that the forthcoming review of financial provision (to which Mr
Baker has committed himself) will look again at both the role and the level of
fees. For example, an increase of fees to perhaps double their present value (with
compensating reductions in the funding for the UFC and PCFC) would
undoubtedly stimulate more effective marketing of courses with improved
recruitment. Any change of the kind suggested will probably require differential
fees for arts and science; and care will also be needed to ensure that no adverse
effects are created for part-time or mature students, who need particular
attention in this respect. But I hope it will be explored.

And so we come to the difficult question of the funding of research. In March 1987, at the Royal Society of Arts, I said this:

> The funding of civil research needs reform. The dual support system is in decay and disarray. The balance between fundamental and developmental research needs to be adjusted in favour of the latter. And a more openly selective, and concentrated, policy of research funding is required. (In spite of the high public profile of NAB and the public sector, most of the really difficult problems in higher educational policy and planning are to be found in the universities: for example, tenure of academic staff, effective management and research funding. It will be an interesting test of any White Paper to see if this is recognised.) [It was not!] The UGC has bravely embarked on a policy of selective (and concentrated) research funding by department, but I believe that this approach needs to be developed both faster and at the institutional level. A country of [the] size and prosperity [of the United Kingdom] may not be able to sustain as many as 45 universities fully funded for research. Perhaps a number between 12 and 20 would be more realistic. Such a select group of universities, adequately funded through a dual support system, would provide for the continuation of 'curiosity research' and much of the fundamental research required. The remainder of the universities would join the polytechnics and colleges as 'teaching-first' institutions, though all of them would be able to compete for research council funds as the polytechnics do now. Such a realignment would not be easy, but the status quo is no longer satisfactory, and the question is an urgent one. If we were to move in this direction, I would expect a substantial portion of UGC funds (say £300 million) to be transferred to the research councils. And it might then be possible to rectify the balance between fundamental and developmental research.

As I see it, the argument of those who contemplate greater concentration and selectivity in research funding runs as follows:

1 Exponential growth in *scientists* (and in the *cost of science*) has to level off. Other countries are facing the same problem. Moreover, the *cost of 'big science'* increases faster than inflation, because of the technology involved. These two factors are probably more serious than the present government's attempt to control public expenditure. But this third point also contributes to the *crisis of science* in the UK.

2 We must therefore improve the distribution of existing resources for science, in order both to make the best use of what we have and also to prepare a case for (limited) extra resources by defeating in advance the obvious Treasury argument that some of our existing resources are being wasted.

3 Some £1,300 million of recurrent public funds (almost one-third of all higher education expenditure) is spent in support of civil research in universities, polytechnics and research institutes, about half each by the research councils and the UGC. But this 'dual-support system' is in decay

and disarray. The balance between fundamental and developmental research needs to be adjusted in favour of the latter. And a more openly
selective, and concentrated, policy of research funding is required.

4   Is this to be achieved by developing the UGC's *departmental approach* ('too
little and too late') or by identifying (and funding) a subset of *research
universities* (as suggested by the Advisory Board for the Research Councils
(ABRC)) or by compromise solutions such as inter-departmental or inter-
institutional *research centres*? 'Big science' today requires a substantial 'critical mass' of research staff and highly expensive equipment. These factors
argue for selectivity and concentration. Any change from the status quo will
have to be planned, and gradual, but we need to know where we are going.
This will require courage, both from strategic planners and from those who
have to endure the results of strategic planning.

5   Funding is the key. So long as the UGC/UFC controls half the budget, and
the research councils (under the ABRC) have the rest, we cannot hope for
decisive leadership or real strategic planning. I would favour the transfer of
some £300 million from the UGC/UFC to the ABRC and require the latter
body to adopt the strategic role in research planning. Other solutions are
possible. But the status quo is a recipe for inaction.

The foregoing argument is an attempt to think out what might promote good
research within existing resource constraints. There is a separate, and strong,
educational argument pointing to the same conclusion, namely that to deliver
increased access to higher education on a cost-effective basis we need a *majority*
of teaching-first institutions (the popular model) to provide skilled brainpower
for the industry and commerce of the future, and a *minority* of research
universities (the élite world) where *research-related courses* provide a model of
higher education suited only to a minority of the most able.

May I, however, make it clear that the debate is about *funded research* (the
distribution of substantial sums of money), not about the free pursuit of
advanced study and research – which should be the duty (and delight) of
everyone who teaches in higher education, whether in universities, polytechnics
or colleges. NAB, which cannot – and doesn't aspire to – provide dual-support
research funding for the polytechnics, believes that a research ethos and
commitment to scholarship is essential to good higher education. When 53 per
cent of students in British higher education are already receiving a perfectly
adequate education in teaching-first institutions, the question is not whether
such a model is possible or desirable, but what balance we should look for
between the teaching-first popular model (polytechnic) and the research-
university élite model, in order to maximise the effectiveness *both* of our research
effort *and* of our higher education. Those who would extend the research-
university model – or even just maintain the status quo – must consider whether
(intentionally or not) they are thereby closing the door yet again to wider access
to higher education and reducing the effectiveness of our research effort.

Higher education, therefore, is likely to be substantially affected and changed
by the review of student awards; the review of research funding; and the review
of marginal capacity and the role and level of fees. When one adds to these

fundamental reviews the Secretary of State's commitment in his letters of 2 December 1987 ('I can certainly give you an assurance that in the course of next year I shall thoroughly review the financial provision for polytechnics and colleges in 1989–90 and beyond') and 18 December 1987 ('The Government will simultaneously be reviewing recurrent and capital provision for the universities') – it is clear that public funding of higher education is likely to face some major restructuring in the months and years ahead. There is now no part of the public funding of higher education which is not under serious review.

The revolution in higher education, of which I spoke at the beginning of this paper, is not just – or even mainly – a matter of the relevant clauses in the Education Reform Bill. The thrust towards access and wider participation, and the fundamental reviews of available public funding, are probably more important and will be – or should be – more far-reaching in their effect. But Mr Baker's new Bill is not insignificant for us. Much of the criticism of its provisions (mostly emanating from the universities) seems to me irrelevant or trivial. But there are three features of it that disappoint me: it is not bold enough; it fails adequately to define higher education; and it is silent on academic freedom.

Like the Greep Paper of 1984 and the White Paper of 1987 the draft Bill is reserved or (at best) tentative on some of the most important issues that face us: in particular, on the question of the integrated planning of higher education, and on the reform of our arrangements for student awards or research funding. We cannot for much longer afford to defer these issues. We need to know where we are going.

In addition, the Bill proposes to amend the 1944 Education Act by inserting the following definition at the relevant point: 'Higher Education has the meaning assigned to it by section 81(1) of the Education Reform Act 1988'. That clause – which releases local authorities from the duty of securing the provision of higher education – refers to Schedule 4 for a list of 'Courses in Higher Education'. And the Schedule turns out to contain nothing more than a list of such items – 'a first degree course, a course for the DipHE, a course for the Certificate in Education', etc. – followed by a general definition that a course is at 'a higher level' if its standard (dangerous word) is higher than the standard of courses leading to the GCE (A level) or the National Certificate or Diploma of BTEC. No vision there. It is a pity that the Bill has missed the opportunity to place on statute (perhaps as a preamble) some more thoughtful and inspiring account of the nature and purposes of higher education.

As for academic freedom, I think the critics are right. It is too important an issue to be left out. Like the definition of higher education, the definition of academic freedom is not easy. Academic freedom, like the freedom of the Press, is one of the marks of a mature, civilised and democratic society. Such a society needs institutions which protect and celebrate the freedom to think, undertake research, and speak openly about issues which may embarrass or irritate the government of the day or the prevailing prejudices of society. Academic freedom should not be taken for granted, not because it is at risk (I don't think it is) but because, like clean water, it is of fundamental importance to our society. In saying this, I am not making a belated defence of tenure in the universities: I favour its abolition and have often said so (and have just abandoned my own).

But the new Bill should have a clause defining and protecting academic freedom in higher education (on either side of the binary line), and I hope that Parliament in its wisdom will provide one.

I said at the outset that we were witnessing a revolution in higher education. Let me end by urging you again not to oppose it but to accept the responsibility for making it work. It is *our* job to create access, and to secure wider participation. It is *our* job to seek the funds we need – from new sources if the old ones prove inadequate. It is *our* job to take the initiative and determine the future pattern of higher education. The restructuring of higher education is not the government's responsibility, it is *ours*.

2

Derek Birley

According to Emerson, 'experience is the only teacher'. That may be so, but there is such a thing as being overtrained. Experience can blunt the sensitivities and become a substitute for thought. It can make you timid: as the proverb has it, 'scalded cats fear even cold water'. It can induce complacency – fifteen years' experience may be the same year fifteen times. Above all, some people are experienced enough to have made the same speech every year for fifteen years.

You can see how this happens; they get into the habit quite early on, with after-dinner speeches, talks to Rotary clubs, homilies to staff, graduation ceremonies and things like that, where the topic doesn't matter. Then comes the dawning recognition that it very rarely makes any difference what you talk about, and the gradual fashioning of a stimulating and thought-provoking address for all seasons.

Scholars are, of course, notoriously economical with their material. Many of the great researchers of our time clearly consider that if a thing is worth publishing it is worth publishing often. The obvious dangers of this approach can be greatly reduced by avoiding the use of original material. In one of my own recent efforts, for instance, there are quotations from the following: Benjamin Franklin, Edmund Spenser, 'Abide with me', Heraclitus, Shakespeare, Matthew Arnold, Edmund Burke, John Henry Newman, Herbert Spencer, the Prince Consort, Samuel Smiles, Lyon Playfair, Karl Marx, Hegel, the author of 'All things bright and beautiful', Sir Keith Joseph, W. B. Yeats, the Charter of the University of Ulster, the Mafia, and Banquo's Ghost. And these were only the acknowledged borrowings.

All of which is a roundabout way of saying: 'Don't be surprised if you've heard some of this before.' Perhaps the warning is unnecessary. For one thing, I'm quite sure that nobody, unless he or she is very green indeed, goes to an education conference expecting to hear anything new. Certainly not from a vice chancellor. (Of course I can't comment on what expectations there might be of the Chairman of the University Grants Committee (UGC), the Chairman of the National Advisory Board and the Secretary of State.)

This apart, it has to be admitted that one of the more serious side-effects of the accumulation of too much experience is a tendency towards what might be called the Isaiah syndrome. If over the years yours has been 'the voice of one crying in the wilderness, "Prepare ye the way of the Lord, make his paths straight"', just because nobody takes much notice you can't suddenly come out in favour of making his paths crooked or holing up at the nearest oasis.

Anyway, as, in preparation for this paper, I read through the files of my past efforts, as experienced persons do in search of general spiritual uplift or more specific opportunities for cannibalisation, I grew more and more depressed. I will try not to pass the depression on: my role model is Isaiah rather than Jeremiah; but I'm bound to say that the familiar features of the landscape twenty years ago – institutions of higher education preoccupied with questions of status, pecking order and resources, remarkably uninterested in philosophical issues and fearful of the slightest hint of change – all these are still with us. Furthermore, what once might have seemed mere nostalgic foibles, amiably idiosyncratic echoes of past traditions, have now become dangerous folly. For the world outside the institutions has become increasingly impatient with our reluctance to change.

This is most clearly apparent in the political world, in which the concept of change has recently been rediscovered and to some extent redefined. I quote as evidence a remarkable fragment that I happened to hear on my car radio as I went home one night a few months ago. This was somebody proclaiming that 'Outdated ideology cannot be allowed to stand in the way of change.' I didn't get the name of the particular speaker. However, it was no rabble-rousing demagogue but a person of high rank at the last Conservative Party Conference, expressing a desire to get rid of reactionary Labour councillors in the big cities.

Now the fastidious, or the cynical, may point out that the verb 'to change' conjugates irregularly (I am firm; thou art obstinate; he is pigheaded) and that its economic applications may be expressed demotically in such homely proverbs as 'one man's change is another man's redundancy'. They may point out that if you want to upgrade a notion, you call it a philosophy; if you want to downgrade it, call it ideology; and if you really want to discredit it, call it dogma. But such sophistry notwithstanding, the citadels of higher learning are, I suggest, in deep trouble when over a quarter of a century successive governments, regardless of the pendulum swing of party politics, have found them resistant to change.

There is, of course, a school of thought that regards education as the custodian of eternal verities, which, especially when viewed from an entrenched position, can be readily equated with received truths. I've never had much patience with the kind of education that does not want to change things. Unless you produce a new generation better than your own what kind of educator are you? This, admittedly, is to beg questions about progress, but why should we go on giving the status quo the benefit of the doubt? There are worse things than living in a turbulent atmosphere.

So if I look to the past it will not be to the good old days before the deluge, but to the locust years. And if I quote what I said at the time it is not to seek belated recognition as a minor prophet hitherto without honour in his own wilderness, but to lament missed opportunities. In any case there was less of the awful warning about these past utterances than a perhaps rather naive call for a sort of collective self-analysis. Not so much a message as a *cri de coeur*, as in Stevie Smith's poem:

> I was much further out than you thought
> And not waving but drowning.

On the other hand, powerful binoculars might have detected that at the end of the signalling arms, waving or drowning, there was sometimes just the hint of a tiny clenched fist. Perhaps the ambiguity of the signals confused or even inhibited potential rescuers. If so, it was just as well. No survivor likes rescuers, especially if they turn up late. As Johnson wrote to Lord Chesterfield: 'Is not a Patron, my Lord, one who looks with unconcern on a man struggling for life in the water, and when he has reached ground encumbers him with help?'

Now I am not suggesting that survival is an end in itself; but if it is not a sufficient condition it is a necessary one. And, unlike drowning, survival is a continuous process. It requires constant attention and it leaves little time for preaching to others. Hardly surprising, then, if survivors' sermons are poor affairs. The main themes of mine over the years have been these – in no particular order: that accountability is not the enemy, but the only reliable protector, of academic freedom; that if you do not apply performance measures yourself, others will eventually impose them; that if you do not embrace planning you will be given bureaucracy; that planning should begin with philosophy rather than organisation and logistics (that is, with 'why' rather than 'how'); that the cosy assumptions of the Robbins Report needed to be challenged; and that the binary policy is not a policy, or even a half-way credible substitute for one. Experience or not, it is very much easier to make assertions of this kind than to attempt to answer the questions the organisers of the conference have asked me to address. The first of them – 'How and why does restructuring happen?' – would need a long lecture or perhaps a book in itself. There may be people among you who can give a confident answer. I can only approach it obliquely.

Ten years ago, or even five, I would have been tempted to say 'Restructuring happens because we are preoccupied with forms of organisation and heedless of philosophy.' Indeed, judging from the files, I seem to have given in to the temptation to say it at every opportunity. Here is Proto-Isaiah as long ago as 1971:

> the emphasis of the central government has been on creating institutions rather than on establishing principles of planning or educational philosophy, tasks which have largely fallen on the not entirely adequate shoulders of the institutions.

And here is a slightly longer extract from a 1973 effort by the same author, notable in retrospect for its foolish optimism:

> In my view instead of brooding over organisational matters, keeping the system at steady state, or setting too much store by statistics, we need a fundamental change in outlook. The prime concern should be with philosophy and objectives and with seeking the radical adjustment of relationships required to allow us to focus on them. There is a planning

vacuum and it can only be filled, in our system, I believe, by our beginning to talk a new planning language, one in which the emphasis is on educational principles rather than accountancy or administration . . . . We may get the change in relationships we need if teachers themselves take the initiative on these lines.

Needless to say there were no such initiatives, and the accountancy was more creative than the administration. There followed some wilderness years, perhaps best forgotten. I can think of no better image for the end of the heedless 1970s than those acrobatic skidding turns performed by Charlie Chaplin. Towards the shuddering end of its headlong outward swing, higher education sought refuge from its real problems by recourse to technical ones.

It was, hereabouts, becoming fashionable – almost obligatory – to blame the government for almost everything; and it brought some of it on itself by reaching into corners hitherto untouched by ministerial intervention. But the bureaucracy also spread, and, as Deutero-Isaiah wrote in 1979, in another stimulating and thought-provoking address: 'Throughout the sixties and seventies the growing complexity of the task of running the expanding social services re-inforced the tendency to think first of resources and organisation and philosophy to the background.' We still held some good cards: 'In education the saving grace is freedom, and in higher education the traditional approach to planning means that the institutions themselves are left free to answer all the teleological questions.' But we were not playing them: 'In practice, however, philosophy always takes second place to the technical problem of the moment. One of the recent favourites has been demography.' Remember Model E?

It would be an oversimplification and perhaps overpolite, to suggest that the new government transformed the situation by putting the philosophical horse before the logistical cart. It certainly changed things. The simple device of calling a halt to all expansion, regardless of merit, which was no more and no less logical than the unreflecting expansion that had gone before, utterly confounded the professional planners. But, according to Trito-Isaiah in 1980:

> Ironically, the earlier preoccupation with organisation and resources had produced no sophisticated planning and funding models. Indeed, since the assumptions underlying the setting-up of the system were of expansion, neither the government nor the institutions had techniques or models capable of dealing even adequately with contraction.

And the following year the UGC gave spectacular evidence of the general inadequacy.

It is not within my remit to expatiate on the philosophical basis that actually underlay higher education at the time – and in large measure still does. So you will be spared a long and critical review of the effects of the Robbins principle. But we can scarcely talk about how and why restructuring happens without spending some time at least on the binary system, if only because it is a major obstacle to restructuring.

It is one thing to say that it exists and that we ought not to waste our time dismantling it (which I take to be the government's present position) but quite another to regard it as a policy; and it is easy to slide over from one position to the other. Thus Mr Peter Scott, in the Leverhulme programme of study in 1983, began by declaring that 'the binary system is the nearest thing we have to an authoritative statement of the purposes of higher education'. Fair enough, perhaps, but he went on to suggest that five stages of developing policy had derived from it – preventing domination by the universities; encouraging vocational and 'relevant' perspectives; discouraging academic drift; putting at least part of the system under social control; and attracting students from outside the main system – and that all of this made it 'both a primary and a qualitative policy'.

In fact, as Lord Crowther Hunt, who had had to grapple with it, pointed out in the same Leverhulme programme, the use actually made of the binary system was inimical to policy-making and planning. He quoted an OECD report which suggested that the system had 'more of elegance and formal parity than of rational estimation of social demand or of long-term projections for highly qualified personnel'. This is hardly surprising. What else can you do with a binary line except invite an equal number of sheep and goats to graze on either side of it?

So there is not only a question of why restructuring happens, but why it does not. To turn to the how part of it, does this mean that I am saying that mergers are a good thing? Up to a point, I suppose I am, and I certainly cannot agree with the assessment of the poet Shakespeare – 'merger most foul as in the best it is' – but I am not yet ready to go on a barnstorming tour of the country for them.

Perhaps the next generation of merging persons will be readier to articulate their principles and practice, but I feel more like one of the Wright brothes than a professor of aerodynamics. Bumble bees, I am told, exhibit the same reluctance to lecture on the principles of flight; no doubt they have a superstitious fear that if they probe the thing too deeply they may suddenly plummet from the skies. In part, though, my own inhibition is because mergers are usually discussed in terms so platitudinous as to be noteworthy even in education. As Sam Goldwyn said: 'Let's have some new clichés.' But chiefly it's because it's hard to separate the particular from the general. Given the haphazard way in which our pattern of higher education has evolved, it is always likely that local idiosyncratic circumstances will obscure issues of principle.

I certainly think we should be cautious about regarding mergers as an instrument of social policy. In the first place, just as the binary system is no real substitute for a policy of higher education, neither is doing away with it. In the second place, to advocate mergers as a way of ending the binary system is like relying on mixed marriages as a way to end racial prejudice. And to come down to particular cases, if expediency is the main reason for retaining the binary division in Great Britain then expediency was the main reason for doing away with it in Ulster.

Regrettably, I cannot indulge in the luxury of documenting this thesis. I shall come back briefly to the second part of it in a while, but in the meantime must be content with making the fairly obvious point that there is no essential connection between mergers and breaching the binary system. Like human marriages,

institutional marriages can be of many kinds. There are marriages of convenience – often paving the way to love – such as those that took place between
the colleges that make up the universities of Oxford and Cambridge. Lower
down the social scale and more recently, the principle has been extended to
great effect, notably when the nineteenth-century red-brick colleges hitched up
with private medical schools. In those primitive times mergers were essentially
federal, fairly painless, relatively voluntary.

More recently, though, as public funding has been extended and the consequences have been rudely pointed out to the recipients, there have come more
awkward financially-based alliances in which the claims of rationalisation have
had to be weighed at least as heavily as those of tradition and inclination. And
among these vulgar couplings most interest has centred on weddings or
rumours of weddings in which the glint of shotgun barrels has been seen,
especially if there has been a hint of miscegenation. 'Would you let your
daughter marry a polytechnic lecturer?'

Those who wish to see Latin preserved as part of the curriculum of our schools
may like to note the motto I proposed for our own merger: *'Aut zonam solvere aut
mori.'* Or, as it might be: 'It is better to marry than to burn at the stake.' These
prurient concerns seemed to have an appeal to some outside observers that had
little to do with educational philosophy.

So we were pleased to be spared the glare of national publicity, once the initial
news value had gone. Fortunately, the *Times Higher Education Supplement*, casting
its searchlight around for desirable new organisational developments, appeared
to think the University of Ulster an unlikely precedent. The grounds it gave
seemed a bit odd: the extra costs of superannuation (fair enough, but hardly
critical) and a nugatory concession on tenure. There were in fact much more
cogent reasons for not using Ulster as a model, notably its four scattered
campuses. But this feature, of course, was not quintessential to the kind
of trans-binary mergers that the *THES*, albeit with modified rapture, was
advocating at the time.

Thus happily spared the limelight, we in Ulster were also spared the dreadful
label 'polyversity' that the *THES* at that time sought to bestow on its candidates. My objection was not only that this was a linguistic monstrosity but also
that it would be bound to typecast any new institution in an unhelpful,
essentially hierarchical way. (Not all enthusiasts for hierarchies are élitist: some
doctrinaire egalitarians seem to like to have things to inveigh against.) To retain
such a self-conscious if not self-indulgent label would have not only been
tendentious, but untimely since the old hierarchy was beginning to show signs of
wear and tear.

More important, though the old guard sought, and seeks, to restrict change to
deckchair rearrangement, it has to face the fact that after the iceberg the *Titanic*
is not what it was. The problem indeed for the first-class passengers is whether
anybody still wants to listen to their special pleading.

To abandon this unproductive metaphor, five years ago a curious paradox
was starting to emerge. While the universities became increasingly preoccupied
with resources and began to clamour loudly (if not very convincingly) for more
money, the government, which had begun by appearing to be solely interested

in costs, was now beginning to interest itself in philosophy and to talk of values.

The intrepid pioneer was Sir Keith Joseph. One would be hard pressed to disagree with Sir Peter Swinnerton-Dyer, who said in a recent address to the Committee of Vice-Chancellors and Principals:

> In his time as Secretary of State, Sir Keith thought harder and more deeply about the condition of British education than any of his predecessors had done for many years. He listened carefully and courteously to all the views put forward to him, and his legacy is his verdict. That verdict plainly is that, from nursery school to postgraduate studies, British education is in need of radical change.

I find a little less compelling Sir Peter's next sentence: 'Against that verdict, under this government, there is no machinery of appeal.' It may be true but if so, it seems unhelpfully late in the day for the UGC to announce it as a slogan. Sir Peter went on, however, to make a more cogent point:

> Sir Keith left behind him a verdict, but little in the way of blueprints for change. If we accept that change is inevitable, we can have a significant influence on the kind of changes that happen. But if we choose to resist change, we shall not prevent or even seriously delay it; we shall merely relinquish our chance to affect what kind of changes take place.

Amen to that, as far as it goes. But does it not ignore yet again not only the teleological questions, but also those intermediate ones that distinguish policy and planning from merely keeping the show on the road? In 1984, Isaiah made a similar point: 'Recent experience suggests that if we want to avoid being regulated in arbitrary fashion then we should take steps to regulate ourselves in purposeful fashion. In other words, we should accept the need for change and try to make sure that it is planned change.' But the paragraph went on to suggest that 'to reject planning, in the cause of freedom, is to risk being enslaved by bureaucracy'.

This was not a reference to the UGC, of which I had little or no experience at the time, and there is not much point in criticising it now, when it is on the way out. But I greatly hope that the new UFC will know the difference between planning and bureaucracy. If not then the old battles may continue, with government on the one side and the universities on the other, but they will be bladder-and-sticks affairs. To an institution of higher education, I suggest, the threat of bureaucratic intervention (which can come from the UGC just as much as from the Department of Education and Science) is at least as great as that of political intervention and its effects can be just as deadly, not least in the loss of institutional self-respect and the consequent forfeiture of respect by others.

But let us get back to our incipient paradox. Sir Keith Joseph, whether as politician or as philosopher *manqué*, certainly reversed the conventional order of things in which university dons were supposed to talk about philosophy and governments were supposed to talk about resources. There was a vacuum and he moved into it. His vista, it is true, opened out onto a bleak landscape, but he surveyed it with unflinching gaze. Take, for instance, his address to the British Academy in July 1984, in which he made the case for a direct government role in policy-making in publicly-funded higher education without destroying liberal values or academic autonomy.

Sir Keith emphasised then (as Kenneth Baker did on his October 1987 visit to the CVCP) that the best way for institutions to ensure their freedom was to become financially independent. He urged the claims of employability of students as a measure of a course's success, and he emphasised that culturally important subjects could not expect exemption from this kind of crude scrutiny unless they reached very high standards. The speech was not to everyone's liking; but it offered an alternative to the treadmill. And as a bonus it offered an approach to planning that put what had gone before to shame: analysis of the issues followed by a statement of the criteria he proposed to use in decision-making.

These criteria quickly put the cosy assumptions of the Robbins Report into perspective. Sir Keith's Green Paper (the mid-term version of the rather gaudier White Paper) started off from the premise that higher education ought to assist in the process of economic recovery, not only for the sake of the country's material well-being but also to be able 'to afford many of the things we value most – including education for pleasure and general culture and the financing of scholarship and research as an end in itself'. Well, to adapt the old song, if that isn't philosophy it'll have to do until the real thing comes along. And it seems a fair bet that in the foreseeable future no new kings are likely to arise up over Egypt that know not Joseph.

Let us now turn to the second question posed by the organisers: 'Are the planned benefits of reorganisation realised in practice?' And let us not quibble about the semantics. The notion of '*planned* benefits' of our own pre-Josephian reorganisation in Ulster might perhaps still cause raised eyebrows; but let me suggest, at least for the purposes of trying to address the organisers' question, that these hoped-for benefits might have been something on these lines: to save a university from closure or a costly, unconvincing and probably temporary reprieve; to do so by associating it with a much larger and more successful polytechnic; to create, if possible, an institution that complemented the work of the province's existing university but was strong enough to provide healthy competition; and to do so cost-effectively.

There was also an unspoken, in-built but highly important, hoped-for benefit in the new set-up – the solution of the unresolved problems of Magee College, Londonderry, the 'failure within a failure' as it has been called. All the travails of the New University of Ulster's taking over this old-established college had resulted in a mere 90 full-time equivalent (FTE) students, few of them following orthodox degree courses, and at the cost of bitter resentment, particularly by Catholics, of the treatment Derry and its aspirations had received from Coleraine.

And there were actual, if not planned, benefits in the outlook and conviction the members of the new institution themselves brought to bear on the task. The government and the Department of Education in Northern Ireland (DENI), I make no doubt, were fully aware that there would be developments of a positive if not necessarily preordained kind. If so, we can add to the targets of this new university the notion of multi-level courses with organised transfer between them; inter-disciplinary emphases in course development and research; a high regard for employability and consequent concern to strengthen links with industry and the professions; a healthy respect for marketing as the basis of planning; and a profound respect for planning itself.

It is far too early for definitive answers about the realisation of these aims, even if I were the best person to consult on such matters. But we can, I think, at least record an encouraging start. We got the show on the road on time and with very little fuss. There may have been a few problems but none troublesome enough to remain distinctly in the memory. We undertook to see that no existing course, or student on it, would be disrupted, and I think we delivered. At any rate, so far as I am aware, none of the many thousands of students involved were adversely affected by the merger *per se*.

We were determined that we would not become a merely federal institution. Logistically attractive though such a notion might have been, given our four campuses, it would simply not have been worth engaging in the upheaval of a merger merely for this. It was axiomatic that courses be offered where students wanted them, not where it was convenient for us to put them. We felt it important to let consumer needs and academic policy determine future developments, not the mere availability of accommodation and equipment or even staff in particular locations.

Nor, on the other hand, did we want to start moving staff around on a big scale for the sake of rationalisation: we hoped to follow the logic of our plans through the in-built efficiencies of the matrix. (Essentially the matrix, in which staff are deployed according to the needs of course provision rather than departmental contention, is supposed to make economies enough to allow the fine tuning needed to meet external professional and internal academic requirements.)

In general we felt that it was of first importance to get the strategy of provision right, and that this, in our case, meant making the faculties, operating across campuses, the main cost centres and the main agencies and instruments of planning. I am glad to say that the early aims of our development plan have been achieved with no mass transfer of the location of courses or of staff. Such movement as there has been has been voluntary; sometimes by promotion, sometimes by personal attraction or convenience.

If our merger had unusual geographical problems, however, we were helped in their solution by the exceptional political and social circumstances which made it possible for us to expand the Londonderry campus. It was political as much as educational policy that ensured government support for a substantial new building programme at Magee College and an increase in the total planned size of the new institution.

In terms of the sociology of the merger, this was a mixed blessing. It undermined the argument of the doubters that this was merely an excuse for cutback, cheered up agnostics, and allowed the planners a little elbow-room. On the other hand, it fuelled ancient prejudices and the attendant anxieties stemming from the peculiar British assumption that A's success can only be achieved at the expense of B.

In practical terms, it put a great deal of pressure on us to recruit the extra students. This was by no means certain, notwithstanding the fervent belief of local civic leaders that here was a vast rich untapped source of supply. Such mythology had to satisfy the astringent tests of the new institution's strategy, which had a weather eye for survival beyond immediate popularity. Well, so far so good. From the 90 FTE we inherited the Londonderry numbers had grown in the autumn of 1987 to some 600 FTE with a built-in growth to over 800 FTE. The students, furthermore, were on the kind of mainstream degree and diploma courses which the local community wanted to see in their city. It remains to be seen whether this initial impetus can be maintained, not only in terms of numbers but, more problematically, whether the courses we are offering can play their part, as we hope, in assisting the industrial and commercial regeneration of the area.

But however you might score such things in the chart of achievement of planned benefits, it can at least be said that the Londonderry campus is busier, fuller, and working to a higher level than ever before – and perhaps than almost anyone thought possible, including the two high-powered commissions that examined higher education in the province in the past twenty-odd years. Whether such benefits could have been achieved without the merger, or without a merger of some kind, are difficult questions, complicated by the fact that Magee College had earlier merged with the New University of Ulster (NUU) without apparent mutual benefit.

It would have been neat, but inconsistent with our aim of putting social and educational principle before the haphazard logistics of existing provision, if we could have matched this development in Londonderry with a reduction in numbers at our overcrowded Jordanstown campus. Not so, and we are, I fear, at present overshooting our overall target numbers.

There is no time, and it would be very tedious for us all, to go into the mechanics of how we intend to implement our development plan, without social engineering and without adverse effect on access and opportunity in any part of the province. Let me concentrate instead on what most people regarded as the most problematical of the tasks we faced: building up the Coleraine campus, the former NUU.

Again, as at Magee – and perhaps I should add, notwithstanding the Magee expansion – we have made an encouraging start. There has been an annual increase in student numbers – I don't want to wave figures around but it was, I read in the newspapers, 12 per cent this year over last year. Equally important, this expansion has been accompanied by a significant raising in admission standards in terms of A-level grades. I will come back to this later. At this point, let me simply say that one highly influential factor is, of course, the vocational and professional attraction of the programmes on offer. We still have some way to go in working out the old and working in the new, but our hope is that, in offering a more purposeful and attractive array of courses, we shall be providing a more stable base for the future.

This is one aspect in which the effect of the merger has been most obviously beneficial. Without going into the chemistry or the metaphysics of the union we can take a tangible example. The Faculty of Business and Management began in 1984 as an almost entirely Jordanstown (ex-polytechnic) unit. The faculty at once committed themselves, in a market-orientated mixture of idealism and prudence, to playing a leading part in the expansion of Londonderry. The notion of developing the Coleraine campus was an additional challenge, less immediately attractive or easy of resolution; and although something could be done through part-time programmes, it needed an investment in full-time provision. This presented a dilemma, both horns of which seemed spiky. Should we risk relocating an existing successful course from Jordanstown; or should we assign scarce extra staffing resources to speculative new ventures or radically changed existing courses? We have decided to do both. It is too soon to be entirely certain how this will work out, but the early signs are promising.

Even such tentative conclusions come up against the extreme difficulty of isolating the effects of the merger as a trans-binary phenomenon from the accidental features of the Ulster situation, and from the effects of changing social attitudes, national government policy, and so forth. This is not just a personal hang-up. In order to give you a more representative expression of opinion I asked eighteen of my senior colleagues, academic and administrative, a somewhat imprecise and unscientific question: what they found easier and what they found harder since the merger. Their replies indicate how hard it is to unravel the various strands. Nevertheless – or therefore – you may be interested in a brief survey of the main points of reply. I have separated the comments into ex-polytechnic and ex-university staff, but you should note a further complication: a very high proportion of the ex-Ulster Polytechnic people had previously been university teachers.

First, the positive side. Of the academics, the former university people thought there was a more coherent, purposeful sense of mission; greater responsiveness to community need; and more students at Coleraine and Magee with better grades. The ex-polytechnic staff welcomed the freedoms given by the Charter; the improvement in status especially in the eyes of industry; the better chance graduates had of getting jobs; removal of Council for National Academic Awards (CNAA) constraints; greater emphasis on research; more money for buildings and equipment; and better-qualified students and in some cases staff. Of the administrators, the ex-NUU people welcomed the speedier implementation of decisions, and the greater delegation of authority, and the former polytechnic people welcomed the fact that, as one of them put it, 'we no longer burn all the unspent pound notes every 31st March'. Individual perceptions varied. One wrote: 'I suppose the simplest thing is that we now no longer require specific Department of Education approval for courses nor do we need to submit estimates which are examined line by line within the Department of Education.' Another recognised this, but said: 'From a Resource Planning perspective everything is more difficult since the merger. We are now locked into a system which is much more complex and unwieldy than that which operated in the Ulster Polytechnic.'

But whereas these matters, more or less intrinsic to mergers, merely evoked mild and conditional comment, the main negative factor everyone mentioned was the specifically local one, the four widely-scattered campuses, the problems of communication, and the reduced opportunities for 'management by walking about'. This may have little or nothing to do with mergers *per se* but it has made it much harder to address the problem, noted by one ex-polytechnic academic, of 'establishing a community of scholarship across the campuses and the former binary divide'.

It is certainly an extra burden, trans-binary merger or not. The inter-campus tensions are slowly disappearing, and have been greatly lessened by the counterbalancing inter-faculty tension, but they are still unproductively there. Rome, as they say, was not built in a day. But until it is we do not, perhaps, score maximum points on the chart of planned benefits achieved.

For what it is worth, also, let me record another agreed negative. No one saw the UGC as likely to – or, some would say, capable of – helping us achieve our distinctive objectives, either social or educational. Their 'tunnel vision' was widely blamed. Once again this may be nothing to do with mergers – standard institutional paranoia? – and perhaps the UFC and PCFC will put all to rights.

To come back to internal problems, some of the negative comments may reflect unfamiliarity with life across the binary line, at least in recent times. Thus, former polytechnic academics, having earlier welcomed the greater freedom to conduct their own affairs, and the removal of the CNAA, found the reachback of the Universities' Central Council on Admissions (UCCA) hand-book a constraint on the speed with which new and properly planned and up-to-date courses could be mounted. They suggested that, in general, our decision-making and committee work had become more ponderous. Adminis-tratively, they found the conventions and constraints of the university system, which came as part of the deal in the framing of the Charter and Statutes of this particular merged institution, cumbersome and an undesirable curb on organisational flexibility.

For their part, the former NUU academics commented adversely on the increased amount of trade unionism of one sort or another – consultation between staff unions and the newly-discovered 'management' of the university, as well as the prominence of trade unionists generally on the Council. One person felt that it was harder to persuade staff to do things voluntarily. Another thought some lay members of the Council were too much influenced by sectional and geographical interests, and suggested that there was a shortage of good lay members anyway. There was criticism of what were thought overelaborate selection procedures for 'minor non-tenured posts, research assistants, etc.', and nostalgia for the greater freedom of the past in this respect. A former NUU administrator noted that the greater emphasis on accountability made for a more elaborate process – more hoops to jump through.

It is for you to judge the extent to which these effects – real or imaginary – are uniquely those induced by trans-binary mergers. My own view is that, though the merger brought some of them about sooner, the changes seem mostly to be of the kind that are being urged on universities anyway, through the influence of the White Paper, and more specifically the Jarratt Report on management.

Which brings me to accountability. We should consider, however briefly, the planned benefits of the merger looked for by DENI, as paymasters. According to our Finance Officer, John Galbraith, whose word I am inclined to take in these matters, DENI's objectives, 'apart from the philosophical and educational ones', were to provide a cost-effective system; to make better use of physical and financial resources by avoiding unnecessary duplication; and to improve the regional dimension. Auditors have recently visited us and their report is awaited. I offer you John Galbraith's impression of how we're faring.

To take the regional aspect first, he thinks the remarkable growth in numbers at Magee College will be recognised as a major achievement. Let us hope so. But the economics of the Coleraine campus, before and after, will clearly be the focal point of any assessment of cost-effectiveness. So far as unit costs are concerned, Galbraith takes three areas (Biological Sciences, Mathematics and Humanities) that were singled out for adverse comment in the Chilver Report on NUU, and points out that the University of Ulster is already below or close to the Great Britain average. The main reason for this is a dramatic improvement in staff–student ratios (also discernible in other areas such as Physical Sciences). As to better use of physical resources, he thinks we have made a reasonable start by increasing numbers at Coleraine and by containing them at Jordanstown. And, rather craftily you may think, he points out as a bonus that the merger has avoided the costs of the co-ordinating body which, without any guarantee of success, would have been needed if the trans-binary system had continued in Ulster.

Accountability, I suggest, is only desirable and, in the context of higher education, only practical, and meaningful, if there are agreed collegial and communal objectives. This applies at all sorts of levels, whether we are talking about governmental erosion of hierarchies, inter-institutional marriages of convenience, required mergers or departmental fusions within institutions.

Again this may not be a sparkling new thought but, as I have tried to suggest earlier, there are some hoary old questions still unanswered that we neglect at our peril. I wish I could reinforce the claims of the quintessential by a few crisp, epigrammatic sentences summing it all up. But you are too subtle and sophisticated an audience to be satisfied with this – and I am too experienced to try. So instead let me conclude with a personal thought or two, unhouseled, unaneled, about our own merger.

The first is that, merged or not, universities and colleges ought to concern themselves, first and foremost, with the well-being of their students – ask themselves whether students are clients or merely products. And the second is that it may be easier in a trans-binarily merged institution, which we may presume will be both large and ready to nail its socio-educational colours to the mast, to offer alongside traditional honours degrees matching sub-degree courses with organised transfer up and down.

The secluded path of recruitment of young persons with good A-level grades to full-time courses has always been the chosen way of most universities, and aspirants to university status. This élitist route, hitherto merely criss-crossed by supply and demand, is now being challenged at its source by utilitarian values, new-style materialistic, hard-nosed interpretations of the cosy professional assumptions of the past. Jack may not only claim to be as good as his neighbour in future, but may be able to prove it through certificates and diplomas. Nor is this any longer out of line with government thinking. (We cannot at this last gasp go into that, thank heaven, but it's there.)

And, notwithstanding the belated and not very convincing official calls for wider access to higher education, and the welcoming echoes, made hollow by suspicions of meritocracy if not opportunism, from some universities, the stern realities are that, one way and another, and *mutatis mutandis*, the race is still going to be to the swift. The warier institutional survivors of the UGC's 1981 performance, in the manner of association football clubs relegated to a lower division, have sought ways of becoming, if not stylish exponents of traditional arts or even crowd-pleasers, at least accumulators of points, and they are led by suitably charismatic managers.

The UGC itself is widely suspected of favouring a super-league, and one furthermore that will turn out to be composed of the clubs with the best sponsorship. The question for many universities is whether to join in the search for corners of excellence the well-founded institutions have so far failed to reach, or whether to look beyond the conventional system to things that students want and need and nobody is so far providing.

The pressures to follow the first course rather than the second are very great, and no less, although with perhaps less logic, if you are in Northern Ireland rather than in the English Midlands. Now I am not entirely sure how a big, and, I hope, indestructible outfit like the University of Ulster is going to deal with these pressures (though I have some idea and some confidence). What seems crystal-clear though, is that if NUU had continued in separate existence it would have found it very hard to live with these pressures. As a small institution rooted in orthodoxy or the new radicalism of the 1960s, not well placed geographically and with little experience outside the academic, it was unlikely to be able to switch successfully to specialism. And as a generalist university it was stuck, despite its efforts to venture into continuing education and wider access, with the tradition it had inherited (and indeed embraced) of the supremacy of the honours degree.

By contrast, whatever its disadvantages, a merged institution of the character and the size of the University of Ulster is able to plan an array of courses at various levels with organised transfer between them. This not only allows a much wider range of options for students – a safety net for those who begin to struggle, more demanding opportunities for late developers – but it is the best possible guarantee of the standard of the honours degree. (If an honours degree is all you have you are at the mercy of market forces: in hard times you either take in fewer students or lower your standards.) This is one feature of the University of Ulster that I would like to see being adopted by other universities.

I cannot claim that we have yet perfected the system. Perhaps we never shall: the claims of the various professions are a major obstacle to delayed choice, credit transfer and the like. But I think it fair to say that we have already used the freedom of being a university to take the notion further than we could as a polytechnic, and infinitely further than NUU did as an unmerged university. Whether we truly succeed or not may ultimately depend on whether we make good use of this facility.

And there, not with a philosophical bang but an organisational whimper, I shall end. I think I can claim that nobody – staff, student, industrialist, professional person, taxpayer or bureaucrat – is worse off as a result of the merger. But I do not thereby conclude that mergers can cure all ills, any more than comprehensive schools have solved the problems of secondary education.

Sooner or later we have to get down to discussing what the ends of higher education – however we organise it – should be. Keith Joseph's questions are more likely to lead us towards an answer than any that have come from government before. Why don't we stop bemoaning what we think might have been, and get down to the task of creating what we can for the young people of tomorrow?

3

Robert Jackson, MP

The topics identified in the conference programme and the large number of papers prepared show that you will be covering the subject of restructuring in its widest sense – veritable *perestroika*. There are indeed many things happening. The other keynote speakers will no doubt have much to say from their own perspective. I should like for my part to share with you various aspects of the government's overall higher education policy. They affect you all.

One of these is of course the Education Reform Bill and the higher education provisions in it. They are quite clearly about restructuring in one of its senses. We are transferring polytechnics and major colleges in England from local authority control. And we are establishing new planning and funding arrangements for those institutions and for the universities in Great Britain. These are important changes. They were foreshadowed in the higher education White Paper (DES 1987) and in our subsequent consultative documents. They have already been the subject of widespread discussion and will continue to be debated both inside and outside Westminster as the Bill makes its way through Parliament.

But it is important to remember that the Bill's provisions do not represent the be all and end all of our higher education policies. The White Paper contained a lot more besides. I should like to deal later with some of the other specific issues it raised. But first a few general words on structure.

Different missions?

The Bill proposes the establishment of two new higher education funding councils – the Universities Funding Council (UFC) and the Polytechnics and Colleges Funding Council (PCFC). It does not require a particularly detailed analysis to discover that the provisions are almost identical for both. The explanation is simple. Both Councils are being established to do the same thing: to allocate funds provided by the Secretary of State to the institutions within their sector. That is what the relevant clauses are about. What differences there are relate solely to the rather more complex constitutional mix in the PCFC sector which comprises not only the new higher education corporations transferring from local authorities but also institutions which are currently assisted as opposed to maintained by Local Education Authorities and the voluntary and direct grant institutions.

It has been suggested by various commentators that the establishment of two bodies with identical functions preludes an eventual amalgamation into a single higher education funding body. This has been a common refrain over a number of years. But I do not need to tell you that things are never quite that simple.

Higher education is a broad canvas which does not readily lend itself to a single ideal structural and managerial model. Witness the diversity which already exists. The post-war growth in higher education has been common to all advanced countries. At the general level, nowhere is there much difference in overall aims and objectives. But each country has developed, or seen evolve, very different traditions in the pattern and extent of provision, and in its planning and funding. So our own historical inheritance in this country is not, in fact, an orderly, unitary system but a heritage of diversity. From the proportion of public funding, this diversity has resolved itself into two parallel sectors differentiated, broadly, by function. I should like briefly to talk about the manner in which this functional distinction has come about, and the question of the extent to which it continues to have valid application to the tasks we have now set for higher education.

In this country the last great period of debate about governance and structure was, I suppose, that of twenty to twenty-five years ago. Its roots lay in the rapidly increasing demand for higher education in the 1950s. The expansion in numbers was accommodated by enlarging existing universities and by creating new ones, both in the transformation of the Colleges of Advanced Technology and in the greenfields expansion. And it was accommodated in the new sector of higher education created by the establishment of the polytechnics.

The decisions of that period set the agenda, even if the more optimistic forecasts of expansion then extant were never wholly fulfilled. Robbins and Crosland built on what was already happening in terms of demand, and on the distinctive contribution of the leading technical colleges. Since then evolution has continued. Each institution has developed in its own way – to use Crosland's language, each has its own distinctive 'mission'. We know how universities vary widely in their history, ethos and range of activities. Similarly there are considerable differences between the institutions now to come within the PCFC sector. There are large, multi-disciplinary polytechnics – larger on average than most universities; there are much smaller specialist colleges dedicated to teaching art and design, or music, or agriculture, or to the training of teachers; and the voluntary colleges with their own important contribution rooted in a distinctive tradition. But how many realise that the polytechnics themselves are by no means uniform? Some have made their mark by pioneering new routes into higher education for those without the traditional qualifications; others have developed formidable teaching skills in fields of growing demand like computer studies and management; and still others have made themselves into among the leading technological teaching institutions in Europe by offering a range of practical skills and, in some cases, undertaking applied research of high quality.

So much for Crosland's concept of distinctive 'missions'. What of his concept of a 'dual system'? The binary line has always been a useful metaphor, and it expresses the reality of the differentiation of the channels of public funding over the past two decades. But it masks the increasing differentiation within each sector which I have spoken about. Sectoral boundaries have less significance as individual institutions become more diverse in their strengths. Differentiation also naturally fosters comparisons, and sharpens competition, between institutions whose strengths lie in the same field. My hunch would be, for example, that comparisons of teaching strength in institutions on either side of the binary line will come increasingly to be made.

As institutions develop in the future some further blurring will no doubt occur. This is because whatever our planning models may be, the reality of life and, above all, the interests and preferences of students will have their effect. One corollary of this is that the successful institutions will be those that build constructively on the traditional strengths they have inherited. There is, for example, much for the polytechnics and colleges to hold on to in the Crosland idea of institutions concentrating on teaching, and especially on vocational, professional and industrially-based teaching courses at all levels of higher education. That is where the polytechnics and colleges are strongest; it is also where the demand is likely to be most buoyant in future years. I believe that there is a growing market for the services of those institutions which cater most successfully for the skills by which society is increasingly inclined to set the highest store. Indeed it is precisely because the polytechnics and colleges have been so successful in what they do best – because they have become self-reliant, self-confident, mature institutions – that we are offering them the new deal foreshadowed in the White Paper and realised in the current Bill. Under this new deal they will, much more so than now, be the masters of their own future. It is not for ministers to prescribe individually or collectively where that future will lie. But the polytechnics and colleges – and, most important of all, their students – may well conclude that the best opportunities lie in continuing to be different from the universities rather than in imitating them.

Precisely where we will be in another twenty-five years in terms of the structure of our higher education is impossible and imprudent to predict. Much will depend on the approaches adopted by the Funding Councils in the new situation. But it is far from certain that their ethos and approach will converge, rather than diverge. Meanwhile the developments foreshadowed in the Bill mark an important step forward, opening up new horizons of possibility without running too far ahead of the complex realities which history has created.

Diversity within the sectors

For its part, the government will be looking to the Councils to foster what is best in what they find; to encourage diversity and the competition and enterprise to which it gives rise. This may require new approaches. For example, the UGC is already applying a new rigour to the research part of its grant, including a judgemental element directed towards high-quality research. The Committee has not yet begun to develop a similarly qualitative approach in relation to the larger part of its grant, namely the teaching element. That is not necessarily because it doubts the principle of selectivity in teaching, but because, as the Chairman said in launching the planning exercise two years ago, they did not in practice see how to do it. He threw down a challenge then to universities on how a suitable methodology might be developed. There have been few, if any, takers. I acknowledge, of course, that this is far from straightforward. The relationship between teaching quality and funding is not simple. The Croham Report pointed out that even if criteria could be established to identify teaching strength, there is no consensus on the uses to which such an appraisal would be put. But I should be disappointed if the UFC and the PCFC failed to address it.

We shall also look to the Funding Councils to adopt forward strategies. There are good academic and financial reasons for an approach which will involve the continuing targeting of resources on strength. This is not a new idea. As I have mentioned, the UGC has recently overhauled its method of allocating recources between universities, incorporating for the first time explicit and public judgement on research strengths subject by subject and university by university. In parallel it has embarked on a series of subject reviews aiming more directly to rationalise provision in particular fields in the interests both of greater efficiency and effectiveness and developing academic strength. The government for its part has allocated some £155 million over the next three years to a targeted programme of restructuring including additional finance for early retirements, some new appointments and the rationalisation of provision. One of the functions of the restructuring programme is to enable the UGC to bring together the *subject* approach adopted in selective funding and rationalisation with a proper concern for the academic health of *institutions* as a whole. And the system of specifying the teaching provision in polytechnics and colleges, based on indicative student numbers which lead to the delivery of funding, is an example of one well-established means of directing resources to those institutions with the best record of attracting students and the highest ratio of graduates to places.

So I return to the theme of diversity. This is already substantial. It is a strength which should continue and develop. To help bring out the best in each individual institution will be one of the tasks of the Funding Councils. We do not want fifty average universities, twenty-nine average polytechnics, and fifty average colleges.

Common themes across higher education

I have concentrated so far on diversity. But alongside that are policies which we believe are common to all institutions. They do not require legislation, but they are no less for that a central feature of the government's view of the future development of higher education. I have already referred to rationalisation and concentration on strength. I should like now to address three more specific issues: contract-based funding; links with and support from industry; and access.

The concept of funding by contract has been misunderstood, perhaps sometimes wilfully. Let me repeat what the Secretary of State has already said several times. When we talk about contracts we are not talking in the commercial sense of legally binding agreements enforceable in law. What we are about is further progress in clarifying responsibilities and sharpening accountability. At the general level this lies behind the establishment of the Funding Councils. But there is a parallel need for greater clarity and accountability in their dealings with individual institutions and for similar clarity and accountability within institutions. The White Paper and consultative document signal a new approach to these matters.

Contracts in the sense of a relationship based on exchange are, however, nothing new in higher education. Institutions are already given public funds in return for which they agree to provide higher education. The nature of the agreement underpinning that provision may be specified to a greater or lesser extent. At the moment this specification is fairly general in the case of the universities, although there the preparation of financial and academic plans as a basis for funding is assuming increasing importance. It is more specific for the polytechnics and colleges, where target student numbers have a much more closely defined relationship with the funds provided and where the targets can be, and are, adjusted to reflect institutions' performance in delivering the provision specified. It is very specific in both sectors where funds are earmarked for specific purposes, a notable example of this being the Engineering Technology Programme. In addition, performance is increasingly a factor in the allocation of resources as in the UGC's judgements of research strengths and, at a more modest level, the operation of the National Advisory Body's special initiatives.

The government's view is that contracting will help us to achieve a clearer specification of what is expected of institutions, and closer links between the level of funding provided and past performance. A clearer understanding with the Funding Councils about how funds are to be used will help us all to clarify our objectives.

To those who doubt our motives I offer this reassurance. We recognise that contracts must accommodate the distinctive characteristics of our higher education. They must *not* be excessively bureaucratic; they must *not* jeopardise the pursuit of research and scholarship; they must *not* deprive institutions of the margin of flexibility they need to seize new opportunities.

As to how contract-based funding arrangements will turn out, the government is still refining its thinking. Much of the responsibility will rest with the Funding Councils. The institutions represented here today are also part of the continuing debate about how the questions which have been raised might be resolved. I hope they will contribute to the limits of their capacity – well beyond those of government.

I turn now to another area in which all higher education institutions have a stake. That is private funding, notably from industry and commerce, where, of course, you are well used to contracts! One of the curiosities of the way the universities at least account for funds, and the way in which they are collected and published nationally, is that the calculation of the precise balance of private and public funding and their relative contribution to general and specific income is no easy matter. But there is no doubt in anyone's mind that the institutions have increased the amount of income they receive from these sources at a rate well ahead of general inflation. Let me offer further reassurances about the government's intentions. It is sometimes said that we encourage private earnings solely in order to spare the public purse. We have made clear that this is not so. We have repeatedly said that we will not abate public support because institutions succeed in raising more private funds. The UGC's allocation method actually rewards success, albeit modestly. What institutions have to gain is the greater independence and flexibility which comes as a consequence of lessened dependence on the state. As well as the additional income, of course.

But the exchange is not just financial. You all have much more to offer and to receive in return. Companies benefit from the services and expertise offered by the institutions. Staff and students benefit from close and up-to-date experience of business priorities and practices.

I want to applaud the efforts made and the gains achieved in recent years. Industry and higher education are increasingly recognising their interdependence and as they work together more closely, so the old misconceptions and barriers continue to tumble. I believe there is a general mood to do yet more.

Finally, I want to leave you with a challenge. The central plank of the higher education White Paper (DES 1987) was the expansion of access. As a policy that has been widely welcomed. But we have at the same time been accused of being too timid. Only another 50,000 students by 1990? Only a small increase in output by the end of the century?

The reality is the substantial nature of what we are proposing. Without very radical changes in our system the actual number of students in higher education is not likely to grow very much in the 1990s. This is a simple reflection of demography. The traditional eighteen- to twenty-two-year old entry group is going to decline by a third. Simply to achieve the government's so-called modest planning targets is going to require a significant increase in the participation not only of the traditional young entry group, but also among older people and those with non-traditional qualifications.

The challenge to institutions is twofold. First the actual process of widening access. This will require fresh thinking on a range of matters: entry requirements and selection techniques; modes of study; more varied and effective teaching to take account of a broader student body; the development and training of staff. I know, of course, that none of this will be new to many of you. But it might be to some.

The second challenge lies in the associated question of quality. The general quality of our higher education is among the best in the world. All institutions must set their sights on preserving the standards now attained, while providing new forms of learning for new sorts of students, many of whom will lack the degree of academic preparation of their predecessors. Let no-one say that this will be easy. It will not. But I believe it should be possible. And the challenges confront all institutions – universities, polytechnics and colleges.

Conclusion

Everything that I have talked about in this paper involves restructuring of one kind or another: planning, funding and students. I find growing mutual understanding and I believe there is now a common agenda to be followed. The initiative in moving forward lies with all of us. That is what this conference is about.

4

Sir Peter Swinnerton-Dyer

It's a considerable risk to ask Christopher Ball and me to speak at the same conference on the same topic, because if we had any sense we would get together in advance and give exactly the same speech – except that, of course, one of us would be standing on his head while doing it. As we failed to get together, I am left with the choice between the two ways of treating this topic: one being what I would hope to see happen if everyone responsible for higher edcuation was sensible, and the other what I expect to see happen in practice. It seems only reasonable that Christopher and I should take one of these approaches each, and Christopher's natural inclination is to believe the best of his fellow men. Moreover, he has just put himself in a position where he must apply for jobs, and to succeed in that he must show his vision, human sympathy and so on; whereas I have a safe job in a quiet fen to go back to. So it seems only fair for me to make the cynic's speech and leave him to make the idealist one. But, of course, I shall be right.

The natural place to start is with the government's attitude to higher education because its members are the most powerful players in the game and their attitude conditions almost everything. Twenty years ago practically everybody felt he or she was entitled to receive government money. By and large that was an attitude which the government shared, so every spending ministry made a list of customers, pencilled in the figures it thought they deserved, added up the total and stood in a queue in front of the Treasury. The Treasury then added up the bill and discovered what level of taxes it had to impose. There was a general attitude that it was the duty of the government to spend adequately and to raise the money somehow. Since 1979 things have changed rather dramatically. We have a government which fundamentally does not approve of public spending and certainly does not believe in giving money away. The most central feature of their policy is not, as Mrs Thatcher sometimes says, to eradicate the concept of socialism, but to eradicate people's idea that they are entitled to government money. Ministers may not put it as bluntly as I have, but once you realise that is their point of view it explains a good many things.

For example, it explains the government's recent emphasis on contracts in higher education and reconciles it with Kenneth Baker's recent statement to the Committee of Vice-Chancellors and Principals (CVCP) that, of course, these contracts would not be legally binding. I am sure that what he means is that the government sees itself as buying certain things from higher education, not as making grants to keep higher education going. It is higher education's job to find enough saleable goods and services to keep itself going, but the government is a reasonably willing buyer. The main things it is going to buy are teaching and research, or perhaps one should say graduates and research. I judge that the emphasis on contracts in the last few months has been one part of the campaign to persuade higher education that it will only get money if it delivers something worthwhile in exchange. We can no longer say, as so many of us have been accustomed to say, or even to believe, that we are intrinsically good and beautiful and are entitled to money simply on the grounds of our goodness and our beauty. For this reason I have never taken so alarmist a view of contracts as most of the universities have, and I observe with some interest that the polytechnics, who are forced to be closer to the hard facts of life than universities are, have also been scarcely at all worried about contracts. Indeed one could reasonably say that the UGC's new funding mechanism is not very far from being contract-based, because the teaching-based component of our grant to a university is essentially proportionate to student numbers (taking subject mix into account) and to a large extent the research-based component depends on the quality of the research that the university has delivered in the recent past. It is true that on this interpretation the research component is a retrospective payment rather than a payment for new goods; but that's a technical issue.

This explanation may persuade you that the government is not as wicked as it is made out to be; though, of course, you may simply conclude that I am a full-time civil servant so I have a certain duty to say things like this from time to time. One could pose the question more generally: is the Department of Education and Science (DES) really such an ogre as it contrives to present itself to us as being, or does it merely contain some jolly bad draughtsmen? Certainly all of us believe there are bad draughtsmen in the DES; the question is whether that is a sufficient explanation for their public image. To answer that one needs to look at what the DES is actually doing in higher education. Given my present job, I must inevitably start with the change from the University Grants Committee (UGC) to the Universities Funding Council (UFC). Of course, nobody knows quite how the UFC is going to work; indeed that will depend a great deal on who its first chairman is, about which all we know is that he will be a distinguished businessman and he will not be Sir Ron Dearing because he is already spoken for.

I do not believe that the transformation from the UGC to the UFC will be nearly so spectacular as people are supposing. I do worry about a couple of problems, but they are niggling problems rather than ones that cause acute agony. One arises from the rooted belief of the government that everything will be all right if only enough businessmen are put in charge of it. Even if one accepts that in principle it may well not be a practicable policy because it is not clear where one can find the necessary supply of businessmen – businessmen for the UFC, businessmen for the PCFC, businessmen for every board of polytechnic governors and, of course, an adequate supply of businessmen for the council of every university, and that's just to cover higher education. There was a time when running a business was so undemanding that a businessman could devote most of his time to public service. There are still a certain number of people who get promoted to a very high level in business before their colleagues realise that, though benevolent and plausible, they are actually not very competent; and there is a grave danger that when government asks for a massive supply of businessmen, business will provide these people, and very few others. So I really am worried whether there will be an adequate supply of able businessmen to fill all these positions.

I am also a little mystified about what the UFC itself (as opposed to its sub-committees) is supposed to do. The Secretary of State seems to me to have given us no clue and the only clear statement that I can find anywhere is the statement in the Croham Report that the UFC will approve the grants to individual universities. But the use of the word 'approve' means that somebody else will work the figures out. I have no quarrel with that; indeed, now that the UGC has designed its new allocation process, we don't work the figures out either. But if approving grants is a typical example of what the UFC are going to do, then they are going to have a remarkably undemanding agenda. The same seems to me true of the PCFC and I will come back to that point in a moment.

Inevitably the UFC is going to have to have a substantial infrastructure of committees, partly because its job, which is in essence the same as that of the UGC's, is almost entirely concerned with details. There is not much scope for grand simple gestures of reform; what has to be done is an endless series of bits of *petit point* work, which has to be done by people who understand the university system and are prepared to devote a lot of time to it. That means the bulk of the work will have to be done in sub-committees dominated by academics because nobody else is going to be prepared to do it. Moreover, the UFC will have to produce from time to time research assessments like the ones which the UGC produced a couple of years ago. I suppose that job could be sub-contracted, though it would not be easy to find bodies which would take on that sort of contract; but short of that, research assessments, too, will require the sort of apparatus of expert committees that the UGC itself has. So I wonder whether the government is not simply re-creating the whole edifice as before with the UFC itself put at the very top. And now there is the question of how much power the UFC itself will really exercise. If it does exercise real power, that creates a bit of a problem in that the chief executive may be almost the only link between the UFC and its sub-structure; so he will be a lot more powerful than the chairman of the UGC is at the moment. I can always be jumped on by my colleagues who understand academic matters at least as well as I do, but the chief executive's colleagues are not going to understand matters nearly as well as he and are probably not going to give nearly as much time to the UFC as UGC members give to it.

The next point about the UFC that everyone seems to worry about is that whereas the UGC is required to report to the government on the financial needs of universities, that has been firmly struck out of the terms of reference of the UFC. I do not think one should take this too seriously. There are a large number of similar bodies, the Arts Council for example, who do not have anything like this in their terms of reference, and the only effect is that since they have no duty to report the needs of their clients privately to ministers they state them publicly instead – and usually in very much more vigorous language. So I expect the UFC to say publicly what the UGC only says privately to government, that higher education needs more money – and the UFC is likely to pitch its bid higher because it knows that its clients are listening.

The other major worry is the power of direction which the Secretary of State has reserved for himself. But in fact he already has that with the UGC and indeed more than that because the UGC is a purely advisory body. We never even get our hands on the money which we allocate to universities; instead we request some DES officer to send out the cheques. Moreover, the UGC can be abolished with a stroke of the pen merely by the Secretary of State saying: 'I cancel the minute by which my predecessor set it up.' The Secretary of State really has even more powers of direction over the present UGC than he will have over the UFC. He has similar powers of direction over the research councils and, to the best of my knowledge, those have never been used. Recently a lot of people badgered him to use them over the move of the Royal Observatory from Herstmontceux to Cambridge. He refused to do so, though that may have been as much a matter of good sense as of self-restraint. Again, eighteen months ago I pressed his predecessor to use his powers in respect of the financial crisis at University College, Cardiff and he would not. So I really do not think that there is any severe risk of his powers of direction being used to excess.

The next new development in or related to the legislation, apart from the legislation against bogus degrees which I think you will welcome, is the new audit arrangements. That consultative paper has put everyone's back up, but that I certainly ascribe to bad drafting. The Secretary of State and Sir David Hancock have made it clear that they do not intend the sort of incessant prying into university affairs that some people have read into these proposals; but after the scandal of Cardiff there really has to be a reserve power to put the ferrets into a university if all concerned in running it appear to have lost either their senses or their backbone.

Then there is tenure. Ministers have felt for a long time that tenure was a matter of high moral principle and the legislation reflects that fact. In due course I think we shall discover that the legislation on tenure makes less practical difference than we now suppose; but given the number of topics I want to cover I ought not to say more about that.

Indeed, I think the universities are going to be far more affected by those parts of the Secretary of State's policy that overtly refer to schools. To start with, the introduction of GCSE will very shortly create a crisis, because what the children actually know when they have just taken GCSE and what the syllabus assumes they know when they start on A levels are very different both in substance and in style. I do not say that they need to know less for GCSE than they did for O levels but that what they need to know is very different. There is going to be a terrible discontinuity and, as we all know, the first cohort of schoolchildren to take GCSE and then A levels is in for a fairly awful time. Mercifully, children are resilient.

Again, AS levels, the other recent reform, are designed to produce more breadth. We do not yet know whether they will or not. I am sceptical because I know how difficult it is for schools to make the arrangements for teaching AS levels; but they are the first of the various ministerial proposals for broadening the sixth-form curriculum to which any Secretary of State has managed to get the agreement of the Examining Boards, and he got that at least as much by their exhaustion as by their conversion. If AS levels do not work, the next reform proposed will not be nearly so moderate. There is a negro spiritual with the refrain 'God gave Noah the angel sign, no more water, the fire next time', and next time reform of the sixth-form curriculum will be the fire and not the water.

Any kind of broadening, indeed almost any kind of change, is going to be used by universities as an excuse for campaigning for a four-year degree. It is inconceivable that any government will find the money for four-year degrees in general, unless it starts making students pay the full cost of their courses, and that is politically unlikely. I am not convinced by the arguments that broader sixth-form studies will necessitate a four-year degree, because they assume that the level of knowledge you should achieve for your BA is a standard established by God. In most subjects, the only sensible definition of the standard of a BA is three years' hard work from what you could be expected to know when you entered the university. There are exceptions, which are, broadly speaking, the professional subjects; but it is difficult to believe that the curriculum in medicine, for example, is incapable of reform, or that lawyers start from an assumption of absolute ignorance, and that really leaves only engineering. A campaign for four-year engineering courses may well succeed; there is a strong case for that even now. But it would be a total waste of time to campaign for four-year first degree courses more generally. The PhD is different because you really have to be already at the frontiers of knowledge if you are to advance knowledge; so I think a four-year PhD course really will be needed, but so many fewer people do a PhD that the financial problems of that change are not insuperable.

I should now go on to a most interesting topic which is not mentioned anywhere in the Bill or in ministers' speeches – that is, the future of the binary line. I think ministers assume that the binary line will go on just as before. I know very few other people who assume that. Some people say it will last five years, some seven and some ten – and that figure is totally uncorrelated with their guess about how long Mrs Thatcher will remain Prime Minister. It seems to me that the two great obstacles to doing away with the binary line will be swept away by the Education Reform Bill. One of them is the fact that until now public sector institutions have been owned in the crudest financial sense by their local education authorities (LEAs), and the other is that the UGC and National Advisory Body (NAB) have been far too busy to think about the binary line. Polytechnics, at least, are being set free from their LEAs, and, as I said earlier, the UFC and the PCFC are going to be extremely similar bodies with very similar-looking agendas and distinctly underemployed. It seems to me inevitable that they will move towards each other and will jointly constitute a strong pressure group for the abolition of the binary line. Even if they do not, Mrs Thatcher will shortly notice that one of them, at least, is superfluous and draw the obvious conclusion. Moreover, there are quite a few trans-binary mergers being talked about; I know of four very obvious ones and you will no doubt know of one or two others, though those one or two may differ from one person to another. Almost any trans-binary merger will do its part towards erasing the binary line. It is true that the merger in Ulster did not, but that may be because people on this side of the water are a little reluctant to see Ulster leading the way.

This leads me to ask what actually distinguishes a university. There is a diversity of possible answers. One is financial autonomy, which universities have and polytechnics do not but very soon will. Then there is academic autonomy, which universities have, provided you forget that about a third of all university degrees have to be appraised by an outside professional body which is not at all reluctant to express its indignation at any changes. Polytechnics are in the hands of the CNAA, but it looks as if the grasp of the CNAA is already being loosened and may well be loosened further. Then there are the various status symbols: the Royal Charter, the office of chancellor, the dignified ceremonies, and all that sort of thing. I find it very hard to see that as a crucial distinction, and there are certainly enough underemployed people listed in *Who's Who* to supply as many chancellors as could possibly be needed, even if every school in the country were given one. And finally, and in practice most crucially, there is the widely repeated statement that universities are equally committed to teaching and research whereas polytechnics were primarily established for teaching. I have phrased that statement with a little more care than the rest of this paper, and, as phrased, you would have to admit that it is true; but the fact that polytechnics were established for teaching has not stopped them wishing to do research and indeed starting to do research. Their complaint is that they are only funded for research on the most niggardly scale.

That inevitably brings me to the notorious report of the Advisory Board for the Research Councils (ABRC 1987) and in particular to the proposal to classify institutions of higher education into Types R, X and T. Sir David Phillips now says that that was never meant to be a policy or a recipe for action, but merely a forecast of what would inevitably occur in due course. It is a bit difficult to square that with the statement elsewhere in the Report that change was not taking place fast enough and I have some difficulty in envisaging Sir David Phillips as Madame Zsa Zsa with a turban round his head gazing into a crystal ball, but one ought to accept what he now says. Even so I do not think we are moving towards that kind of classification, though we are moving towards a considerable degree of selectivity in research funding. In fact there are very few institutions of higher education all of whose departments are of high quality in research. By a merciful symmetry, both Cambridge and Oxford had one department that was rated below average by the UGC, and there are only three multi-subject institutions funded by the UGC that did not have at least one below average department. That is a somewhat inadequate basis on which to produce Sir David Phillips's fifteen Type R institutions, the more so as Lampeter is one of the three. I do not believe that the ABRC proposals will ever be implemented, but I do not see selectivity in research funding ever being swept away; and I think that in the medium term the polytechnics will inevitably be brought within the same system.

I would like to say a little more about this. Let me start by saying that almost everyone who talks about research talks about it either entirely with laboratory subjects in mind or entirely with non-laboratory subjects in mind – mostly the former. There must be some sensible statements to be made which apply equally to laboratory and non-laboratory subjects, but there are few of them and they tend not to be among the statements that people actually make. But if one is to think about research one must separate those two groups very firmly. The ABRC Report was overwhelmingly concerned with laboratory subjects and so are most of the speeches about research which I have heard since. So let me start with non-laboratory subjects. What are the resources that are needed for research in non-laboratory subjects? The dominant resource is the time of academic staff; therefore, to enable academics in such a department to do more research, the crucial thing is to diminish the amount of teaching they have to do. In effect that means providing a better staff–student ratio, which is a matter of putting more money into the department; but it also means stopping the department using that extra money to increase the diversity of options in their courses. In other words, it involves putting in more money but it also requires the department to behave sensibly. The other crucial resources are probably travel grants and access to adequate libraries. Libraries are at the moment a major problem, because they are getting more and more expensive. I, and I think most members of the UGC, hope increasingly desperately that what can best be called economical remote reading will soon become available, so that academics can consult material in other libraries without having to leave their own campus.

That would radically change the availability of library resources, both for laboratory and non-laboratory subjects. What laboratory subjects need in addition, and what they regard as the crucial resource, is what the UGC used to provide for the dual support system – the well-found laboratory. In the old days the UGC provided well-found laboratories in every experimental department in every university. The underlying idea was that grants from Research Councils descended at random as if from heaven; and it was necessary to provide a well-manured soil wherever they might land, so that they would grow and flourish. From the point of view of the Research Councils that system worked splendidly, but it was an extravagant procedure and there is no possibility of our being able to maintain it. We must therefore contrive that the well-found laboratories are those in which the Research Councils are most likely to put their money – in other words those where good research is most likely to go on. That involves a substantially greater degree of co-ordination both of judgement and of action between the UGC and the Research Councils than has been customary in the past. Such co-ordination is not easy. We did our best to produce it mechanically by means of the DR component (the dual support element in the funding formula, which matches expenditure arising from grants from Research Councils and Medical Charities) in our research-allocation formula; but that has unfortunately been taken by a number of people in the Research Council system as a lightly disguised way of allowing them to write cheques on the UGC's bank account. That is not the only thing wrong with DR, but it is quite serious enough in itself; and I judge that, though DR will go on for the lifetime of the UGC, it is one of the things the UFC will have to look at at a very early stage in its life. Nevertheless, the UFC will have to go on providing the well-found laboratory in the good departments because you cannot simply wave a magic wand and overnight produce a good environment for research. Similarly, the UFC will have to provide what I can only call a not-too-badly-found laboratory in the middling departments so that although it may cost the Research Councils a little more to put their grants there they will find an infrastructure which they can build on; and equally the UFC will have to provide something in those weaker departments which have to be given an opportunity to pull themselves up by their bootstraps. How much that something is depends on how much money the government provides.

None of this is as radical as R, X and T. It is also different in another way, in that I have been talking entirely about individual departments and not about institutions. But I think the ABRC view that one should concentrate on entire institutions is pure muddle-headedness. It is true that a good physics department will find it useful to have good electrical engineering and good applied mathematics, for example, in the same institution; but it is of no importance to the physicists whether the institution has a good history department or not. The converse is equally true, so for research purposes I do not see that it makes much sense to talk about entire institutions.

I have time for only one more topic and that inevitably has to be rationalisation. The last few times I have heard Sir David Phillips speak in public, he has started by quoting the statement in the Robbins Report that no multi-subject university should have less than 5,000 or 6,000 students. No one has been so unkind as to ask him what practical advice he draws from this except perhaps that we should obtain a time machine and rerun the last twenty years rather more intelligently. It is certainly true that if the university system were suddenly handed over to ICI or GEC to run, the first thing they would do would be to close a dozen universities, so as to have what in their language I can only call production units of economical size. That option is not available to the UGC because it is politically unacceptable; indeed I think it would be politically unacceptable to any government and any conceivable Secretary of State for Education. Thus one of the UGC's major problems is that of providing in an increasingly parsimonious world a sensible future for small universities. In the long run one could hope to build them up to a more economic size but the only way of doing that is to have available a lot more funded student numbers; and the moment when the relevant age group is about to fall by 30 per cent over five years is the worst possible moment to be faced with this particular problem. What handicaps a small institution is not its overall smallness but the consequent smallness of its individual departments; this simultaneously means that they are undersupplied with expertise and that their staff have to work too hard in order to cover a syllabus whose size is independent of the number of students. A small university can be cost-effective and very distinguished if it limits its range of subjects. The most obvious example of this, though not the only one in the United Kingdom, is Essex. But it is not easy for a university to contract its range of subjects very much even if it is persuaded that that is necessary for its survival; it is also a pretty uphill task to persuade it since it is always in a position to appeal to the great traditions of the past – even if the past stretches back only twenty-five years. We have been trying to nudge small institutions in the right direction; in particular, we have been trying to nudge the small university institutions both in Wales and in Scotland into a much greater degree of co-operation. This will probably be helped if we are able, which I hope we shall be, to provide audio-visual links between them. That sort of remedy may not be ideal but we have to make the best we can of the situation in which we find ourselves; it is no good saying where we would have started if only we had been in an ideal world. Moreover, the existence of these small universities is a very considerable constraint on subject rationalisation because subject rationalis- ation tends to move staff from the small to the large institutions, and the small institutions cannot afford loss of student numbers. None the less, as you will know, we have a policy of subject rationalisation – or, to be more exact, several policies, because there is a diversity of subjects and different kinds of subject have to be handled in different ways. There are, for example, the subjects with small student demand, almost all of them non-laboratory subjects. There the important thing is to have some departments large enough to be centres of excellence; and because there is limited student demand, and a centre of excellence under the Thatcher government's funding regime needs a reasonable number of students to be adequately funded, small subject rationalisation has to be essentially a matter of concentration. Then there are the manpower-limited subjects. We have already reviewed one or two of these and we are in the middle of reviewing what is clearly going to be a most sensitive one. That is dentistry, where the Department of Health and Social Security tells us how many dentists it wants us to produce each year. Three years ago it asked us to cut numbers by 10 per cent, and last year they asked us to make another 10 per cent cut. It is fairly evident that it will never ask us to increase numbers again, so we are threatened with having uneconomically small dentistry departments.

The large humanities do not appear to be in need of rationalisation because the situation is reasonably satisfactory already. In this context I regard mathematics as a humanity because the critical tests are whether it needs expensive apparatus and whether research is done by teams or by individuals; on both these tests mathematics looks like history and not like physics. But in the large sciences research increasingly needs substantial teams and access to very expensive apparatus. A couple of years ago I would have said that such apparatus cost between a quarter of a million and half a million pounds. It now looks like costing between a quarter of a million and a million pounds, and these figures are going to continue to rise. Such pieces of apparatus are very impressive and will do an immense amount of work; but one cannot cut them up into ten pieces and give one of those pieces to each of ten universities. Thus if the UK is going to have internationally respected research in an area which needs expensive apparatus we are committed to concentrating that research very considerably so that adequate use can be made of these powerful but very expensive objects. There are exceptions to this because there are major devices which can be used remotely. Supercomputers are the most obvious example, and telescopes are another; but those are very exceptional. If we are to maintain world-class departments in these highly instrumented research areas there will have to be a considerable degree of concentration. How much depends on what is the minimum size of department that is likely to be able to be internationally distinguished and that really does vary from one subject to another. According to the Oxburgh Report on Earth sciences, a subject which perhaps demands the largest departments, the minimum is about thirty academic staff. As of now there are only two UGC-funded universities with a group of that size and only one of those two groups is actually outstanding; so that is a subject in which something fairly drastic will need to be done.

Part 2

The Papers

5

Reconstructing Higher Education Policy

Rob Cuthbert

Introduction

This paper has two broad aims. First, I propose briefly to explore the conceptual connections between values, policies and policy-making. Second, I plan to use the rudimentary conceptual framework so derived to reassess the policies expressed in the Department of Education and Science White Paper, *Higher Education: Meeting the Challenge* (DES 1987), and subsequently embodied in the Education Reform Bill. I will argue, in particular, that this reconstruction of higher education policy fails to be radical enough to achieve the access targets identified in the White Paper. Increasing access to higher education depends on redefining administrative boundaries to incorporate all post-secondary education within a more coherent structure, as Trow (1986) and others have argued.

Concepts

Too often, even in higher education, we talk about values and policies without examining exactly what we mean by those terms. So let me begin with some definitions, borrowed from Maurice Kogan's various writings.

On *values*, Kogan (1974, p. 97) says: 'I take a basic value to be a self-justificatory "ought" – a moral entity which requires no justification beyond the fact that its proponents are prepared to defend it as morally right and acceptable.' This is a helpful starting point, but this notion of 'value' alone is a 'flabby' concept which might sprawl across an argument if not disciplined within a framework which puts some boundaries around its use. Without a framework, arguments tend to degenerate into mere assertion and counter-assertion of values, for example: 'The Bill is welcome because it promotes choice', or 'This is a bad Bill because it promotes inequality.'

Kogan attempts to sharpen the concept of value by differentiating *basic* values from *secondary* values, the latter being 'concepts that carry the argument into the zone of consequences and instruments and institutions' (Kogan 1975, p. 54).

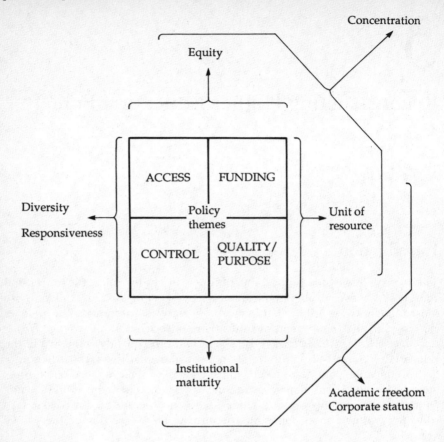

Figure 5.1

Such a distinction is, however, difficult to operationalise and may become circular. For the time being it is sufficient to use the notion of basic value as the end point of any argument or debate, where differences are reduced to the assertion of one set of values over another.

To this we need to add an action-based concept – *policy*. In Kogan's (1975, p. 55) words: 'Policies are the operational statements of values.' We have learnt from *Yes Minister* that it is politically convenient for each new policy to appear to spring to life from the spontaneous brilliance and deep concern of the Secretary of State. But policies have their antecedents; actions are connected with other actions; each policy builds on or removes from what has gone before. How, then, are we to understand the interconnectedness of policies?

Kogan's approach was to differentiate four *value bases* for policies: educational, economic, social and institutional. This has some intuitive plausibility, but it still builds an argument with sand – the values slip through your fingers and become something else as policy tides wash over events.

There are 'grand theories' of policy-making which deal with concertation of economic and political interests in the corporatist state, and develop the concept of 'policy community' to explain policy making behaviour. Crispin and Marslen-Wilson (1984) provide a useful critique of the applicability of such notions to educational policy-making. My ambition is much more limited: to find some middle-range explanations which look at the common substance of higher education policies. What questions do all policies deal with? What issues must they all address?

This was my starting-point – a desire to make better sense of what was happening in higher education policy-making, which seemed chaotic and confused, a maelstrom of access, quality, efficiency, autonomy, independence, choice, market forces, standards, privatisation, diversity, responsiveness, equity, institutional maturity . . . . How could all these things be comprehended? Some diagrammatic juggling led me to the representation in Figure 5.1. There seem to be four central issues which, in different combinations, underlie most if not all higher educational policy-making, and can therefore be used as the basic building blocks for analysis. The four issues, which in the diagram I label 'policy themes', are:

Access: who benefits from higher education and how many people benefit?
Funding: how much should the government spend on higher education, who else should pay for higher education, and how much?
Control: how is higher education activity regulated and by whom?[1]
Quality and purpose: how should we construe the nature and purposes of higher education and what standards should it meet?

I was aware, in juggling with these ideas, that there was some congruence with Kogan's four value bases; I had failed to realise my debt to Toby Weaver (1982) until I was reminded of it by McNay (1987). Weaver, of course, also identified four key questions – curriculum, access, structure and resources – in his elegant analysis of 'policy options for post-tertiary education'. The four themes are, of course, interrelated. Figure 5.1 is no more than a modest attempt to connect the themes to values and issues in recent higher education policies – a kind of *template* to lay over any policy of interest.

Thus, for example, diversity, a central concern of the binary policy, may be seen as depending on decisions about who should benefit from higher education, and how it should be controlled – that is, *access* and *control*. The unit of resource, Robert Jackson's 'metaphysical concept' much used in inter-sectoral comparisons, depends on decisions about standards (*quality*) and *funding*. The recurrent obsession of the Department of Education and Science (DES) with concentration of higher education in fewer and larger institutions can be construed in terms of *quality* and *funding*, but has obvious implications for *access*, and so on.

The Education Reform Bill

Let me now put my 'template' over the Education Reform Bill, the 'Gerbil'. (This creature is an interestingly ambiguous piece of symbolism. In the wild, gerbils survive in a hostile desert through having sharp teeth and being able to move very quickly. But caged gerbils are condemned to run on treadmills, endlessly dissipating energy, perhaps becoming leaner and fitter, but without ever making progress. Worse, in cramped conditions, gerbils will cannibalise their young!) Consider the contents of the Bill in terms of the four themes of quality, funding, control and access.

Quality

On *quality*, perhaps few would argue with the proposition that the Bill and the White Paper are instrumental and utilitarian in their assumptions about the nature and purposes of higher education. It is perhaps a little odd that a Government which lays so much stress on the rights of the individual should exclude individual growth and development from its statement of the purposes of higher education. I am not opposed to the idea of a 'useful education', but I would construe it perhaps rather more broadly than Christopher Ball (1985). To define quality as 'fitness for purpose' may be too narrowing: one crucial purpose of higher education is open-ended individual development, and this individualistic notion ultimately defies the simplistic application of collectivist managerialism, with its quantified objectives and measured accountability. There must be a balance of approaches, reflecting both preferred values and judgements about how the present proposals threaten (or not) those values. But the debate about quality and purpose fairly soon reduces to such assertions about basic values.

Funding

On *funding*, the White Paper tells us that 'Higher education is expensive' (this being the opening sentence in the chapter on quality!) and seeks a 'lessened dependence on public funds'. I would not personally object to some degree of user-supportedness in higher education funding, and it is certainly consistent with the economic/utilitarian notion of quality to encourage industry and commerce (perceived as clients) to pay more for the services they receive. But user-supported enterprises operating in a market rarely, if ever, hand over control of the enterprise to their users – they rely on exit, voice and loyalty to judge their success or failure (Hirschman 1970). So it is inconsistent to propose, as the Bill does, to hand over *control* to 'persons experienced in industry, commerce and the professions'.

Control

Control, I have argued, offers a fundamental choice between markets, bureaucratic and clan structures. Markets are efficient where the product exchanged is clearly specified, and price can adequately regulate the trans-action. Bureaucracies are efficient where a structure of legitimate authority is needed to minimise the costs of exchanging more ambiguously defined services. Clans are structures which depend on shared values to minimise the costs of transactions between individuals. The utility of the distinction is this: if you believe that higher education has a narrowly-defined purpose, then it will be consistent to believe also that the market will be an efficient form of control. So there is a deeper consistency in general government policy in terms of quality and control.

Finally, on control, the ultimate merging of the two proposed Funding Councils has been much mooted during this conference. The DES is reported to have explained the interim need for two bodies to the Treasury by using the analogy of Rugby League (the polytechnics and colleges) and Rugby Union (the universities) – different codes but similar games. This is a rich analogy indeed; consider:

- in rugby league, teams need fewer players to achieve the same result;
- scoring a try provides more points in rugby union;
- rugby league draws bigger crowds than rugby union;
- rugby union depends much more on the public schools for its raw material, whereas rugby league allows more ordinary working people to play;
- in each code, women have only recently been allowed to join in, and are still largely excluded from the big league;
- a lot of players in rugby league have two jobs, and see the game as a useful way of supplementing their main source of income;
- a lot of players in rugby union have a deep love of the game in spite of some mismanagement at local and national level;
- earning money in rugby league is a sign of success, but in rugby union it is still frowned on;
- in both codes, the bar is a major source of income!

Access

The White Paper's proposals on access were widely welcomed. It has also been noted that there are no parallel proposals for a commensurate increase in funding, despite the fact that provision for the new students is likely to be more rather than less expensive. In short, the inconsistency between access and funding aspects of the White Paper policies is well recognised.

There has been rather less comment on the problem, if such it be, that 'access' students are often drawn to the 'unfavoured' areas of humanities and social science. This is of course an *advantage*, because these disciplines are relatively cheaply provided – but there is nevertheless a further conflict between access and quality/purpose aspects of the policy.

There has been even less comment on an equally significant inconsistency – between the access and restructuring aspects of the policy. By removing polytechnics and colleges from local authority control the Bill will create a new boundary – administrative, not educational – between higher and further education. Though the effects of this change are a matter for speculation, such evidence as there is suggests that this change will disrupt links between further and higher education. When Napier College and Glasgow College of Technology transferred from local authority control to become Scottish central institutions, there was a significant breakdown in relationships with local further education colleges, which took some time to rebuild (Stevenson 1988). This was despite the relative goodwill which characterised the transfer, a state of affairs unlikely to be universally repeated in the English changes.

Nevertheless there will no doubt be many areas where higher education links with schools and colleges will be sustained and developed. The access targets will stand or fall on the success of those links. Christopher Ball (1987) has described non-advanced further education as 'the royal road to higher education', and Martin Trow (1986) has argued that if the British system is ever to become a mass system of higher education the essential step is to reconstrue *all* post-secondary education as higher.

The Thatcher government's reforms do nothing to promote this, indeed they hinder it. The proposed separation of the planning of full-time and part-time higher education outside the universities also increases the likelihood of academic apartheid between different kinds of higher education provided in different places for different people. There is, in brief, an overwhelming inconsistency between the proposals on access, and the proposals for quality and purpose, funding and control.

It is noticeable that the structural debate at this conference has been about whether, or when, the UFC and PCFC might merge. A genuine commitment to increasing access should pose a different structural question: when will a *third* Funding Council be established to deal with all non-advanced further education? Such a Council might perhaps be called the Local Authority Post-Secondary Education Council, to generate a suitably symbolic acronym (LAPSE). We might then look forward to a merger of all three Councils, followed by the establishment of an effective regional structure for funding and controlling higher education (redefined as post-secondary in the American sense).

It is unlikely that many particpants at this conference will take this suggestion seriously. There are many barriers to co-operation between further and higher education: ignorance of those in higher education about what further education is and does; higher education institutional cultures, values and attitudes; geographical; financial; political (for example, LEA opposition, in future); and credential (here the future work of the National Council for Vocational Qualifications at higher education level will be crucial). Of these perhaps the greatest barrier is ignorance. Despite the work done by increasing numbers of people in higher education to promote access, it remains true that these few are swimming against a strong tide of indifference or outright hostility in universities and polytechnics.

There is one other possible route to increasing access, which has also attracted relatively little attention. This is higher education on company or employers' premises, under employer control – what in the United States is known as the 'corporate classroom' (Eurich 1985). In the UK this form of provision is either underrepresented, undervalued or unnoticed. No doubt some of the learning in corporate classrooms should also be recognised within a new definition of higher education.

Conclusion

Taking a broad view of higher education policy over the last twenty years, using the simple policy 'template' proposed above, we can see a steady shift in emphasis. Where once we were concerned with bottom-up control, growth and effectiveness, qualitative assessments of performance, education and the individual in society, we are now concerned with top-down control, contraction and efficiency, quantitative assessments of performance, training and the worker in the economy. There has been, in other words, a shift in emphasis from access and quality to funding and control.

There may be a dangerous paradox lurking for the utilitarian tendency: if higher education is managed as if it were primarily aimed at promoting economic efficiency, even this objective might be defeated, for want of a more fruitful balance in emphases. And alongside this balance there should be a balance in terms of access. Tyrrell Burgess was wont to say that higher education is the vocational training of the middle classes, while vocational training is the higher education of the working classes. We should redefine higher education as post-secondary, and aim for higher education for everyone.

Note

1 The fundamental choice here is, I contend, between three forms of regulation or organisation: markets (regulated by prices); bureaucracies (regulated by legitimate authority); and clans (regulated by shared values). This argument and its implications are developed in Cuthbert (1987).

References

Ball, C. (1985) 'The triple alliance: what went wrong? what can be done?', *Oxford Review of Education*, 11 (3), 227–34.
Ball, C. (1987) 'The future provision of AFE in colleges with a substantial amount of non-advanced work', paper presented to the summer meeting of The Association of Colleges for Further and Higher Education, Norwich, 4–5 June.
Crispin, A. and Marslen-Wilson, F. (1984) *Education and the New Block Grant*, final report of an ESRC-funded research project, London University Institute of Education, Department of Educational Administration and Policy Studies in Education.
Cuthbert, R. E. (1987) 'Efficiency and the market mechanism in further and higher education' in H. Thomas and T. Simkins (eds), *Economics and the Management of Education: Emerging themes*, Barcombe, East Sussex, Falmer Press.
Department of Education and Science (1987) *Higher Education: Meeting the Challenge*, Cm. 114, London, HMSO.

Eurich, N. P. (1985) *Corporate Classrooms: The Learning Business*,Princeton, NJ, Carnegie Foundation for the Advancement of Teaching.

Hirschman, A. O. (1970) *Exit, Voice and Loyalty*, Cambridge, MA, Harvard University Press.

Kogan, M. (1974) 'Social policy and public organisational values, *Journal of Social Policy*, 3(2), 97–111.

Kogan, M. (1975) *Educational Policy-making*, London, George Allen & Unwin.

McNay, I. (1987) 'The emergence of the regional factor in the structure of higher education', paper presented to the SRHE Conference Restructuring Higher Education, December

Stevenson, W. (1988) 'The Scottish central institutions' in R. E. Cuthbert, (ed.), *Going Corporate*, Blagdon, Avon, The Further Education Staff College (Management in Colleges Series).

Trow, M. (1986) 'Academic standards and mass higher education', paper presented to the Higher Education International Conference 'Quality Assurance in First Degree Courses', Birmingham, 6 September.

Weaver, T. (1982) 'Policy options for post-tertiary education', *Higher Education Review*, 14(2), 9–18.

6

TVEI: A Major Secondary Sector Curriculum Initiative and its Consequences for Higher Education

Malcolm T. Deere

Introduction

The Technical and Vocational Education Initiative (TVEI) began its pilot phase in September 1983 in fourteen Local Education Authorities (LEAs). By September 1987 all but a handful of LEAs had started their pilot phase. By the same date eleven LEAs progressed to extending TVEI, and over half of the others had submitted proposals for extension.

The purpose of pilot TVEI was to test and explore ways of managing the education of fourteen- to eighteen-year-olds so that certain aims and criteria were met. These included the requirement that the scheme was for all abilities, that it should consist of coherent four-year programmes from fourteen to eighteen, and that more students should seek to acquire formal qualifications.

TVEI is therefore about curriculum, about management, and, subsequently, it has also come to be about in-service training (INSET). Its planning and delivery has remained in the hands of the LEAs, working in partnership with the Manpower Services Commission (MSC). It has rapidly evolved into an educational philosophy that has not been narrow – as early criticism obviously feared – but one that has added new dimensions to general and integrated education.

Curriculum

While, initially, TVEI applied to a minority slice of curriculum time, it has spread continuously into a larger number of fields, so that the terms 'technical' and 'vocational' have been liberally interpreted. It has achieved in terms of *structure*, a move towards larger cores, extending beyond mathematics and English into information technology, business and technological awareness and capability, and integrated extra-classroom experience. This has resulted in fewer options, better articulation between core and options, and more cross-curricular activity.

More radically, there has been greatly increased interest in modular or unitary structures, stemming from the advantages of shorter-term learning goals, easier updating of syllabus material, logistically improved ability for in-service training of teachers, and, importantly, flexibility in constructing student programmes.

The reason why the case for modularity still remains, to some extent, 'not proven' probably lies in the potential disadvantages. These include the risk of lack of coherence, more complex accreditation, additional marking load, and therefore additional expense.

Lastly, in terms of structure, there has been the adoption by schools of the kind of curriculum framework used in further education, for example City & Guilds of London and certain BTEC programmes.

Accreditation

Under this heading we have seen a better matching of assessment development to curriculum assessment. It is important to emphasise that this has been largely within established arrangements – there have been few new 'courses'. In part this has been reflected in the recognition of new teaching and learning styles, and supported self-study. This move has been assisted by the General Certificate of Secondary Education (GCSE) rather than hindered by it. Additionally, INSET for TVEI has been in harmony with INSET for GCSE.

This thrust has both prompted and been benefited by developments within the Examination Boards themselves. A practical outcome has been recognition of the need for more appropriately trained examiners, so as to spread more widely the responsibility for the quality of assessment.

As an example of less-expected outcomes, the contract-based relationship between the MSC and the LEAs has had a positive effect on LEA–school relationships. In terms of accreditation, this has focused the LEAs' attention and resulted in improved development and training. This has in turn tended to cause the Boards to recognise their own broader role.

Students

The increased attention paid to learner-centred learning, supported self-study and extra-classroom work has further developed interest in profiling and records of achievement. This goes far beyond providing a recording document, but operates as a prompt to negotiation and to create feedback to teaching. It also emerges as a potentially valuable managing and planning tool. While this requires considerable supporting INSET, it does result in better-motivated, discriminating and independent students.

Management

Much of the foregoing amounts to curriculum management – indeed, the more flexible the curriculum becomes, the more powerful its management needs to be. Beyond that, there is evidence of other management-type development. First, there are new institutional linkages; schools are planning curriculum together, and departments are joining together to deliver it. The further education and schools sectors are also collaborating: in joint delivery pre-sixteen as well as post-sixteen; in joint INSET; and in resource-sharing. Second, the basis of the TVEI programme is different. Funding is targeted against clear and mutually developed objectives, and it is made available through a contract. There is ample evidence that this idea of contract funding has filtered down into LEA–school relationships.

The sixteen to eighteen phase, and progression

It is against this background that I now explore the sixteen to eighteen phase, and begin to consider its implications for higher education. Most LEAs delayed consideration of the sixteen to eighteen phase, and acceleration has been slow. Nevertheless, there are strong undercurrents. There is, as noted, a clear requirement for programmes to be continuous and progressive from fourteen to eighteen. Joint planning, joint INSET, and joint delivery materially assist this aim, but the aim itself needs elaboration.

Progression includes the following strands:

- Core studies, including extra-classroom work, need to carry on beyond sixteen.
- Teaching and learning styles, including student-centred learning, have to be taken forward.
- Curriculum frameworks and structures offer a good vehicle for progression. This is especially important for GCSE, where a similar ethos and arrangement are necessary.
- Profiling and records of achievement offer the kind of opportunity to mark progression that we cannot afford to miss.
- As students' attitudes develop, so will their expectations, and they are the better equipped to express those expectations.

As these strands of progression begin to inform post-sixteen development, so the shape of the curriculum begins to emerge. First, there is a core. It is likely to contain pastoral and academic guidance to a greater extent (based on profiling as a concept). It will include the development of 'awareness' and 'literacy', economic and technological. It will also extend to the development of basic skills, particularly those to do with information, and of capabilities, such as working in groups, and connected with the concept of enterprise. Lastly, in some places the capability will extend to the handling of large-scale assignments.

In terms of the structure within which the core will operate, modularity is receiving cautious support, for the reasons given earlier. In one LEA, units are being used to build a limited number of A, and AS, levels. In another, a partial modular structure is being developed, based on 60 per cent core within, say, science, with flexible extensions beyond the core.

In yet another Authority the Certificate of Pre-Vocational Education (CPVE) is being used as an overarching structure to provide complementary General Studies components for A-level 'packages', and to begin to cross-relate the individual A levels. In the North West of England, a group of LEAs is working with a university to provide 'enhancement' to A-level programmes.

Such enhancement, or the desire to link core studies more closely into mainstream courses, requires proper curriculum planning and control. One relevant device is 'analysis and exemption'; this compares – in matrix form – the required elements of a student's complete programme with the courses that the student intends to follow. The outcomes of this potentially very powerful exercise are as follows:

- it maximises the usefulness of existing provision;
- it identifies the need for compensating elements, and enhancement oppor- tunity;
- it develops academic tutoring as well as pastoral tutoring;
- it deepens the subject teacher's insights into specialist courses;
- it begins to identify overlap and mutual reinforcement between, say, parallel A levels.

These developments are existing, but they require two parallel support systems. Staff need development to increase, first, confidence, and second, competence; to handle more appropriate teaching styles, and to manage the flexible curriculum. Students require better arrangements to manage the transition at sixteen (and this has to begin well before sixteen), together with adequate guidance.

Extension

The extension of TVEI increases the scale of the operation. The developments so far described are to be delivered to all secondary institutions within the LEA, for complete year groups from fourteen to eighteen, and across the curriculum.

The contract-based funding has to be the subject of bids, judged with rigour at least equal to that of the original pilot proposals. In the context of this paper, such bids need to include:

- a compliance with the government Paper *Better Schools*;
- a compliance with the MSC/DES TVEI Extension Curriculum Criteria, which extend beyond *Better Schools*;
- an *entitlement* curriculum, particularly with respect to science and tech- nology, and to certain core skills;
- built-in inducement to cross-institutional working;
- continuity into the sixteen to eighteen phase, not least to meet student expectations developed pre-sixteen.

More recently, it has become necessary for LEAs and institutions to be able to manage the curriculum to meet the requirements of the national curriculum. In that connection, it is worth noting that the Bill refers to reserve powers in respect of the sixteen to eighteen phase.

Experience so far, with a number of LEA proposals for extension, points to some future radical change. They relate to consortium working, and to very significant changes in curriculum structure (for example, larger cores, entitlements, and ways of controlling those entitlements). Such structural changes are bound to progress into the sixteen to eighteen phase, for a number of different reasons, some of them (for example, the Higginson Committee on the future of A levels) not directly connected to TVEI. There is evidence that the Higginson Committee is listening to, and noting, LEA news on the curriculum.

The implications for higher education

The curriculum changes so far described now show clear evidence of successful innovation. As one year at a time is introduced to such innovation, it will not be long before the eighteen-plus age group is affected. Quite apart from this, if the participation rate beyond eighteen in full-time education is increased, this alone has implications. In any event, one does not expect dramatic change in respect of paper qualifications.

Underpinning this movement are the following strands:

- the concept of *progression* will not be allowed to stop at the age of eighteen;
- ideas of *induction* and *transition*, now clearly emphasised at the age of sixteen, have just as much validity at eighteen;
- curriculum structural change, aimed at better coherence in whole programmes (rather than say, simply sets of A levels) cannot be ignored;
- the broader base of *total* assessment available at eighteen (for example, record of achievement, the results of assignment work, and student views on the results of that work) offers to higher education more evidence on which to base selection;
- such evidence can be linked to the criteria of students' attitudes, outlooks, and expectations, and their capacity for independent study.

Finally, it is worth nothing that, as *genuine* fourteen to eighteen programmes emerge, a degree of 'non-age relation' will also emerge.

Some targets for further development in higher education

As a result of the curriculum and management thrusts discussed here, certain targets can be identified. Most of them have come, not so much from TVEI, as from discussions within higher education itself.

- The basis of targeted funding against mutually agreed objectives (the basis of TVEI) is extendable into higher education. Indeed, the very recently revealed Enterprise programme in higher education is just such an example.

- Additionally, there is scope for the funding on this basis of active curriculum development at undergraduate level, together with the associated staff development that this implies.
- Thus, the exploration of a programme of core studies at undergraduate level offers some promise to some universities and polytechnics, beyond that implicit in the Enterprise programme.
- Such a core programme could be the first manifestation of positive action to broaden the base of first-year undergraduate studies;
- A major feature of TVEI has been vertical planning, whereby schools and colleges reciprocate in the planning of fourteen to sixteen and sixteen to eighteen programmes. This could be extended usefully to bring together sixteen to eighteen and post-eighteen deliverers, working to improve progression across the age-eighteen gap. To take just one example, higher education experience of modularity would be very valuable to schools and colleges.
- Further exploration of credit transfer (as so far carried out by the CNAA, for instance) would be valuable. There is the reservation, similar to that for modularity, that coherence and longitudinal progression would need to be preserved.
- One would wish to see a shift of admissions policy on to a broader base, to match the breadth of development between fourteen and eighteen. A first step might be the development of targetted staff training for admissions tutors.

To sum up, we are seeing major changes within the fourteen to eighteen phase of education. This is structural, and it is going to develop further still. Our central targets have to be the increasing of the participation rate post-eighteen, and the achievement of linked planning between sixteen and twenty-one, to match and overlap the work in hand that is concerned with fourteen- to eighteen-year-olds.

7

Contracting and the Funding of Research in Higher Education

Anthony J. Pointon

Introduction

With the issuing of the government's higher education White Paper of April 1987 (Department of Education and Science 1987a) and the discussion document of the Advisory Board for the Research Councils (ABRC 1987) the following month, it appears certain that some restructuring of the system of funding research in higher education cannot be long delayed.

Although the White Paper reaffirmed the government's intention to continue to fund research in higher education, it was the concept of contracts introduced in that Paper which raised the questions about the future method of that funding. The possible forms of contract – by course, by programme area or by institution – were discussed in a Consultative Paper issued in May 1987 (DES 1987b). It was clear from this that the wish of the government was to change the funding of higher education away from a system of grants designed to maintain institutions which then, in return, educated undergraduates and postgraduates. Contracts would represent instead an exchange of funding for the delivery of a given number and type of qualified persons; this concept is implied, though not spelled out explicitly, in the Education Reform Bill, published in November 1987, major parts of which followed from the White Paper.

The question which derived from the contracting principle was whether such a system could encompass all the activities in higher education, research in particular. The Consultative Paper (DES 1987b) itself admitted that the 'institutions' role in relation to the advancement of scholarship or the early exploration of new curricula is susceptible neither to very precise specification, nor – in the short term – to the establishment of tests of performance', and went on to conclude that 'while contracts will play a major part in regulating relations between the funding bodies and institutions, that relationship cannot be wholly contractual'. These statements suggest that there will or could be two distinct types of funding – one formula- or contract-based, the other based on perceptions of institutional need (and possibly institutional performance).

This concept would be very different from the system which currently operates through the National Advisory Body for Public Sector Higher Education (NAB), where the funding is, at least theoretically, on a straight per-capita basis – with no base funding for institutions or departments or, in general, for identified activities. In mathematical terms, the total funding F for the teaching function under NAB can be written as

$$F = \sum_i n_i f_i = \sum_i n_i w_i f = Nf \qquad (1)$$

where f is a unit of resource, n_i is the number of students of type i, w_i is the weighting factor (which runs from 0.15 for an evening humanities student to 2.1 for a full-time computing student), and $N = \sum_i n_i w_i$.

A problem which arises for the funding of research and scholarship on the basis of provision separate from the contracts for teaching is that these two activities are regarded as the *sine quiberus non* of teaching quality across an institution. Indeed the Robbins Report in 1963 claimed: 'There is no borderline between teaching and research'; while, twenty-one years later, in a policy statement on research, the Council for National Academic Awards (1984) stated:

> Institutions are, therefore, expected to continue to develop forms of research and comparable activities at a level and of a quality appropriate for the support of all their CNAA courses. For Honours and taught Master's degree courses such development is essential and without it academic approval may be withdrawn.

(This statement, since CNAA is the main validating body for approximately half of higher education, has to be taken as a fact: withdrawal of approval for courses has occurred on this basis.)

Before an attempt is made to consider the future funding of research, it is necessary to review the present situation.

The nature of research

A major difficulty in discussing research in higher education is the dual nature of the activity which, in the absence of a precise definition, ensures misunderstanding. In the White Paper (DES 1987a) research has three strands: basic research (concerned with the advancement of knowledge); strategic research (which has potential for application in wealth creation); and applied research (which is directly related to wealth creation or improvement in society). On the other hand, CNAA (1984) gives a list of activities under this heading – fundamental research; applied research; consultancy; professional practice; scholarship; creative work; and related activities – all of which could be included, without being derogatory, as contributing to staff development.

Because scholarship is wholly necessary to sustain liveliness and quality in teaching, while research *per se* can be considered as a separate activity, it is possible to have a contrary view that, in some cases, research may actually detract from the teaching function. Flood Page (1987) has posed the question, for example, 'should colleges be places of learning rather than of teaching and research?' The 1985 Green Paper on higher education in the 1990s (DES 1985), stated, in rebuttal of claims made by the University Grants Committee (UGC), that 'there is no evidence that all academic staff must engage in research'. There was no reference to the need, or otherwise, for all staff to engage in scholarly activity, either in the section on 'Academic Standards' or in that on 'Staff Development'. (The Leverhulme Seminars in 1982 also failed to justify the need for all academics to participate in research *qua* research. ABRC (1987) appears to question whether the British research effort requires the participation of all academics.)

An attempt is made in Figure 7.1 to illustrate the overlap between the various activities which contribute to scholarship in higher education. The contribution of scholarship (including those parts of other activities which are subsumed in scholarly activity) to the teaching function is taken for granted. In particular, the contribution of research to the training of research personnel is stressed. The interrelation between research and scholarship does not mean that they should share the same funding mechanism, or that they should each be expected to have the same effect on the teaching function.

The present funding of research

Dual funding

Dual funding for research exists in the polytechnics and similar colleges as well as in the universities, in principle if not to the same extent.

In the polytechnics, a 1971 CNAA survey concluded that the proportion of the total budget spent by institutions on research ranged from 0.7 per cent to 15 per cent, although the range may have reflected in part institutions' perceptions of the questions asked. In 1979, the Committee of Directors of Polytechnics (CDP) found a range of 6–10 per cent (Clayton 1987). For the universities, a UGC survey in 1979 concluded that 30 per cent of the total funding received from the UGC was expended on research (Clayton 1987): the ABRC divided this figure further, taking 15 per cent as being for research *qua* research and the other 15 per cent for scholarship. Clayton (1987) showed that, for 1985–6, the universities expended around 40 per cent of their UGC grant on research, mainly on staff time and the provision of 'well-found' laboratories. (Some departments estimate a spend of around 60 per cent on research.)

Clayton's survey for the polytechnics showed a spend of about 10 per cent of the NAB funds, with some departments having a figure of about 15 per cent; most of the expenditure was on staff time. (For the higher education colleges, the research spend was less than for the polytechnics.) Clayton found that research expenditure accounted for considerable sums in all areas of the budget, as is shown in Table 7.1.

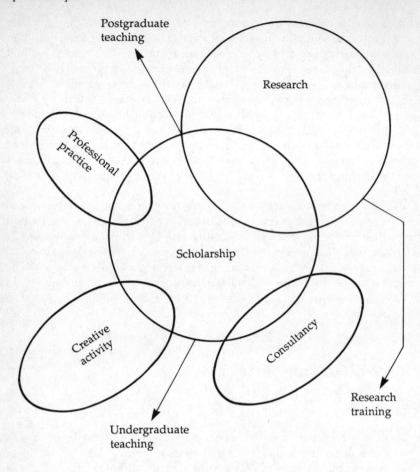

Figure 7.1   Interaction of the various activities

Table 7.1   *Percentage Expenditure Attributed to Research*

	University	*Polytechnic*	*HE College*
Computing	73	10	3
Library	50	10	5
Premises	40	7	2
Administration	38	4	1

Source: Clayton (1987)

NAB

For the year 1985–6, the NAB (1984) proposed that the sum of £20 million should be set aside for a 'research initiative' whereby money would be allocated for specific research projects in institutions under its aegis. In the event, £2.5 million was allocated (or 0.4 per cent of budget) and this was to be used for selected projects in the areas of science or technology or production which were industry-related (*Bulletin of the NAB*, Spring 1985). Twenty-one institutions benefited from the allocation, the most favoured receiving £150,000. In particular, the funds were not to be used for the support of projects linked to the teaching function (since the NAB Research Group held the view that the function of research of 'sustaining the quality of teaching should be expected to be funded by the basic pool allocations to institutions' – *Bulletin of the NAB*, Spring 1985); nor were they to be used to supplement capital allocations, so that no item costing more than £6,000 could be purchased, even though the NAB had referred to the level of capital provision as a 'disgraceful state of affairs'.

The difference between the sums allocated by the NAB and the costs of the research projects proposed for funding meant that successful institutions had to choose between funding about half of their proposed projects in full or spreading their allocation to sustain and enhance the general research activity. It is of note that institutions which followed the second course reported (in private communications) increased success in the attraction of external funding, as if some multiplier operated in the generation of research funds; this point will be discussed below.

It is estimated that in 1988–9, about 1 per cent of the NAB budget will be dedicated to selected research programmes (as extrapolated from the NAB figures in the *Bulletin of the NAB*, Summer 1987) and this will represent some £30 per full-time equivalent (FTE) student across the whole sector. Although the funding is still relatively small – and may be considered to be allocated away from scholarship towards research – its purpose as a declaration of intent is clear.

External funding

There are three sources of external funding of research in higher education: charitable trusts; commercial interests (among which must now be included government departments); Research Councils (which form the second arm of dual funding). The Science and Engineering Research Council (SERC) accounts for some 75 per cent of all research council funding. Its 1986–7 *Annual Report* shows that, at 31 March 1987, the value of research grants current in the universities was £316 million: the corresponding figure in the public sector, including the Scottish central institutions, was £21 million, which, as a proportion, represents an increase of 50 per cent over five years.

The distribution of grants to universities shows a considerable skew, with about 70 per cent of the grants going to 15 institutions. While the polytechnics only receive 4 per cent of the total number of *research* studentships, compared

Table 7.2 *Recurrent UGC and Research Income for Selected Universities, 1983–4*

University	UGC	RC	Other research
Leeds	3,947	296	631
Leicester	3,740	436	552
Liverpool	4,801	353	505

Source: Answers to Parliamentary Questions 37–8, 3 December 1985

Table 7.3 *Recurrent NAB and Research Income for Selected Polytechnics, 1983–4*

Polytechnic	NAB	RC and other
Leeds	2,067	35
Leicester	2,253	107
Liverpool	2,145	–

Source: As Table 7.2

with 95 per cent for the universities, they receive 20 per cent of the *advanced course* studentships which generally provide for taught Master's courses.

A comparison between the base funding and the total external research funding can be taken from Parliamentary answers for universities and polytechnics separately in terms of the funding per student. Tables 7.2 and 7.3 give the information correlated for 1983–4. Once again the question appears to be whether there is here a multiplier between base funding and externally negotiated contracts: there appears to have been no research on this question.

The contribution of externally funded research to the teaching function

It tends to be taken as axiomatic by researchers (and others) in higher education that research of all kinds makes a positive definite contribution to the quality of teaching. The existence of dual funding in the universities illustrates this belief. The NAB accepted the view of its Research Group that one of the justifications of research was 'its importance in sustaining the quality of the teaching activity' (*Bulletin of the NAB*, Spring 1985) and this echoed the view of CNAA (1984).

It is possible to consider the contribution of externally funded research to the teaching function under two heads. The first of these is the *indirect contribution*. Where there is a rapidly developing subject or discipline, external contracts may prove to be the only way in which academics can keep abreast of their subjects; such contracts may therefore represent a considerable subsidy to the teaching function. The second is the *direct contribution*. There are five direct contributions which external contracts may typically make to teaching, namely:

the contribution of research staff to teaching; the contribution of research students to laboratory supervision; the contribution of research technicians to honours projects; the contribution which research equipment may make (after a delay) to the relevance of laboratory teaching; and the contribution to the training of research personnel. (There may be negative contributions if the research activity actually distracts staff from the provision of teaching and from the pursuit of updating which can require a substantial part of non-teaching time in some subject areas.) The Committee of Vice-Chancellors and Principals (CVCP 1972) produced a survey which, *inter alia*, showed that research staff gave 30 per cent of their time to teaching.

Her Majesty's Inspectors identified in 1984 a shortage of scientific teaching equipment in institutions, having seen 'examples . . . of research equipment which had been applied to undergraduate laboratory teaching thereby introducing sophisticated instrumentation and measuring techniques' (DES 1984a). (A similar assessment was made in an HMI report on science teaching (DES 1984b).)

A more quantitative survey was carried out by the Association of University Teachers at Bristol University (AUT 1984) in which it was estimated that external contracts contributed around 25 per cent of their value, either immediately or after a delay, to the teaching activity (not including any charges for overheads or profit). The survey did not take into account the indirect contribution, nor the subsidy which the contract may have received from premises, library provision, well-found laboratories and academic staff time: however, it is clear that there is a non-negligible contribution from external contracts to the teaching activity. (The Secretary of State, in a speech on 30 October 1987, has given the assurance that such contributions to the institution's funds will not be set off against their income derived from UFC or PCFC (DES Press Release 322/87).)

Against the positive aspect of external contracts in general, some institutions have found that large research council grants may be too expensive in terms of the subsidy which they require, particularly in terms of the running and maintenance of sophisticated equipment.

The future of research funding in higher education

The funding of teaching in higher education has largely taken place on the basis of contracts over the last few years. In the case of the NAB, funding has been substantially based on Equation (1) above, with little provision for base or contingency funding. (In that equation, the unit of resource has been calculated, not on the basis of the sum(s) needed to maintain quality, but by dividing a politically decided quantum of money by a politically determined (weighted) number of students. The task of the CNAA and HMI has been to validate that calculation from the point of view of whatever quality results.) The system used by the UGC is not so public and involves additionally an assessment of the amount of research funding an institution within its remit deserves on the basis of past performance.

With the introduction of contracting, the question arises how the actual costs of educating a graduate will be determined and, from the point of view of the present paper, how the cost of scholarly activity (or research) to support the teaching function will be estimated. In deciding whether there will be any funding for research/scholarship at all, the differing implications of the Education Reform Bill and of ABRC (1987) must be examined.

In the Bill, a duty is laid symmetrically on the Universities Funding Council (UFC) and the Polytechnics and Colleges Funding Council (PCFC) with regard to research. For the UFC, Section 92(5)(a) imposes a duty for 'the provision of education and the undertaking of research by universities' while Section 93(5)(a) requires funding by PCFC for 'the provision of education and the undertaking of research by institutions within the PCFC sector'. Additionally, the new higher education corporations which will run institutions under the PCFC shall have power 'to carry out research and to publish the results of the research' (Section 85 (1)(c)).

In their White Paper (DES 1987a), the government 'recognises that a system of contracting must be so designed as to avoid damage to aspects of the work of institutions, such as the advancement of learning, which cannot be readily embraced by specific contractual commitments'. (It has already been mentioned that the Consultative Paper (DES 1987b) extended this acknowledgment to scholarship.) The problem posed in the area of scholarship and research by contract funding was referred to by the Secretary of State in a speech to the CVCP on 30 October 1987 (DES Press Release 322/87) when he said: 'In particular, contracting must not jeopardise the pursuit of research and scholarship. Nor should it be of a kind that deprives universities of the margin of flexibility they need to seize new opportunities for teaching and research.'

The possibility which emerges of funding scholarship and research separately from the contracts for teaching poses the question whether these activities are truly interdependent. If the teaching process depends for its effectiveness and quality on the scholarly activity of the academic staff, then contracts must take that fact into account. Otherwise the funding of scholarship can be arbitrary and without reference to the needs of students.

Here the ABRC (1987) proposals for the categorisation of universities (and presumably other institutions not mentioned by ABRC but which account for just over half of all undergraduate teaching) are significant. The idea of dividing institutions into those which have advanced research facilities across all disciplines (Type R), those which have no advanced research facilities (Type T) and those which are 'mixed' (Type X) appears to make assumptions about the distribution of high-grade research which are not sustained by the assessments of the UGC: it also appears to rest solely on the needs of laboratory-based research (and expensive research at that) and to ignore the non-interaction within institutions of research in different disciplines.

However, the definition of the Type T institution as one 'offering undergraduate and MSc teaching with associated scholarship and research activity but without advanced research facilities' does not bring it into conflict with the concept of contract funding provided that the contracts are for integrated provision of that 'scholarship and research activity'. The three-way classification only becomes relevant if research and scholarship are to be subjects of contracts separate from those for teaching: then there would be introduced a degree of arbitrariness and inflexibility which would effectively undermine the purpose of the contracting principle.

If, outside of the contracting system, the Research Councils decided to set up in association with higher education institutions specialist centres which they funded entirely, then this could be done in a flexible manner in terms of future use of staff while, at the same time, the Councils would be able to know the exact cost of the programmes which they were funding.

A possible funding system

In determining the funding system which will include provision for scholarship/ research related to teaching, it is necessary that institutions preparing contracts shall have regard to the need for accountability for both internal (UFC/PCFC) funds and external funds; the need to include provision for scholarship but not for research *qua* research; the need to allow flexibility to the Research Councils; and the need to ensure that the higher education system remains in being both economically and in terms of quality. (Although the government may adopt a customer-orientated stance towards higher education, all actual statements indicate the wish to maintain the system in being at a high quality and a high level of competitiveness internationally.)

The drawing up of a contract would need then to take account of five elements of cost: funding for the institution, f_I; funding for department i, f_D^i; funding for course j, f_C^j; funding for lecturer k, f_L^k; and funding for student m, f_S^m; where student m may be full-time or part-time, undergraduate or postgraduate – although, naturally, groups of students will be funded together. In calculating the contracted sum for the institution, Equation (1) would be replaced by

$$F = f_I + \sum_i f_D^i + \sum_j f_C^j + \sum_k f_L^k + \sum_m f_S^m \qquad (2)$$

Equation (2) would allow for marginal costs, whether greater or less than the average costs, to be estimated. Although, in principle, the funding for research and scholarship to support the teaching function could be included within any of the elements f_I to f_S, it is the funding of the lecturers which would be normal commercial practice: commercial concerns make provision for the updating and development of their activities through support given to their staff. By funding scholarship through f_L, the resources for this purpose will be identified and there will not be short-term fluctuations in the investment in quality as student numbers change year on year.

It is possible that the government for its part will wish to transpose the funding formula into one more closely resembling Equation (1), perhaps even with the number of students (input) replaced by the number of graduates (output). However, if managers do not have the information on which to assess their real costs, then competing institutions risk academic if not economic bankruptcy.

The advantages of the proposed system, that is, including scholarship with the contract system, are that: the true cost of the teaching can be assessed; the true cost of research projects can be known; enterprising institutions can enhance their status and their level of research activity; there will be flexibility in the research status of institutions; and external research contracts can be costed against their benefit to the teaching activity. The alternative will be to continue that degree of arbitrariness which led the authors of the Green Paper (DES 1985) to explain that some institutions cost more than others 'by virtue of more generous provision and land, premises, staffing and equipment'.

References

Advisory Board for the Research Councils (1987) *A Strategy for the Science Base*, London, HMSO.
Association of University Teachers (1984) *Contribution of External Research Contracts to Teaching*, Bristol, AUT.
Clayton, K. (1987) 'The measurement of research expenditure in higher education', University of East Anglia, February.
Committee of Vice-Chancellors and Principals (1972) *Report of Enquiry into Use of Academic Staff Time*, London, CVCP.
Council for National Academic Awards (1984) *Research and Related Activities: A Policy Statement*, London, CNAA.
Department of Education and Science (1963) *Higher Education*, the Report of the Robbins Committee, Cmnd 2154, London, HMSO.
DES (1984a) *Engineering in Polytechnics*, a report by Her Majesty's Inspectorate, London, HMSO.
DES (1984b) *Research in Science in the Polytechnics in Relation to the Undergraduate Experience*, a report by Her Majesty's Inspectorate, London, DES.
DES (1985) *The Development of Higher Education into the 1990s*, Cmnd 9524, London, HMSO.
DES (1987a) *Higher Education: Meeting the Challenge*, Cm. 114, London, HMSO.
DES (1987b) *Contracts between the Funding Bodies and Higher Education Institutions*, Consultative Paper, London, DES.
Flood Page, C. (1987) 'Digging up the roots: Some unanswered questions', paper presented to SRHE Conference 'Restructuring Higher Education', December.
Leverhulme Seminars (1982) *Research into Higher Education Monographs*, Guildford, SRHE.
National Advisory Body for Public Sector Higher Education (1984), Private communication, Summer.

8

Selective Funding of Research and Development: A Case Study of CNAA's Development Fund

Alan Crispin and Jeffrey Weeks

Introduction

Barely a week passes without one reference in the higher education media to selectivity in the funding of research. Selectivity may be defined either as choosing specific areas or issues as worthy of investigation or, alternatively, identifying certain institutions as designated research institutions in comparison with others (Advisory Board for the Research Councils 1987). Of these two approaches, the Development Fund of the Council for National Academic Awards (CNAA) concerns the former and this is reflected in the particular emphasis of this paper.

It is sometimes forgotten that selectivity is not an invention of the past year or so, designed to signal the imminent arrival of the proposed funding councils (Department of Education and Science 1987). Research councils and most funding agencies have often operated partly on the basis of selectivity: for example, the initiative by the former Social Science Research Council (SSRC) to examine central–local government relations between the late 1970s and early 1980s or the recent directed programmes of the Science and Engineering Research Council (SERC) in areas like information technology. Such initiatives have often been accompanied by guidance, albeit sparse for fear of offending academic autonomy, into the sorts of issue the funders consider to be important.

More recently, however, the issuing of very *detailed* briefs inviting researchers to tender have become more common; the *Enterprise in Higher Education* initiative of the Manpower Services Commission (MSC 1987) is a striking recent example of this genre. Such briefs specify the precise area or issue and may outline the objectives, purpose and rationale for the study as well as procedures for applying. The CNAA, through its Development Services Registry, has also deliberately adopted this approach, particularly since autumn 1985 – that is, from the setting up of its Development Fund. As an approach it is not without dangers, some of which will be outlined later. Yet despite such dangers it is argued here that selectivity is not merely an inevitable response to diminishing resources but also an approach that has inherent strengths.

The CNAA's involvement in developmental work

The Development Fund: Background

In 1981 the CNAA decided to engage directly in developmental work in order to monitor and evaluate its policies and practices; to assemble and analyse information and data relating to pertinent issues; to carry out pilot studies to underpin new policies and procedures; to develop proposals for research and developmental projects; and to inform itself of relevant projects (and their results) undertaken elsewhere. These activities led to a number of publications and workshops.[1]

This work was significantly expanded by the establishment in December 1984 of a Development Fund covering the period 1985–8. The Fund is primarily intended for educational development initiatives in polytechnics and colleges which result in improvements in the standard of courses and which are of direct and substantial benefit to institutions. To oversee the Fund a Development Fund Sub-committee (DFS) was formed in 1985 with members drawn from institutions, industry and other major interests.[2] Further details of this initiative are contained within an interim review report of the Fund (CNAA 1987). The work supported by the Fund built naturally on that already under way. In particular a number of (then) existing applied research projects had a developmental orientation and it was this aspect that the Development Fund was created to enhance, though it was recognised that an element of applied research would be retained. For these purposes £540,000 was to be set aside annually, deriving from the interest on £6 million.

Response to the Development Fund

It was clear from the first announcement of the Fund that there was an extensive interest in conducting applied research and development work in and on PSHE. In response to an open invitation for outline proposals in March 1985, some 580 were received, covering a wide range of topics and ranging in proposed cost from a few hundred to several hundred thousand pounds.

Evidence of the vitality of ideas in institutions has continued to grow. This is borne out by substantial responses to the various other initiatives announced by DFS as well as a regular flow of enquiries and unsolicited proposals from institutions and researchers. By the end of 1987 around 850 proposals had been processed of which roughly one in nine received approval.

Faced with such a response, processes for selecting projects for funding became crucial. Applications needed, of course, to contribute to or underpin the

CNAA's general policies and priorities. Rather than simply reacting to each proposal as received, it was decided to proceed by selecting issues or areas for priority support. This decision led to a sequence of other developments which in their totality represent no less than a *complete project system* from the design to the dissemination phase. The uniqueness of this approach resides not in any single component but rather in the total package as developed. The description and analysis of this project system, predicated upon selectivity, constitutes the core of this paper.

The Project System

Essentially the system constructed may be represented as follows:

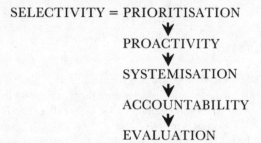

SELECTIVITY = PRIORITISATION
PROACTIVITY
SYSTEMISATION
ACCOUNTABILITY
EVALUATION

Prioritisation

The initial 580 project proposals, referred to above, constituted a data base which allowed the identification of possible projects and sources of expertise. They provided data for a detailed examination of key issues and problems as identified in and by institutions (overwhelmingly public sector). All proposals were classified according to quality, cost and areas of interest. This information was related in turn to major issues for the future of higher education identified in a Green Paper (DES 1985), the report of the Lindop Committee (Committee of Enquiry 1985), and the CNAA's own policy statements over the previous seven years. On the basis of this exercise, and its own views and experience, DFS was able to identify priority areas, develop projects with individual proposers, and plan further initiatives. Perhaps not surprisingly, therefore, only five of the original 580 proposals were funded immediately.

Briefly, the priority areas thus identified covered access; open learning; aspects of teaching, learning and curriculum development; credit accumulation and transfer; assessment; data bases on students in higher education; internal validation and evaluation processes; and higher education and work. It was agreed that these would be subject to review and revision in the light of changing circumstances. The proposals in DES (1987) confirmed to a large degree the appropriateness of the above priority areas.

A proactive policy

Having established priorities there emerged the adoption of a proactive policy rather than one of simply reacting to each proposal as submitted. This policy involved a close interaction between proposers, members of DFS and CNAA officers. Eventually, the following basic pattern of initiating projects emerged:

(a) identification by DFS and project committees of the need for work to be done, data to be gathered, etc.;
(b) drafting a project brief;
(c) tendering the brief to CNAA-related institutions;
(d) selection of successful applicant(s);
(e) determining any conditions or objectives to be attached to the project before funding is confirmed and negotiating with project teams their response to these conditions.

Systematisation

Processes, procedures and mechanisms inevitably have to be systematised. This has occurred both formally and informally. Regarding the former, the system developed is of a conventional nature – that is, 'vertical' or hierarchical. Thus individual project steering groups (where they exist) report to the relevant CNAA project committee which in turn reports in general terms to DFS.

Probably of greater interest – and possibly of equal importance – are the informal or 'horizontal' systems that have emerged, in particular the networking and brokerage functions that have developed as the Fund has moved into full implementation. Linking related projects, for example, has been one of the most important and rewarding features of the whole initiative. We return to a discussion of these functions on pp. 76–7.

Accountability

Dispensing public funds demands clear accountability which extends beyond mere financial probity. In the context described here accountability has been, if anything, enhanced since once committee members become involved in the detailed construction of a project brief and in the choice of the successful applicant, an element of responsibility, even 'ownership', is introduced. Such 'ownership' reinforces the requirement for accountability and results in a strong emphasis on monitoring and evaluation of projects. Three mechanisms for monitoring have been employed:

(a) Each project was assigned a *link officer* from the Development Services Unit to liaise with researchers and to monitor project progress and finances.
(b) Related projects were grouped and assigned to an appropriate CNAA *project committee* which requires regular reports from, and on occasion attendance by, project directors and researchers at meetings.

(c) Advisory *steering committees* were established for a number of the larger projects usually based in the institutions.

These mechanisms were designed to ensure that each project continued to conform to agreed objectives and any detailed conditions set out in the initial contract.

Evaluation

The 90 or so projects under the Development Fund are at various stages, with most not being completed until the end of 1988, or even 1989 in some cases. It is not possible, therefore, to provide a final evaluation of outcomes. It has been possible, however, to evaluate the processes and procedures adopted, and to describe interim outcomes. Completed projects are required to submit an evaluation report, within three months of the end of the period of funding, which is then submitted to the relevant project committees for consideration. Special 'reading groups' of CNAA members and officers with sometimes external assessors have been convened from time to time to provide detailed scrutiny of final project reports. It is intended that an external and independent assessment of the Fund be carried out around late 1988. This will seek to draw out salient generalisable lessons of relevance to CNAA's future developmental activities. It is relevant, in concluding this section, to refer to the importance attached to project outcomes and their dissemination as being crucial to any evaluation; this is discussed further on p. 77.

Main features and strengths

Selectivity, then, has been accompanied by a series of developments as described above. The vigour of certain of these developments, for example the proactive mode of initiating projects, was unforeseen. The extent to which such developments inevitably follow the adoption of a selective policy is briefly discussed in the concluding section to this paper. For the moment, let us examine the main features and strengths of the system as described.

The developmental emphasis

Defining developmental as opposed to a research activity is admittedly difficult. Yet it is frequently possible to differentiate in practice between these activities even if definitional problems remain. Traditionally, the emphasis throughout social science has tended to be on research rather than development. In contrast, it is arguable that the presence of a selective system, as described here, encourages and indeed enhances the developmental. This is because of the inevitable emphasis on *tangible* outcomes, along with a more 'hard-nosed' value-for-money approach. It is also worth noting that the impact of other funders such as the MSC, Department of Trade and Industry (DTI) and

Further Education Unit (FEU) has also redressed the balance somewhat towards the developmental.

The collaborative emphasis

Without doubt this is one of the key features of the CNAA system. We refer here to collaboration between CNAA link officers and projects, and between the projects themselves and the project committees (referred to on p. 74). The role of link officer extends from designing projects to being a full member of the project team, from setting up networks to editing and writing reports. Such examples of their role will indicate that link officers do *not* operate merely as research secretaries or bureaucrats. They are involved, indeed immersed, in project work. Above all, they support and contribute to the conduct of projects and visit them on a regular basis.

The rationale for such linkage is worth spelling out. First, the arrangement optimises the likelihood of outcomes of relevance to CNAA and Public Sector Higher Education (PSHE). Second, it reduces the project failure rate and improves the final product. Third, link officers act as a support or a resource rather than simply as a monitor.

The relationship between individual project directors and project committees is still evolving at the time of writing. Each of the six current project committees has adopted different procedures but all involve project directors in their meetings in one way or another. Thus, one committee may invite all directors to a seminar following a morning business meeting, while another may invite only those projects nearing completion and final reporting. Yet another mode is to assign individual project committee members to specific projects – linked CNAA members if you like. Such linked committee members operate alongside link officers. It is too early to say whether this particular mode leads to duplication of role and to unnecessary interference in projects.

Networking and brokerage

Both these features fit readily into a collaborative mode of operation. With around 850 proposals received, CNAA's Development Services is well placed to act as a networking agency. Formally, networking is best exemplified by those projects which comprise a number of participating institutions. Thus the project aimed at encouraging the teaching of design within undergraduate business studies courses, jointly funded by the CNAA and DTI, is being undertaken by groups in seven different institutions. Typically, such groups are required to contribute to workshops organised at the beginning of, during and at the end of the project. Informally, networking usually centres around the link officer, with resultant activities being many and varied. The officer will endeavour to facilitate contacts between projects involving in some cases even unsuccessful applicants who have expressed continuing interest or who offer certain expertise.

Brokerage goes further than networking. It suggests negotiation, entre-preneurship and proactiveness, often but not exclusively in the context of finance. Thus, by negotiating jointly-funded projects, the CNAA has enlarged existing projects and funded new ones. As another example, attaching condi-tions to contracts has ensured the wider participation of other institutions where deemed necessary and in one particular case the CNAA has even specified the consultant to be involved.

Most project proposers do not initially expect the funding body to be as interactive as set out above and on p. 74. It clashes to some extent with the conventional ethos of academic autonomy, yet in practice most people appear to welcome it. That so few should express reservations with the collaborative approach is perhaps not altogether surprising since what is essentially being offered is support and help. It is also relevant to mention that the approach particularly commends itself to staff from institutions or departments which do not have a tradition of research or developmental work.

Targeted funding

Selectivity in the context of research does not necessarily lead to targeted funding but adding prioritisation and the other elements outlined on p.73 does. Indeed, an example of targeting, in the CNAA context, has already been described on p. 73. The claim here is that the system as developed – includ-ing the role of link officer – enhances targeting of funds, which in turn increases the likelihood of value for money. The CNAA, of course, is not a research council and hence targeting is a defensible and even inevitable mode or goal of operation.

Dissemination of outcomes

The most common outcome remains that of a publication produced and distributed by the CNAA, based on the final project report and involving the link officer as editor, distributor and even, in some cases, author. But the dissemination of outcomes means more than simply publishing a report. There has been a growing emphasis on workshops, seminars, small working or interest groups and the like. Indeed, in spring 1987 it was decided to allocate part of the remaining moneys under the Fund for such purposes. The driving force has been the desirability of effecting changes at course and institutional levels. In this respect it is desirable to link projects and their outcomes to the work of the CNAA committees responsible for validation, review and subject development. It is this linkage which holds the greatest promise to introducing and implementing change where necessary.

Dangers in the selective approach

In operating the selective system described here a number of dangers have emerged. First, the setting of priorities can introduce an element of rigidity and inflexibility by excluding good ideas in other areas. In practice, this danger is less real than potential. Provided priorities are reviewed there is little danger they will ossify. In any case, even among priorities practice has shown that greater weight is given to some than others and that such weighting changes over time.

Second, selectivity which is accompanied by any reduction in funding can lead to *exaggerated accountability*, that is, an excessive emphasis on accountability, monitoring and evaluation. Yet it cannot be forgotten that research and development remain *risk* activities requiring risk capital! Some failure has to be tolerated and expected. One manifestation of this exaggerated accountability may be the tendency to spread relatively modest amounts of money over numerous small-scale projects. In the context of developmental-type activities there may be some justification for this approach. But whatever the nature of the activity administrative costs need certainly to be borne in mind given such sub-division.

Third, there is the intriguing question of 'ownership' of projects – intellectual and psychological – as referred to on p. 74. We have observed that those members involved in devising projects continue in most cases to display a close subsequent interest. They have expended time, effort and interest, and thus wish to contribute to a project's successful outcome. Conversely, a project committee may react unenthusiastically if required to provide oversight to projects in the absence of any prior involvement. The point here, of course, is that 'ownership' leads to the exercise of control of projects which in practice means even greater emphasis on accountability (for example, the view that *all* projects must report to *all* meetings of project committees). Thus such ownership, coupled with the danger of exaggerated accountability, as outlined above, means that care has to be taken not to restrict unduly the researchers' autonomy.

The fourth danger is the familiar one of making funding decisions on the basis of previous 'track record'. Hence there is little encouragement for the inexperienced or new applicant. Although this is a well-known and well-aired problem it is likely to be exacerbated by the operation of a selective system as described on pp. 72–3. After all, if attention focuses on accountability, evaluation and dissemination of outcomes the tendency is to support those with proven track records. To do otherwise would be imprudent. One solution is to earmark funds to provide 'seedcorn' money or to pump-prime developments. To these ends the CNAA allocated £180,000 or 11 per cent of the Development Fund to support a small grants scheme.

Concluding comments

Does a selective or directive approach inevitably lead to the establishment of a system as described in this paper? Part of the answer lies in whether certain conditions prevail, for example reduced funding, an accent on accountability, evaluation and dissemination. It also partly depends on the *nature* of the funding body. Thus, viewed as a chartered body concerned with academic standards –

as opposed to a research council – CNAA has little need to justify its selective approach to funding. Conversely, research councils, for example, are unlikely to go entirely down the selective path despite the claim that research funding is harder and harder to come by, 'with the Economic and Social Research Council (ESRC) increasingly insisting that it comes up with the ideas' (Rusbridger 1988).

We suspect that what is pertinent is the proportion of funds earmarked for unsolicited proposals as opposed to selective funding. Nevertheless, where selectivity occurs – either in totality or in large part – developments such as those described earlier will manifest themselves.

Whether the CNAA system will be replicated exactly elsewhere is debatable given the uniqueness of some of its features, in particular the collaborative networking and brokerage functions adopted by CNAA committee members and link-officers.

Notes

1 List of publications available from CNAA, 344 Gray's Inn Road, London WC1X 8BP.
2 This sub-committee was replaced in October 1987 by the Committee for Information and Development Services.

References

Advisory Board for the Research Councils (1987) *A Strategy for the Science Base*, London, HMSO.
Committee of Enquiry into Academic Validation of Degree Courses in Public Sector Higher Education (1985) *Academic Validation in Public Sector Higher Education* (the Lindop Report), Cmnd 9501, London, HMSO.
Council for National Academic Awards (1987) *The Development Fund*, CNAA Development Services Publication no. 15, London, CNAA.
Department of Education and Science (1985) *The Development of Higher Education into the 1990's*, Cmnd 9524, London, HMSO.
Department of Education and Science (1987) *Higher Education: Meeting the Challenge*, Cm. 114, London, HMSO.
Manpower Services Commission (1987) *Enterprise in Higher Education*, Sheffield, MSC.
Rusbridger, A. (1988) 'Who needs sociologists?', *Guardian*, 16 February.

9

The Management of Institutional Adaptation and Change under Conditions of Financial Stringency

John Sizer

Introduction

This paper arises from a research project, funded by the Department of Education and Science (DES) which was concerned primarily with nine British universities' responses to, and the impacts of, the University Grants Committee's (UGC) grant letters for 1981–2 dated 1 July 1981, and also to the events leading up to the issue of the letters during the period 1 August 1979 to 1 July 1981.

The research project examined the responses of nine universities both to events leading up to the UGC's grant letters of 1 July 1981 and to the letters themselves; their impact upon the organisational structures, management style, planning and resource allocation processes, etc; and upon the teaching, research, academic and administrative services, and related activities of institutions. Each participating university prepared a detailed case study in four parts:

Part I   Background information.
Part II   Build-up to receipt of the UGC's grant letter for 1981–2, dated 1 July 1981.
Part III   Responses to the UGC's grant letter for 1981–2.
Part IV   Impacts of the UGC's grant letter for 1981–2.

In a comparative analysis (Sizer 1987a), which was summarised in a Final Report to the DES (Sizer 1987b), the responses of, and different impacts on, institutions which faced substantially different percentage cuts in recurrent grants and/or student numbers were considered and summarised, together with the implications for future policy formulation by the DES, UGC and Committee of Vice-Chancellors and Principals (CVCP) and for the effective and efficient management of universities. The characteristics and treatment of the nine universities which participated in the project are summarised in Table 9.1, including required changes in full-time home and EC student numbers compared with UGC 1979–80 targets and 1980–1 actuals.

In this paper the managerial guidelines for the management of institutional adaptation and change under conditions of financial stringency drawn from the comparative analysis of the nine case studies are presented. Some are contrasted with the Jarratt Report on Efficiency Studies in Universities (CVCP 1985), with a UGC analysis of universities' responses to the Jarratt Report (UGC 1987) and with some other developments since the research project was completed.

Managerial guidelines for managing financial reductions

If vice chancellors and principals are to be successful in developing and implementing a plan for significant reductions in core funding, possibly accompanied by similar student number reductions, which recognises the need to protect the institution's strengths and requires selectivity in the allocation of resources, the analysis of the case studies suggests they should consider carefully whether to employ the following managerial guidelines.

1 Build, and ensure support from, a strong and cohesive managerial team with clearly defined responsibilities, capable of the sort of extra dedication, involvement and utilisation of imagination which characterises a first-class team. Assess the needs for, and acquire, appropriate management and leadership training and development for *all* members of the team. Avoid members of the managerial team having both top-down managerial roles and bottom-up representative roles.

Comment: This guideline appears to be consistent with the Jarratt Committee's recommendation that universities should recognise the vice chancellor not only as academic leader but also as chief executive (para. 5.5 (d)), which implies the increasing use being made of pro-vice chancellors as members of a managerial team, and the need for pro-vice chancellors and other senior academics, from whom the next generation of vice chancellors will be chosen, to be given the opportunity to improve their managerial skills through appropriate training and development. However, during the period of the research none of the nine vice chancellors and principals were formally recognised as chief executives, though a number adopted an executive style of management. The Jarratt Report also comments on the conflicts that arise when deans play dual roles as representatives and academic leaders of their Faculties and are also playing a key role in developing and implementing university policies.

2 Recognise the importance of understanding the external environment, in particular:
   (a) being aware of external factors and influences at work and being able to interpret these authoritatively within the institution;
   (b) being able to relate to and work effectively with external bodies; and

Table 9.1 *Summary of Treatment of Participating Universities*

Nature of university	Nature of treatment		
	Relatively well	*Middle range*	*Relatively harshly*
Ancient/civic		*Sheffield* (Medical School) 6,860 students* 1979–80 0% students (–8%)† –14% recurrent 11% overseas	*Aberdeen* (Medical School) 5,140 students 1979–80 –4% students (–5%) –23% recurrent 7% overseas
			Hull 5,070 students 1979–80 –17% students (–18%) –20% recurrent 7% overseas
Newer		*Sussex* 3,890 students 1979–80 – 5% students (–7%) –21% recurrent 12% overseas	*Stirling* 2,470 students 1979–80 –18% students (–26%) –27% recurrent 8% overseas
Technological	*Bath* 3,190 students 1979–80 +2% students (+1%) –7% recurrent 8% overseas	*Heriot-Watt* 2,430 students 1979–80 –13% students (–17%) –13% recurrent 12% overseas	*Aston* 4,670 students 1979–80 –22% students (–18%) –31% recurrent 17% overseas
			Salford 3,940 students 1979–80 –30% students (–30%) –44% recurrent 14% overseas

* Full-time Home and EC students
† (%) changes compared with 1980–81 actuals

(c) keeping a finger on the pulse of the local business and wider community.

3   Employ computer-based models for financial forecasting, student number and staffing projections, and support management at all levels with computer-based financial planning and control systems, management information systems, and performance appraisal procedures.

4   Develop detailed departmental profiles.

Comment: Appendix F of the Jarratt Report contains a detailed specification of the content of departmental profiles.

5   Recognise, when faced with the prospect of financial reductions, the need to build up financial reserves so as to provide the maximum flexibility to adapt to reduced financial circumstances. If advance warning is received of a possible range of financial reductions, prepare financial contingency plans to see the institution through any short-term financial crisis, and consider carefully whether the contingency plans should be made available in the university.

Comment: Sizer (1987b) explains why a number of the nine universities were ill-prepared for coping with the contents of the grants letters of 1 July 1981; only two had financial contingency plans in place. In the absence of clear indications of the possible range of financial reductions and strong external pressures, there may be a natural reluctance to develop contingency plans. In May 1986 the UGC did provide a longer-term funding horizon; it has requested detailed financial forecasts from institutions including sensitivity analyses of key assumptions and has pressed institutions to prepare contingency plans. Increasing use is being made of computer-based financial forecasting models. Whether to make contingency plans widely known within a university remains a difficult judgement (see Sizer 1987c; 1988a).

6   While recognising that a vigorous political campaign of protest, and appeals to a central funding body following the announcement of significant reductions of grant, may assist in maintaining internal cohesion and morale, separate the political campaign from the development of academic and financial plans. Do not delay the planning process while awaiting the results of appeals.

7   Ensure that the chairman and lay members of Council/Court understand fully Council's/Court's responsibilities and the role they have to play in support of the vice chancellor or principal in ensuring the institution faces up to the need to set priorities, to make hard choices, and to develop an integrated financial and academic plan; and subsequently in monitoring its implementation and, if necessary, ensuring appropriate corrective action is taken.

Comment: The role of lay members of Councils/Courts in the development and implementation of plans to reduce expenditure and, in some cases, student numbers, varied between institutions. Where they played a significant role it was in supporting a vice chancellor or principal in ensuring the institution faced up to the need to set priorities, to make hard choices, and to develop an

integrated academic and financial plan, and subsequently in monitoring progress as members of Council/Court Committees. Generally they were not
involved in detailed planning and implementation. In the Jarratt Report
concern is expressed about the relationship between Councils and Senates. The
decades of expansion up to 1981, it is suggested, placed Senates in the
ascendancy in these relationships; and the relative decline in Councils' in-
fluenc. increased the potential for Senates to resist change and to exercise
natural conservatism. It may well be, the Report states, that a degree of tension
between them is necessary in the circumstances now facing universities, and can
be creative and beneficial in the long term, but it can only happen if Council
asserts itself. A number of institutional responses to the UGC's questionnaire on
the implementation of the Jarratt Report disagree with these comments (UGC
1987). They question the notion of 'a degree of tension' being 'creative and
beneficial' in the long term. Senior lay members doubt whether it has significant
validity. They do not regard good relationships as an indication of weakness or
loss of influence. The Jarratt Report also recommended Councils to assert their
responsibilities in governing their institutions notably in respect of strategic
plans to underpin academic decisions and structures which bring planning,
resource allocation and accountability together in one corporate process linking
academic, financial and physical aspects. The Report recommends the establishment of a planning and resources committee of strictly limited size, com-
prised of members of Council and Senate with the vice chancellor as chairman,
appointed by Council and reporting to both bodies. All members should
recognise that they are there to pursue corporate interests of the university and
not to represent sectional interests. The UGC's analysis reveals a variety of
institutional responses to the Jarratt recommendation. Many have implemented the recommendation, others question it. One university which
effectively managed severe cuts in recurrent grant over the 1981–4 period rejects
the recommendation as inappropriate to the challenges which the university
will continue to face. Demands will inevitably be made on time, energies and
commitment of individuals allied to the need to master complex briefs. It is
argued that a mixed committee would almost certainly find difficulty in
sustaining continued attention to detail and consequently would foster the
creation of sub-groups, and attenuate the lines of communication between the
planning committee and departments. Another technological university, which
faced a similar situation in 1981, has an advisory group to the vice chancellor,
without lay members, which has served the university well; the university sees
no reason to change. A third technological university with a reputation for
sound planning and management has a long-established committee with no lay
members. A number of other universities appear to follow managerial guidelines 1 and 7. The questioning of the role of lay members as members of a
planning and resources committee is consistent with concerns expressed elsewhere about the assumptions in the Jarratt Report about the role and supply of
lay members. Some universities have difficulty in attracting able, active industrial and business people, particularly outstanding younger executives. There is
a heavy reliance on lay members who are retired and professional people.
Concern is expressed about the conflict between increasing demands on the

time of industrial and business members and the greater involvement implied by Jarratt. These demands will be further increased if Councils establish audit committees as proposed by CVCP (1987) and DES (1987), and also by the granting of corporate status to polytechnics and some other institutions of higher education. Should the role of lay members be equated with that of non-executive directors; should they advise on overall policy and strategy and ensure institutional planning is consistent with the institution's objectives and strategy, financial health and circumstances, monitor implementation, but not be involved in the detailed formulation of strategies and action plans and their subsequent implementation?

8 Involve an influential, respected and informed group of senior academics in obtaining agreement to the planning process, in the preparation of a plan and its subsequent implementation.

9 Communicate and consult extensively with departments, staff and student unions in order to obtain agreement to the planning process, its timetable and the criteria to be employed in evaluation, and to identify them with the philosophy of the plan.

10 Within a tight, step-by-step timetable, employ a top-down, bottom-up, top-down approach to the preparation of the plan, with an extensive information-gathering exercise preceding the top-down proposals, extensive consultation about the proposals and a willingness to give serious consideration to bottom-up responses, leading to top-down plans for approval by Senate and Council. Do not rely on faculty or school self-evaluation; recognise there may be a reluctance to make hard choices and a preference for equal treatment and maintenance of the existing range of subjects.

11 While recognising the need for widespread communication, consultation and participation in the preparation of plans, accept that extensive argument, debate and controversy may have to be tolerated as part of the process of gaining acceptance of hard and difficult choices.

12 When preparing top-down proposals:

(a) Recognise the impact of financial reductions on the university's capacity to undertake research and concentrate on a limited number of fields. Identify those departments and units whose past research performance and future potential warrant their being selectively supported.

(b) Employ small, specialist *ad hoc* groups when it is necessary to identify, and evaluate quickly, policy options and to propose plans for the implementation of strategies for complex or specialised areas.

(c) Recognise, if actions have not been taken previously, opportunities exist to reduce costs and generate additional income in non-academic areas.

(d) Establish a central development/innovation fund to provide for flexibility in implementing the plan.

(e) Avoid raising expectations and making unrealistic promises, which may create debts to be paid that subsequently may prove to be embarrassments and lead to discontent and dissension.

13   Make positive efforts, and involve all staff, to promote continually the external image of the university and to secure additional income. Develop and implement a planned and co-ordinated public relations policy programme directed at communicating to appropriate audiences the institution's distinctive characteristics, strengths and appeal.

14   Develop positive personnel policies and procedures. Involve unions in the development and implementation of these policies. Recognise that at an appropriate stage in relations with unions careful consideration should be given to whether it would be helpful to commission an independent review of the university's financial position. As far as possible employ the concept of a single pool of staff and regard early retirement as one element of a policy which encompasses unpaid leaves of absence, vacancy review procedures and staff training and redeployment. Avoid equating voluntary redundancy with academic incompetence. Respect the dignity of individuals, adopt personal approaches to agreeing early retirement arrangements, and encourage continuing association and identification with the university. Recognise the negative aspects of intimating the possibility of compulsory redundancies and only contemplate this in the last resort.

15   Ensure that planning, resource allocation, accountability and monitoring of performance are effectively integrated. As far as possible develop plans for responsibility centres, allocate resources, devolve financial responsibility and accountability and provide incentives to generate additional income, directly to responsible heads of department, and subsequently monitor their performance. Avoid intermediate planning and resource allocating bodies, such as faculties, which may be unwilling to make hard choices and implement selectivity, and cannot subsequently be held accountable for their actions.

Comment: This guideline is consistent with the main thrust of the Jarratt Report. Futures analysis and the formulation of institutional objectives and strategy, as the Jarratt Report argues, should lead to the development of departmental mission statements and plans, which identify the role and mission of departments, set out their objectives, strategies and action plans, the resources required to implement the action plans, and the progress measures, including performance indicators, against which performance will be assessed and monitored. These longer-term departmental plans have to be translated into annual action plans and budgets. Thus the Jarratt Report recommends '[budget] delegation to appropriate centres which will be held responsible to the planning and resources committee for what they have achieved against their budgets' (CVCP 1985, para. 5.5f). The key word is 'achieved'. In their progress reports to the UGC some institutions appeared to confuse resource allocation with budget delegation, and viewed accountability in the narrow, financial sense of comparing actual with budgeted expenditure. A budget is *not* simply an allocation of resources derived from a resource allocation model, but a financial quantification of an action plan to implement a strategy to achieve a set of objectives. Accountability is concerned with whether the head of the responsibility centre has successfully implemented the plan for which resources were provided, that is, with what has been achieved, not simply with what he has spent. Accountability also implies incentives and rewards for good performance as well as sanctions for unsatisfactory performance. Has sufficient consideration been given to the incentive, reward and career structures for successful heads of academic departments and other executive heads?

16 Ensure that plans and decision-making processes are sufficiently dynamic and flexible to allow for externally generated developments, and for initiatives to be taken quickly in response to external opportunities.

17 Recognise the changing, more demanding, and at times conflicting managerial and representative roles of heads of departments, and the need for periodic replacement. Plan for succession and provide appropriate managerial and leadership training and development for current and future heads of department. Ensure heads of department do not neglect staff appraisal and development by implementing formalised departmental and university systems. Ensure as far as possible that heads have appropriate administrative support.

Comment: The case studies show that:

> The roles of Chairmen and Heads of Departments changed substantially as a result of the financial reductions. They were under constant, and at times conflicting, pressures from the administration and their own staff. They became more involved in planning and resource allocation issues and in protecting their department's interests. Their staff management role became more demanding and critical. Their own teaching, scholarship and research inevitably suffered. Some were unable to cope with the extra demands and the additional stress. They had insufficient time to respond to staff development needs and required more administrative support. There was a widespread belief that headships should rotate about every four or five years if the leadership commitment was to be maintained, and the pressures coped with (Sizer 1987a, p. 127).

Subsequent developments have increased the pressures on, and have highlighted the changing roles of, heads of departments. They are being pressurised to move from a collegial and consensus style of academic leadership and management to an executive style of management. The Jarratt Committee recommends the appointment of heads of departments by Councils on the recommendation of the vice chancellor after appropriate consultation, with clear duties and responsibilities for the performance of their departments and the use of resources. It is heads of departments rather than departments that are to be held accountable for plans and budgets, as in guideline 15 above. Furthermore, heads of departments will have a central role in the new procedures for staff appraisal agreed by the Association of University Teachers (AUT) and the CVCP, which inevitably will change their relationships with departmental colleagues. It is unfortunate that staff development and appraisal has resulted from a national salary agreement rather than, as the Jarratt Report emphasises, from its recognition as a key responsibility of every manager. The

Jarratt recommendation stimulated a larger proportion of universities during 1986–7 to develop for the first time formal statements of the duties and responsibilities of heads of departments, and others to review existing statements. Some have recognised that it is also necessary to define more clearly the duties, responsibilities and accountability of deans. There is a tendency in the responses to the UGC's questionnaire to lose sight of the word 'performance' and the phrase 'responsibility for the use of resources'; few refer to their lines of responsibility and accountability for the development and implementation of departmental plans, for performance against agreed action plans and progress measures of performance. Those responses that recognise the integrated nature of the Jarratt recommendations tend to be those that have established, or are establishing, management development programmes for heads of departments. Some of these responses express concern about the increasing load being placed on professors as they assume more and more responsibility as line managers in addition to their crucial roles as creative teachers, researchers and academic leaders. This concern reinforces the need for appointments as heads of departments to be for a fixed term, which implies large, managerial units and multi-professor departments, planned managerial succession, training and development and appropriate administrative support for heads of department. A number of universities have grouped small departments together to form larger, budgetary units. It also raises questions about whether outstanding academic leaders should be forced into an executive style of management mould, that is, whether executive styles of management will stimulate or inhibit excellence in teaching, research and scholarship within academic departments. The Jarratt Report recognises that there is a danger that the managerial role may crowd out the teaching, research and scholarship leadership role of the eminent and the able professorial head. It takes the view that it is preferable to retain the managerial and academic leadership functions in one person, but where this is not practical the head of department must possess the requisite managerial skills and be encouraged to delegate some part of the responsibility for academic leadership to others. However, will all eminent and able professors be willing to play second fiddle to a less able academic who has executive management skills? For example, would the eminent professor be agreeable to his/her head of department formally assessing his/her performance? If the performance of all professors in a department is not appraised by the head of department would this not only be inconsistent with his/her executive role, but also undermine his/her position within the department? Given the crucial roles of heads of departments and the increasing pressures they face, urgent consideration needs to be given to the provision of incentives, rewards and career structures, as well as to management development programmes.

18   Advise academic departments, schools and faculties to examine relationships between the component parts of their student–staff ratios – average student contact hours, average class size, and average lecturer hours, and the structure and content of their courses – and to consider the impacts on these ratios of modularisation, increased flexibility and joint courses.

19   Recognise that further reductions in the UGC's recurrent grant and other

unexpected financial setbacks may occur and, after testing the sensitivity of the financial plan to variations in the key assumptions, develop a contingency plan. If revisions to the plan are necessary, employ the top-down, bottom-up, top-down approach to secure agreement and commitment to the changes.

20 Communicate extensively with all departments, staff and student unions regarding progress in implementing the plan to maintain a shared commitment to its successful implementation.

The leadership and managerial role of a vice chancellor or principal

The case studies and comparative analysis (Sizer 1987a) are supportive of the conclusion of the Jarratt Report that the effectiveness of a vice chancellor or principal is crucial to the success of an institution. The Jarratt Report considers that vice chancellors and principals will have to adopt a clear role of executive leader and have the necessary authority to carry it out. It also recommends executive styles of management with clear lines of authority, responsibility and accountability. 'Positive and decisive leadership' and 'high quality manager of change of appropriate academic standing' (Sizer 1982; 1986) are used in the comparative analysis and Final Report in preference to 'executive leader'. Some, but not all effective vice chancellors and principals adopted the role of executive leader and implemented executive styles of management. Leadership, managerial and political skills are equally crucial but, as the Jarratt Committee observes, and university responses to its recommendations recognise, no single leadership style may be appropriate in all circumstances. As Harvey-Jones (1985) has observed:

> The test of our leadership must be whether all the various organisational and bureaucratic management tools are 'on switches' or 'off switches'. We need to ask repeatedly whether the effect on our people is to get them willingly and freely to accept the challenge or to turn their wit, ingenuity and energy to defeating the intent of the systems with which we seek to manage them.

The case studies provide examples both of different leadership styles, and of where institutional leaders created environments of 'on switches' and of 'off switches' and combinations thereof. They confirm that the leadership challenge is particularly demanding in a self-governing community of scholars where the vice chancellor or principal has few executive powers. This is particularly the case in institutions with long-established strongly decentralised faculty structures. The leadership skills required to move from faculty 'on switches' and university 'off switches' to common university/faculty 'on switches' will be considerable, and it is doubtful whether the desired changes can be achieved rapidly unless the vice chancellor or principal possesses exceptional leadership and managerial skills. Furthermore, it must be emphasised that in the absence of UGC restructuring funds to oil the wheels of change, vice chancellors and principals with exceptional leadership skills, who employed the managerial guidelines identified, and who were supported by a first-class managerial team, could not have successfully managed the reductions in grant faced by many institutions during the 1981–4 period.

Those concerned with the successful implementation of strategic change must not only take account of the context within which the change is occurring but also employ the appropriate managerial processes. Background papers, prepared by the Project Director, and the case studies provided the context, and the comparative analysis highlighted the importance of managerial processes, and the managerial guidelines should assist in determining the appropriate managerial processes. The analysis suggests that a Jarratt-style executive vice chancellor could create a climate of 'on switches' but also 'off switches'; as a high-quality manager of change he should activate the 'on switches'. Such an executive vice chancellor or principal should be careful not to lose sight of the fact that new innovations, new initiatives and outstanding teaching, research and scholarship occur through the creativity of individuals in academic departments and research centres. They and their students create excellence. Vice chancellors and principals have to take the leading role in creating the environment in which such excellence flourishes and in which mediocrity withers and dies. They should be concerned to ensure that heads of departments' executive roles do not crowd out their teaching, research and scholarship leadership roles. Thus Keller (1983, p. 126) observes:

> Leadership is that intangible ability to touch people's nerve endings and cause them to act. It is what a university president must provide, quietly or with fire in his breath, if he is to dignify the enterprise, rouse the disparate faculty and staff into a united drive towards excellence, and defend the work of higher education with cogency and ardor against unknowing or unappreciative assailants.

Taylor (1986) has argued that the Jarratt Report is long on rational/analytical principles, and short on behavioural and political aspects. Sizer (1987a) describes, and the managerial guidelines address, some of the behavioural and political aspects of managing financial reductions. They complement the guidance on management processes contained in the Jarratt Report. They are consistent with Sir Alex Jarratt's view (1986, p. 746) that the planning process

> is essentially one of debate, based on good material, in which everyone can fight his or her corner but then accepts the final outcome as a contract to which each of the parties to that debate then work. This *is* consensus management, but to be effective it requires disciplined thinking and presentation, openness in discussion and, finally, the ability to take decisions that will be respected and implemented.

Executive styles and institutional culture

The Jarratt Report, as Sir Alex has maintained, is a framework of guidance not a blueprint to be applied uncritically. This paper has suggested that in deciding how best to implement this framework of guidance when managing institutional adaptation and change under conditions of financial stringency, careful consideration will have to be given to the role of lay members, to the pressures that executive responsibility places on heads of departments and to the need for incentive, reward and career structures. It also suggests when considering how to implement an executive leadership role that a vice chancellor will have to evaluate carefully the trade-off between Sir Alex Jarratt's view of the planning process, particularly the need to secure acceptance of the need for change and participation in its planning and implementation, given the pressures to change institutional culture towards an entrepreneurial and market economy model, and the advantages to be derived from being able to exercise the authority of formally being executive head as opposed to being recognised as first amongst equals. Outstanding leaders, high-quality managers of change, may not need formal executive authority, which is no substitute for exceptional leadership and managerial skills.

However, does executive management as advocated in the Jarratt Report equal consensus management? Is Sir Alex's view consistent with the emphasis in the Report on the executive role of vice chancellors, on clear lines of responsibility and accountability, particularly on the responsibility of heads for the performance of their departments? Can heads of department be executively responsible and practice consensus and collegial management and fulfil their academic leadership roles in their departments? At the present time executive styles of management cannot be considered in isolation from the government's wish to reduce its commitment to funding higher education and its expectation that institutions, through an increased entrepreneurial and market-oriented focus, will build up alternative funds. Thus there are pressures on institutions to change their 'culture' from a free, oligarchic and consensus model, supported by administrative styles of management, to an entrepreneurial and market-economy model with executive styles of management with an emphasis on securing value for money in terms of economy, efficiency and in particular effectiveness (Sizer 1988b). Important dimensions of effectiveness are not only quality of teaching and research but also responsiveness and relevance to the changing needs of society in general and the economy in particular, selectivity in the allocation of limited resources available for research, and hard choices concerning small, weak departments. In these circumstances it may be difficult to equate executive management with consensus management. Thus it is important to differentiate between widespread consultation as part of the process of executive management and consensus management, which at worst implies decision-making by the majorities in committees not by executive heads after widespread consultation.

Conclusion

The managerial guidelines arising from the research project should assist university leaders, high-quality managers of change, to identify and activate the 'on switches', to touch people's nerve endings, to secure acceptance of the need for change, and commitment to its planning and implementation. However, they cannot guarantee success, particularly for those who do not possess the necessary leadership and managerial qualities and skills. As the Jarratt Report emphasises, those responsible for appointing vice chancellors and principals should recognise the need to include leadership and managerial qualities, expertise and ability in their search and selection criteria. University leaders should assess their need for leadership and managerial skills training and development, skills which they will find essential if they are to manage effectively institutional adaptation and change under conditions of financial stringency.

References

Committee of Vice-Chancellors and Principals (1985) *Report of the Steering Committee for Efficiency Studies in Universities* (the Jarratt Report), London, CVCP.

Committee of Vice-Chancellors and Principals (1987) *Financial Management and Accounting*, July.

Department of Education and Science (1987) *Accounting and Auditing in Higher Education*, London, Department of Education and Science.

Harvey-Jones, J. (1985) 'Switching on – not off', *Management News*, May, p. 4.

Jarratt, Sir Alex (1986) 'The Management of Universities', *The Royal Society of Arts Journal*, October 1986.

Keller, G. (1983) *Academic Strategy: The Managerial Revolution in American Higher Education*, Baltimore, MD, The Johns Hopkins University Press.

Sizer, J. (1982) 'Assessing institutional performance and progress' in L. Wagner (ed.), *Agenda for Institutional Change in Higher Education*, SRHE Monograph 45, pp. 33–69, Guildford, SRHE.

Sizer, J. (1986) 'Efficiency and scholarship: Uncomfortable or compatible bedfellows?', *Higher Education Review*, 18(2), 45–54.

Sizer, J. (1987a) *Institutional Responses to Financial Reductions within the University Sector, Part II, Comparative Analysis of Universities' Case Studies*, London, Department of Education and Science.

Sizer, J. (1987b) *Institutional Responses to Financial Reductions within the University Sector, Part I, Final Report*, London, Department of Education and Science.

Sizer, J. (1987c) 'Universities in hard times: Some policy implications and managerial guidelines', *Higher Education Quarterly*, 41(4), 354–72.

Sizer, J. (1988a) 'British Universities responses to events leading to grant reductions announced in July 1981', *Financial Accountability and Management*, 4(2), 79–98.

Sizer, J. (1988b) 'In search of excellence: Performance assessment in the United Kingdom', *Higher Education Quarterly*, 42(2), 152–61.

Taylor, W. (1986) 'Problems and Prospects for Change in University Management', *Management and Efficiency in British Universities: The Implications of the Jarratt Report*, Proceedings of Public Finance Foundation Seminar, London, Public Finance Foundation, pp. 79–83.

University Grants Committee (1987) *Report to the Secretary of State on Universities' Responses to the Jarratt Report*, London, UGC.

10

Contractorisation in the Field of Higher Education: An Account of Three Years' Experience of a Major Educational Contract

F. R. Hartley

Introduction

The British government referred in the White Paper published in April 1987 to a future funding of universities and polytechnics based on a contractual approach. In May a rather less glossy paper amplified slightly some ways in which contracts might be established. It is not the intention of this paper to argue for or against a contractual approach, but rather to describe the experience of the last three and a half years gained at the Royal Military College of Science (RMCS) of running what is believed to be the largest contract in the field of higher education in the world.

RMCS, whose origins go back to 1772, was established to provide the scientific, engineering and more recently management education necessary to enable the Army to design, procure and fight with the technologically advanced equipment necessary to engage in successful combat. Up until 1984 the College was run as a wholly Ministry of Defence (MoD) establishment with both military staff and civilian academic staff. Civilian academic staff were first introduced some 120 years before in 1864.

In 1982 the MoD decided that, rather than continue to run the College itself, it would invite a university to take over the academic task of the College under a contractual agreement. In the first instance the contract would last for five years. All forty universities in England and Wales were asked by the MoD whether or not they would be interested in being invited to tender for such a contract. It is very interesting in the light of the universities' current doubts about the idea of contracts that twenty-five universities replied indicating their interest in the proposal. When it is remembered that RMCS is a military college and that 'matters military' are not always top of the popularity stakes in universities, that was a very high response rate. The twenty-five interested universities were reduced to a short list of five who were invited to tender. Of these two dropped out when the realities of what was involved in a military college dawned upon their Senates, one had internal difficulties with a very senior member of staff and had to withdraw, while two submitted formal tenders; and it is a matter of history that Cranfield Institute of Technology won the contract and now operates the RMCS. The senior person responsible to the Vice Chancellor for running that contract is the author in the role of Principal and Dean since 1984. However, the author's knowledge of the RMCS is based on twelve years there, from 1975 to 1982 as Professor of Chemistry and from 1982 to 1984 as Acting Dean or senior academic.

How the contract works

Course programme

The RMCS runs a wide range of courses at undergraduate, postgraduate and professional mid-career level, all in the area of science, engineering and management (Table 10.1). These courses are of three types, A, B and C. Type A courses are restricted to students nominated by MoD, and are equivalent to the bespoke courses run by some universities for specific companies. Type B courses are courses run for the MoD but to which the RMCS is encouraged to recruit extra, so-called private-venture, students to bring them up to capacity. Such students pay to attend the courses. Type C courses are courses the RMCS offers to the world at large and for which it recruits students.

All courses, as in any university or polytechnic, are designed by a Course Committee and submitted to the Faculty Board for approval (see Figure 10.1). The RMCS represents one of the six Faculties of Cranfield Institute of Technology. Once approved by the Faculty Board, courses leading to degrees of

Table 10.1   *Courses Run at RMCS*

Level of course	No. of courses	Type of course*
Undergraduate degrees (BSc and BEng)	6	B
Postgraduate taught degrees (MSc and MDA)	8	B
Postgraduate research degrees (MPhil and PhD)	~ 70 students	B
Staff courses	4	A
Professional mid-career short courses	92	A, B, C

* A, students nominated by MoD only; B, MoD courses to which private-venture students may be admitted if places are available; C, private-venture courses.

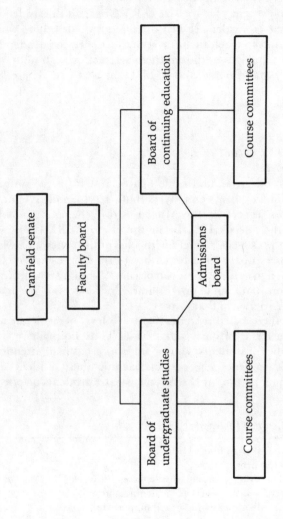

Figure 10.1 Academic Structure within RMCS (Cranfield)

the university are submitted to Senate for approval. Thus a programme of courses is established and this programme is continually updated by the modification of existing courses, the insertion of new courses, and the deletion of obsolete courses. Thus establishment of the programme of courses follows exactly the same procedure as at any other university.

It may be helpful to get a feel for the size of RMCS. If all the students were reduced to the full-time equivalent (FTE) of undergraduates there would be almost 1,300 of them and to teach them there are just over 100 academic staff and about 200 support staff. In addition, there are just over 30 military staff primarily for the Army Staff Course, and 70 MoD support staff. There are also 86 research staff.

Annual cycle of the contract

The contract is based on an annual cycle (Table 10.2). In the autumn the Director of Army Training talks to employers (both service and civilian within the MoD and overseas, especially the Ministries of Defence of Canada and Australia, to identify their needs. He talks informally to the RMCS as well. In February the Director presents Cranfield with a list of the courses he wishes to be run and the numbers of students he wishes to send on each course. The programme is examined to ensure that it can be run. Assuming it can, Cranfield agrees in March to run that course programme which refers to the academic year commencing on 1 August of that year.

The programme is then costed by reducing it to a level of academic activity which is quantified in terms of Postgraduate Full Time Equivalent Students (PGFTEs) – the number of students who would be present if all attended for a full year like an MSc student. The cost of teaching these students is then determined. If subsequently the MoD sends a few extra students on one course

Table 10.2   *Annual Contract Procedure*

1   Sponsor specifies course programme required
2   Contractor agrees to run programme
3   Programme is costed in terms of amount academic activity (PGFTEs)

PGFTE $\times$ academic SSR $\times$ average academic salary	$\pounds a$
PGFTE $\times$ non-academic SSR $\times$ average support staff salary	$\pounds b$
Insurance	$\pounds c$
Rental of buildings, equipment, books and computers	$\pounds d$
Maintenance, utilities and cleaning of premises	$\pounds e$
Maintenance and replacement of equipment	$\pounds f$
Private venture repayment	$\pounds g$
Special earmarked items	$\pounds h$

Annual contract sum $\pounds(a + b + c + d + e + f - g + h)$

4   Detailed negotiation between sponsor and contractor over final annual sum

and a few less on another this is ignored, assuming of course it is possible to fit the extra students into one of the classrooms. Thus although the contract seems to be very detailed, it is actually operated fairly flexibly.

Once the number of PGFTEs has been determined a staff–student ratio (which itself can be the subject of negotiation) is applied to determine the number of academic staff. This number is then multiplied by a sum of money representing the agreed average cost of an academic member of staff which is a fixed point on the senior lecturer pay scale; this yields a sum of money (£a in Table 10.2). The same procedure is repeated for the non-academic staff (£b). Then the cost of insurance of both staff and buildings (£c), the cost of renting the buildings, equipment, library books and computers (£d), the cost of maintenance, utilities and cleaning of the premises (£e), and the cost of maintaining and replacing the equipment (£f) are all added in to produce a grand sum. From this grand sum is subtracted an amount in relation to the use Cranfield has made of the buildings and equipment in support of private venture work (£g), any earmarked sums for special items (£h) are added, and the result is the cost to the MoD for running the course programme. Readers will not be surprised to learn that these costs are not usually acceptable to the MoD's Contracts Branch and detailed negotiations follow until a finally agreed sum of money emerges.

This brief description raises many questions. An important one is probably: 'What happens if there are sharp changes in the course programme?' If the MoD wants a lot more than the previous year, and that has generally been the case so far, the response depends on 'can it all be achieved?' If the MoD wants a lot less then clearly there would be a staffing problem. Recognition of this has led to penalty clauses in the contract whereby in the event of staff becoming surplus due to a reduction in the programme, the MoD would be required to fund the consequent redundancies. This acts as a major deterrent to unnecessary short-term fluctuations in the MoD's requirement.

A second important question is 'what happens when major capital items such as buildings or equipment are needed?' In such a situation Cranfield makes a bid to MoD and if granted then a special sum, earmarked solely for the purpose specified, is granted.

Measurement of performance

An important implication of a contract is that it enables an agreed task to be performed for an agreed sum of money. How does the MoD determine whether or not the task has been performed satisfactorily? In simple terms, the MoD had little idea as to how to do this and so it turned the question on its head and asked Cranfield to demonstrate that it had performed satisfactorily. Essentially what was done was to define a series of criteria of performance which are basically very similar to the performance indicators since developed by the universities.

There is also a Contract Monitoring Board at which the principal and the vice chancellor present an annual report on the year's work to very senior members of the MoD. The discipline of producing an annual report was something the present author introduced; it has proved very valuable internally in assessing what has been accomplished in the past year, and where the RMCS is going in the future. It covers teaching, research and consultancy in terms of quantity and quality, reports from the schools, and plans for the future. The idea of a Contract Monitoring Board may sound frightening to those who have never experienced it. Actually it has proved very valuable because it provides an occasion on which the sponsor is forced to think about what the College is doing, whether or not it is what is wanted and whether or not its performance is satisfactory. This avoids the sponsor and contractor drifting slowly away from each other over a period of time without either realising it has happened and then the sponsor becoming disenchanted and wanting to make radical changes. It was perhaps the lack of this discipline that allowed the DES and the universities slowly to drift apart to the point where the government wanted to effect a major change of direction rather than a steady evolutionary change. At the end of the Contract Monitoring Board's meeting Cranfield knows just where it stands, where it has been successful and what must be done for the future. The meeting also provides an opportunity to discuss any contractual problems with the sponsors.

Time-scale

The initial contract was for five years from 1 August 1984. Colleges running three-year undergraduate degree courses cannot change direction suddenly. So during the third year of the contract the MoD had to consider the future. The contract has been a resounding success at RMCS. The College is a vibrant, exciting place to be in with twice the students and five times the research of three years ago and so the MoD has extended the contract for a further six years from 1989 to 1995 and arranged that at each annual review from 1990 onwards the contract shall, subject to satisfactory performance, be extended for a further year, so that it always has between six and five years to run (six at the beginning of a year, five at the end).

What are the implications of a limited-term contract for the conditions of employment of the staff? Cranfield entered the contract confident that it could fulfil the contract to the complete satisfaction of the MoD and that it would therefore be renewed. Accordingly the staff at Shrivenham are employed on exactly the same terms as all other Cranfield staff, who under the Statutes can only be removed for 'good cause', defined as conviction of an offence considered to render a person unfit for duty; physical or mental incapacity; scandalous or disgraceful conduct; or conduct considered to constitute failure or inability to comply with the conditions of holding a post.

Pros and cons of a contract

What are the pros and cons of a contract (Table 10.3)? In the case of the contract

Table 10.3 *Pros and Cons of a Contract in the Field of Higher Education*

Pros	Cons
1 Enhances flexibility	1 Less security for staff, but this leads to greater responsiveness
2 Enhances responsiveness	
	2 Contractual negotiations can be long and drawn out
3 Annual reviews of performance	

under discussion, there are two pros. First, the contract has provided the flexibility to develop new courses by entering easily into further contracts with new sponsors as well as annually negotiating the development of the main contract. Consequently, the RMCS is now far more responsive to the needs of its customers than it was before. An important con would appear to be that the contract gives far less security for the staff. In fact this leads to a major advantage in that it stops the staff collectively becoming complacent and unwilling to face change. As a result it has enabled the College to be more responsive to the needs of customers.

An important advantage is the annual review of the RMCS's performance which the Contract Monitoring Board gives. It has already been emphasised how important this is in flushing criticism out into the open, as those for whom the RMCS works have seriously to consider whether or not it has met their needs.

The final disadvantage of a contract is that negotiations can be long and drawn out. The MoD penalties for delaying reaching agreement are high (75 per cent funding from the expiry of one contract until agreement is reached over next year's rate). But at present there is still a learning curve for both sides to be surmounted.

Summary

This paper has attempted to present a fair view of how one contract operates. In the particular situation of the RMCS, the contractual approach has completely revitalised the college and allowed it to grow dramatically. It has enabled it to become a vibrant and exciting place to work in, which in the mid-1980s is not true of all higher education institutions. It would be wrong to argue that what is right for one very special college is necessarily right for all, but it is demonstrably true that one sizeable contract has been shown to work, and to work well. So perhaps as a result of this experience universities and polytechnics need not be quite so fearful of the concept of a contract as once they were.

Acknowledgement

The recent success of the Royal Military College of Science results from the vision of General Sir Richard Vincent and Lord Chilver of Cranfield, but above all is due to the hard work and dedicated service of all the staff. It is a pleasure to thank them all for the work on which this paper is based.

11

The Roles of Academic Education and Professional Training in the Development of the Modern Accountant

K. Srinivasan and C. McCallum

The purpose of this paper is to make a contribution towards the current debate about the way in which academic education and professional training need to be combined in the development of the accountants of tomorrow.

The education of accountants can be seen as very important because its recipients are (in many cases) destined for status, responsibility, power and independence. What form should it take? One crucial issue which has been constantly under consideration over the last thirty years has been the balance between academic education and practical training. Traditionally, accountancy education has consisted mainly of experience gained 'on the job' supplemented by success in professional examinations (often achieved with the assistance of commercial correspondence courses). In recent years this form of education has come under increasing criticism.

> If accounting education of the traditional kind is open to one criticism above all others, it is that it has been too much concerned with the mechanical application of well-tried procedures to stereotype situations and too little concerned with improving the student's capacity to think for himself, to handle new situations and to solve new problems which confront him (Solomons 1974).

Increasingly, therefore, in recent years professional education has been seen by many as ideally consisting of academic education allied with professional training. The difficulty lies in obtaining a mix of education and training which will satisfy the interests of professional accountancy bodies and the large accountancy firms along with those of society in general and seekers of accounting education in particular.

The traditional problems associated with accountancy education have been those of exclusiveness and severity. The two ways in which professional bodies have been able to maintain standards in the past have been by limiting initial access to the best academic achievers at school and by ensuring that the standard of the professional examinations has led to the failure of a large number of candidates; neither of these methods is remotely acceptable to modern educationalists or the government.

Accounting education is relevant not only to professional education bodies and accountancy firms. Commercial and industrial organisations employ accountants. As far as these organisations are concerned they have no particular loyalty to or vested interest in the accounting profession. They look on all their staff, including accountants, as members of a team working towards corporate goals. Managers in commerce and industry have sometimes argued that course curricula have paid far too little attention to accounting in a commercial or manufacturing setting and have been overinvolved with the needs of professional firms.

If one turns from the needs of employers of accountants to those of people who undertake accounting education, matters become even more complicated. Many students who obtain degrees or diplomas in accountancy or become members of the British professional bodies do so because they aspire to careers in cognate areas (banking, general financial services, management, etc.); others are looking for careers at technician level.

The recent Scottish experience

The Institute of Chartered Accountants of Scotland (ICAS) has always maintained a keen interest in accounting education. Historically, ICAS has participated regularly in discussions with Scottish universities and central institutions on educational matters. By drawing on some of its members who work in commerce and industry and others who are in professional practice, ICAS makes a genuine effort to ensure that all interested parties have an opportunity to be involved in educational initiatives and discussions. Most of the other major British professional bodies have also played an active role in recent educational developments in accounting in Scotland.

By the early 1970s there had been many calls for an 'all-graduate entry' into the accountancy profession in Scotland. 'Relevant' (accountancy) and 'non-relevant' (other) degrees were both seen as acceptable since the value of a degree to prospective Scottish Chartered Accountants (CAs) was the academic rigour it was supposed to guarantee. In accordance with the ideas expressed above, many partners in accounting firms were particularly supportive of the non-relevant degree as a basis for entry because it provided an opportunity for them to recruit talented youngsters who had not looked to accountancy as a career when they had left school but wished to change course following a successful completion of a first degree in some other area. These students were, however, required to complete a one-year full-time postgraduate diploma before they were eligible to obtain trainee contracts as chartered accountancy students. The most economical way (in terms of time) for a student to become a CA was to complete a three-year (ordinary) degree in accounting and join a professional firm for a three-year training period during which a two-part ICAS examination had to be completed. Thus, the total education and training package lasted for six years via the 'relevant degree' route.

ICAS decided against an all-graduate profession at this stage. Instead, three major British accountancy bodies, ICAS, the Association of Certified and Corporate Accountants (now CICA) and the Institute of Cost and Management Accountants (now CIMA), working under the auspices of the Scottish Council for Administrative and Professional Education (SCAPE, later SCOTBEC and now SCOTVEC) and with the collaboration of other higher educational institutions and representatives from commerce and industry, launched the Scottish Higher National Diploma (SHND) in Accounting. This was a two-year full-time course. The holder of the SHND in Accounting was qualified to seek a position as a CA trainee with the one proviso that the training contract with a chartered accountancy firm had to be of four years' duration. During the training period the SHND holder sat the same two ICAS examinations which were taken by graduates. The total education and training package for the SHND holders lasted for six years (the minimum possible period).

In its early years, the SHND in Accounting was a successful course in two ways. First, it attracted competent and motivated students who did not wish to commit themselves to three years' full-time study after leaving school, either because they were mature students or because they had financial commitments and responsibilities. Second, students who completed this practical and technique-orientated course successfully were welcomed by accountants in professional practice who had sometimes complained in the past that graduate trainees knew a lot but did not seem to be able to do very much in the early days of the training period.

By the mid-1980s, however, the SHND in Accounting was experiencing the following difficulties. The majority of students were unable to cope with the steadily increasing content of accounting syllabuses which had to remain satisfactory to the three accountancy bodies involved. Students who somehow struggled through the course were experiencing considerable difficulties in coping with professional examinations in later years. There was a growing feeling that with Scottish central institutions also offering degrees in accountancy, students of the required calibre were no longer available in plentiful supply. By the end of 1987, ICAS had effectively withdrawn its support for the SHND in Accounting.

There are three important questions which should be asked based on the SHND in Accounting's record to date in Scotland. First, is it acceptable that decisions taken by professional bodies can go against national education trends? ICAS has moved towards all-graduate entry at a time when the government is committed to widening the education base and offering greater access. Second, when several professional bodies work together in developing or designing a course, is it not essential that they show considerable restraint in stipulating topics which should be included in the course curricula? If those responsible for a particular course are asked to gear their syllabuses to suit the needs of several bodies, academic planning is extremely difficult. Third, should there be any attempt to prescribe the course content of accountancy degrees?

Academic education and professional training in accountancy

It is generally agreed that a person who is to be satisfactorily equipped for a career based on accountancy should undergo three types of experience. First, some form of full-time or other concentrated study seems desirable. Second, work experience is crucial. Third, society expects professional competence from its accountants; therefore, the validity of education and training programmes have to be tested by establishing the extent to which their alumni are professionally competent.

Is 'academic education' the same as 'full-time study'? The former sounds detached from the reality of the world of business and commerce. If accountancy graduates were actually receiving academic education in this sense, professional bodies (and business organisations) should legitimately be concerned with the relevance of such an education to the accountants of tomorrow. In reality, however, the way in which degree courses are designed and operated (particularly in the public sector of higher education and increasingly in universities) is very different.

Figure 11.1 represents a typical academic development process in higher education institutions. The current thinking and interests of the professional accountancy bodies have a significant impact on the various stages of this process. Course design is influenced in three separate ways. Informal communication, which takes place among staff in all higher educational institutions and representatives of professional bodies, provides a continuously available channel for inputs of 'professional' thinking. Secondly, at the initial design stage, demand considerations play an important part. Planners are likely to take cognisance of the fact that many students undertake courses in accountancy with a view to obtaining professional qualifications. The extent to which a degree

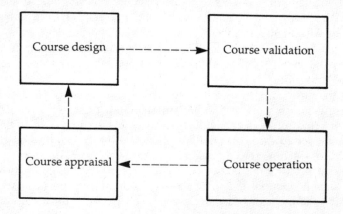

Figure 11.1   Typical academic development process in higher education institutions

provides its graduates with exemptions from the various stages of professional examinations may have a significant bearing on its marketability. Finally, many of the members of staff in the accountancy departments of colleges and universities are themselves members of professional bodies. Their background, outlook and loyalty all combined to ensure that they are unlikely to ignore professional trends and needs during the process of course design.

Any lack of involvement felt by professional bodies at the design stage is amply compensated for when degree courses are validated. The CNAA validation process almost guarantees in practice that the members of visiting parties or subject boards are well aware of the views of professional bodies. Additionally, nearly all the major accountancy bodies appear to have opted for the process of accrediting degrees in the way in which various branches of the engineering profession have been doing for some time. What do professional bodies look for during accreditation visits? Recent thinking identifies the following important areas: 'the academic environment, course content, standards of papers, qualifications of staff and facilities and resources available' (ICAEW 1987, p. 18). Here again, the existence of a number of professional bodies complicates the issue for course planners particularly where course content and examination papers are concerned.

The involvement of professional bodies in the operation of courses is comparatively limited (there is no reason for this state of affairs to change) although examination papers can be structured to meet with the approval of a particular body. The role of the profession in the fourth stage of the process as defined above (that is, course appraisal) is, however, becoming an increasingly active one. 'Subsequent performance in the final examination of students with specially approved degrees will be evaluated and will eventually form part of the accreditation process' (ICAEW 1987, p. 18). Most educationalists cannot but have serious doubts on the validity of gauging the success of a course by considering student performance at subsequent professional examinations which may test different attributes. In any case, it is arguable that the success (or otherwise) of students taking examinations some years after completion of a degree course depends more on their recent training experience and extent of examination preparation than the quality of past undergraduate study. Not all professional examinations always provide fair and clear tests, either. The recent moves by the Institute of Chartered Accountants in England and Wales (ICAEW), and the existing ICAS practice of publishing in an education bulletin a table showing how students of various colleges and universities perform in professional examinations cannot be without significance. They represent a conscious decision to appraise courses; it is very important that suitable criteria for such appraisal be established.

ICAEW has, however, adopted a rather different philosophy. A flexible approach is advocated. Students may either take a discrete route (along the lines followed by ICAS trainees) or pursue an integrated programme which consists of concurrent study and work experience. The reason given for ICAEW's choice is illuminating: 'The needs of training offices differ, so the optimum solution is to allow offices to select the scheme most suited to their particular requirements' (ICAEW 1987, p. 10). It would clearly not be correct to assume that the interests and needs of training offices (professional firms) always coincide with their trainees' educational requirements.

In summary, then, ICAS supports the concept of accountancy as an all-graduate profession which is best served by an academic underpinning (a degree) followed by an emphasis on practical work experience (supplemented by part-time study); the final seal of approval is given following the successful completion by students of tests of professional competence. ICAEW's more flexible approach is aimed at satisfying the varying needs of the professional firms and allows youngsters with differing initial education qualifications (many below degree level) to contemplate careers in chartered accountancy.

Both these approaches have strengths and weaknesses. ICAS have made a decision that under normal circumstances those who are not prepared to undertake and complete a degree course successfully will not be given the opportunity to become CAs. As long as the academic freedom of individual colleges and universities continues to be respected, high achievers at school who have been mentally and intellectually stretched by the ICAS programme will form the basis of a high-quality intake into tomorrow's profession. ICAEW's proposals have the merit of flexibility; additionally, the broad basis of entry places less emphasis on the ability of our traditional education system to identify all prospective accountants. The possible weaknesses of each of the two approaches can be identified with reference to the other's strengths. Thus ICAS is, perhaps, being unnecessarily restrictive. ICAEW's latest proposals do not offer guidelines on what is considered to be the best way to educate an accountant and society may not be served by the decision being left to training offices.

By the late 1980s there had been further changes in the way in which some people thought about accountancy education. This reflected developments in general educational thought. Concepts such as criterion-referenced learning and definition of outcomes have been used in course design at the National Council for Vocational Qualifications (NCVQ) and the equivalent Scottish body. Targets and learning objectives are being specified. Can the same process work at higher levels of education? Should we attempt to list all the things an accounting graduate should know or (more specifically) all the things that he or she should be able to do? Of course, we return to the particular problem faced by accounting academics. If every accountancy degree were to contain what a number of professional bodies chose to call 'essential' we would have academic chaos and student fatigue.

The irony lies in the fact that the Council for National Academic Awards (CNAA) has been loosening its reins on public sector institutions for some time. It would indeed be unfortunate if professional accountancy bodies were to step into the breach and exert an excessive influence on the content of degree courses.

Qualified accountants are expected, quite rightly, to give value for money. As accountants we would argue, for instance, that a tax consultant should save the client at least as much as the fee charged and that the benefits of an audit should outweigh the cost. This does not mean, however, that because society may judge the value of an accountant largely by what he/she can do, the entire education and training process should consist of a series of narrowly defined and essential modules which must be digested by all would-be accountants. We believe that accounting education should be vocational, but it need not, must not, be non-academic.

References

Institute of Chartered Accountants in England and Wales (1987) *Training the Business Professional*, a Consultative Paper, London, ICAEW.

Solomons, D. and Berridge, T. M. (1974) *Prospects for a Profession*, Advisory Board of Accountancy Education, London.

12

Opening Access to a Modern University

Keith Percy

Introduction

The University of Lancaster, situated in the North-West of England, opened its doors in 1964 and currently has just over 4,000 students. It was one of the 'new' universities, committed to curriculum and teaching innovation. However, on a number of occasions in the 1960s and 1970s, the university considered seeking 'Responsible Body' status from the Department of Education and Science (DES) so that it would be part-funded to provide extra-mural classes and courses for adults in its geographical area. On each occasion it backed off from the prospect – mainly on financial grounds but also because of doubts in the minds of some senior decision makers in the university about the value of what they understood to be 'traditional extra-mural studies'. In 1977 and again in 1978 at the annual Christmastime gathering of the university's Court (with an attendance of hundreds, mainly lay representatives of the community) there was a call from the floor for a regional adult education commitment by the university. On each occasion the university's response was to set up a working party. The report of the second working party led eventually in autumn 1979 to the tentative internal appointment, initially for one year and on a half-time basis, of an 'organising tutor for extra-mural studies' to explore what, if any, extra-mural role could be developed by the university. From that appointment grew the work of the present Extra-Mural Studies Office of the university and the approaches to opening access which have characterised its work in the 1980s.

This paper does not set out to be a chronology of that work or to be an even-handed documentation of all its aspects. Rather, it examines a thesis which is fundamental to the development of the Extra-Mural Studies Office at Lancaster: that a university is a remarkable and unique community resource (both in its physical facilities and in the store of intellectual expertise which its academic staff, postgraduates and others represent) and that resources should be made available to adults in the local region in ways other than, and additional to, courses leading to the award of a degree, particularly if the normal mode of attendance for degree courses is full-time. Those universities which accepted

'Responsible Body' funding from the government have usually taken the line of creating an annual programme of specially designed courses and classes of 'liberal education' often taught to adults in the evenings at a distance from the university campus. That route has largely not been open to Lancaster; the policy, rather, has been to question the hegemony of the degree format and to acknowledge that adults may wish to 'study at university' in a variety of ways which make sense to them, but which are not traditional to adult education. The thesis of the paper, therefore, is that opening access to a modern university is more than a question of preparing and admitting non-traditional adult students to degree study.

It is also the case, and it is not an accident, that the Extra-Mural Studies Office at Lancaster has maintained a heavy commitment to empirical research into the education of adults. It was evidently appropriate for a unit which was briefed to be 'non-traditional' to have access to systematic knowledge about current practice in the provision of education to adults and to be able to evaluate its own practice. Thus, the bias of the research work of the Extra-Mural Studies Office, most of it externally funded, has been towards surveys of provision and evaluation studies. More fundamentally, the main research interest, which pre-dated the creation of the Office and helps to explain its orientation, is in learning by adults in non-formal and independent settings and in the images and roles of 'learning' perceived by adults in all sectors of society.

There are grounds for a real claim, then, that the developments in provision, and the research programme, of the Lancaster Extra-Mural Studies Office stem from a common source and that, to some extent, they have been interdependent in the period 1979–87. Table 12.1 provides a summary overview of development in provision initiated by the Extra-Mural Studies Office and of the main research programmes undertaken.

Table 12.1   *Chronology of Research and Development in the Extra-Mural Studies Office at the University of Lancaster*

Year	Development	Research
1979	Open College of the North-West	Independent study
	Educational Guidance	Open College*
1980	Open Lectures	Post-Initial Education in North-West*
	Mature Students' Study Skills Programme	Prime-use Accommodation*
1981	Summer Programme	Open College*
	Town-Centre Lectures	Community Schools*
	Part-time Part 1 Degree Study	
1982	University of the Third Age (U3A)	
	Part-time Part 2 Degree Study	
1983	Unemployed Adults	Distance Learning*
1984		Unemployed Adults
1985		Accreditation of Prior Learning*
1986	Occasional Students	Voluntary Organisations*
1987	Community Learners	Open College/Unemployed Adults*

* Externally funded research.

What follows in this paper are attempts to indicate the findings of research (most of which has been conducted at Lancaster) which have contributed to the philosophy which underpins extra-mural studies at Lancaster; to give an account of three of the attempts to open access undertaken there, together with statistical and evaluatory information; and to discuss the implications of this work for current debates about opening access to higher education.

Research

Four studies, three of them conducted from Lancaster, contain important indicators for the theme of this paper.

Independent studies in higher education

A study, based on investigations conducted at North-East London Polytechnic and the University of Lancaster in the mid-1970s (Percy and Ramsden 1980), reported on the early successes and failures of the two pioneer schemes in the country through which, to put it briefly, students designed the content of their degree courses and chose the appropriate modes of assessment. It was significant that mature students appeared to be attracted to the schemes of independent study in disproportionate numbers. They appeared more likely to have clear ideas about key issues and/or questions around which their studies could be organised and to possess the confidence to strike out on their own; some mature students seemed to have built up very high expectations of academic life before entry, to have become disillusioned with normal departmental teaching to the point of rejection and thus turned to a scheme for independent study as the only way in which they could continue to learn in the university or polytechnic environment. Some mature students taking independent studies had developed dominant, almost obsessive, particular intellectual interests during their adult life and were looking to degree study as their chance to study them freely; in some cases they needed to draw on a disparate range of non-cognate disciplines which was not available in a conventional scheme of study.

Independent adult learning

The work of Allen Tough and associates in North America (see, for example, Tough 1979) into the phenomenon of independent learning among adults is well known. It has been replicated in all five continents – although in the United Kingdom the comparative investigations have been limited in scope (see Brookfield 1980). Despite problems about Tough's methodology and questions about social class differences which have not, so far, been resolved adequately, it seems clear that most adults (almost to exist satisfactorily in modern society) are engaged regularly in 'learning projects' 'in which the learner's *primary* intention is to gain certain knowledge and skill' (Tough 1979).

Such learning projects may not be perceived as 'learning' by the adult; they may be unsuccessful or partial; most of them will be self-directed (Tough says over 70 per cent). If Tough is right, the statistics normally quoted about the small percentage of British adults who, in any one year, participate in formally provided adult education courses and classes, represent only the tip of an iceberg of adult learning. If he is right, adults are learning all the time; they just do not do it in ways recognised by professional adult educators.

Post-initial education of adults

In 1979–81, a major survey of educational provision for adults in the North-West of England was conducted from the University of Lancaster (Percy *et al.* 1983a). The brief (from the then extant Advisory Council for Adult and Continuing Education) incorporated the terminology of 'post-initial education', terminology which failed to gain popular currency. However, a more important point is that the survey was briefed to be as wide-ranging as possible and, despite the needs to develop research methodology, not to confine itself to the courses and classes made available to adults by the formal providers such as local education authorities, colleges, adult education centres, universities, Workers' Education Centres, etc. It was to look for systematic adult learning wherever it could be found.

The research project surveyed voluntary organisations; private and commercial educational agencies; employer-provided in-house job training; community development organisations; trade unions; local and regional authorities other than LEAs, as well as the more obvious providers of systematic adult learning. It calculated that over 20 per cent of the adult population of the North-West of England in 1979–80 was participating in 'post-initial education provision' (previous surveys produced estimates varying between 10–15 per cent). The research project further suggested that 20 per cent of this participation was in organised learning provision made available by voluntary organisations and that there were indications that elderly people and working-class adults preferred the less formal ambience of voluntary organisations to that of taught adult classes often located in educational institutions. The project concluded that 'we are, in fact, a learning society . . . . Empirically . . . learning adults are the norm, although they may not know, or wish to acknowledge, that they are involved in "education"' (Percy *et al.* 1983a, pp. 230–31).

Learning in voluntary organisations

A study conducted from the University of Lancaster in 1986 (and financed by the Unit for the Development of Adult and Continuing Education) sought to enquire further into the learning activities of adults in voluntary organisations (Percy *et al.* 1988). The notion of a voluntary organisation is not a clear-cut one but can be held largely to refer to organisations which are controlled by voluntary members and are neither statutory nor commercial. It includes, therefore, major national and regional organisations as well as small local clubs and societies. Voluntary organisations in the study were categorised as being mainly identified with one or more of six 'orientations', which were labelled as: interest; service; advocacy; social; vocational; and community. The findings of the research project are relatively complex and tend to differentiate between adult learning in voluntary organisations with different 'orientations' and in different locations. General conclusions, however, are that pursuit of learning goals is an inherent aspect of adult participation in voluntary organisations (although most adult participants would not put it that way and would not recognise such terminology as applying to them). Adult learning in voluntary organisations is as much non-formal and informal as it is formal. That is to say, adults may be found to be participating in a recognisable programme of teaching or training (in which there is a 'teacher' and they are 'students'); but, just as likely, they are to be found learning what they need or want to learn by observing another person, by asking questions, by doing, by trying something out, checking and trying again. In voluntary organisations the roles of 'teacher' and 'student' are much more interchangeable than in educational institutions; adult teaching is demystified; what adults learn and how they learn it is much more within their control – more 'democratic' as some of them put it.

Provision

Overview

It would be transparently facile to make any claims that the developments initiated by the Extra-Mural Studies Office at the University of Lancaster since 1979 have been based directly upon the outcomes of research. Financial constraints, internal politics, personal circumstances and other factors would all conspire to make this unlikely – apart from the fact that research into education rarely has such clear-cut findings that policy and provision implications are self-evident. However, sufficient should have been said in the previous sections to indicate a set of tendencies or strategies with regard to the behaviour and perceptions of adult learners which may be held to be emerging from the conclusions of the research projects. There is no philosophy or body of principles here, more a set of working hypotheses which, as the work of the Extra-Mural Studies Office developed, it seemed sensible (as well as challenging) to take into account. The working hypotheses may be summarised as follows:

1   The extent of systematic adult learning is significantly greater than that which can be identified as participation in classes and courses put on in a prearranged format by educational providers.
2   Adults may see, and define, what they 'want to learn' in terms and modes which are not the familiar ones of the vocabulary of professional educators. Terms such as 'subject', 'disciplines', 'courses', 'assessment' and 'drop-out'

are not wholly relevant. Some adults have particular and dominant interests and goals and will make use of educational provision in ways not predicted by educators; indeed they will not share notions of educational 'progression' with which educators are comfortable.

3   Indeed, some adults may not have notions of 'what they want to learn' and the terminology of 'education' and 'teaching', etc., may actually be alienating. Nevertheless, such adults may, in practice, be both learners and teachers.

4   Educational institutions (perhaps universities in particular) may appear intimidating and remote to many adults and they may prefer to learn in other settings which are less formal and more 'democratic'. Thus the predominant mode of access to higher education (again, in particular, access to universities) which requires the giving up of three years and a wholesale commitment to full-time degree study can scarcely enter the consciousness of most adults.

5   With particular regard to universities, it seems sensible to provide as many different modes of access to university teaching as possible, recognising that adults will have a range of motivations and circumstances that will make degree study (especially in the full-time format) appropriate only for some and that the time and commitment which adults will wish to invest in the experience of being 'university learners' will also vary greatly. However, adult learning aspirations and motivations often change. If a system of access is flexible, an adult making only a minor commitment to, say, a scheme of open lectures may acquire sufficient interest and confidence to apply eventually to be a degree student.

Table 12.1 shows the chronology of the extra-mural developments at Lancaster. Taken separately, none of the developments is innovative in the sense that it has not been tried elsewhere in some British university or polytechnic. The early emphasis on educational guidance for any adult who approached the Office and on the provision of study skills introductory programmes and in-course workshops for mature entrants to degree programmes related both to the spirit of the working hypotheses above and to notions of good practice developing in the adult education world in the 1970s. The targeting of some publicity and support on elderly people (University of the Third Age (U3A)) and unemployed adults also reflected national initiatives and concerns. The role of the Extra-Mural Studies Office in making successful proposals for the development of part-time first degree study at Lancaster pre-dated developments in many universities, but the provision is of only a limited variety. The Occasional Students' Scheme (which allows adults to gain access to undergraduate courses, including tutorials, laboratory work, essay and examination assessment, without being registered as degree students), and the Community Learners' Scheme (through which individual adults are matched with a university 'expert' in a specialism or area in which they are pursuing individual learning programmes and want guidance) stemmed directly from the working hypotheses outlined above.

However, in this paper, it seems worthwhile to discuss more fully three other

Table 12.2   *Age of Participants in Open
Lectures, 1986–7 (per cent)*

21–34	20
35–49	23
50–59	21
60 +	32
No response	5

partly contrasting areas of development in which the Extra-Mural Studies Office at Lancaster has been involved and to consider what we know about the adults who have been gaining access to university educational facilities through them. The three areas are: (a) the Open Lectures Scheme, which was based on the idea that adults might wish to attend university undergraduate lectures without being registered as undergraduates; (b) the Open College of the North-West, which started almost four years before the inception of the Extra-Mural Studies Office but in which the Office has played a substantial research and development role; (c) the Lancaster University Summer Programme of residential holiday courses for adults and their children which the Extra-Mural Studies Office created primarily, but not exclusively, to generate income.

The Open Lectures Scheme

In 1980, the Senate of the university agreed that undergraduate lectures should be 'open' to members of the public. Each department annually would determine how many of its lecture courses would be 'open'; admission to lectures would be dependent on space being available and would be to formal lectures only (seminars and tutorials were excluded); members of the public would have to undertake a simple form of registration procedure in the Extra-Mural Studies Office. The provision was to be advertised as a university 'scheme'. After a lively debate, the Senate voted that (despite the prevailing financial climate) admission to 'open' lectures should be free of charge, as a gesture of community goodwill. In the event, almost all departments opened some, at least, of their undergraduate lecture courses and almost 500 daytime lecture courses were thus available. All took place on the university campus, which is three miles outside the small town of Lancaster at the end of an expensive bus route. Since 1980, the pattern has been established that each year approximately 60–80 members of the public register in the Extra-Mural Studies Office for the open lectures scheme. However, it is well known that, after a year's familiarity with the scheme and with chosen departments, some members of the public circumvent the formality of revisiting the Extra-Mural Studies Office to register and deal directly with departmental offices. There are no fees to collect; virtually no administrative or other problems have arisen with the scheme over seven years; and there is no need to police what is happening. Thus the actual number of participants in open lectures can only be guessed at and may well be over 100 annually.

An end-session survey of open lectures participants in the first year of

Table 12.3 *Employment Status of Participants in Open Lectures, 1986–7 (per cent)*

Full-time employment/self-employed	7
Part-time employment	9
Unemployed	14
Not seeking employment	58
No response	12

operation, 1980–81, showed that the most popular courses of lectures were in the departments of history, sociology, philosophy and English literature. About two-thirds of participants attended first-year lectures. However, there were members of the public admitted, for example, to third-year specialist lectures who, in response to the survey, showed that they had considerable experience in the subject (and this might, or might not, have been accompanied by relevant qualifications). Of respondents to the survey, approximately one-third claimed that they had attended over 90 per cent of the lectures in the chosen course(s) (in some cases such courses lasted over three terms). It was possible for these members of the public to make use of the university library but only a minority did. There seemed to be several different, but often overlapping, motivations for attending open lectures. The majority talked of 'keeping their minds alive', 'being interested in the subjects' and 'hearing the experts'. A few claimed to be doing 'research' or pursuing a 'special project'. Several wrote enthusiastically about 'seeing what it was like', 'sitting alongside those real students', trying out 'the university experience'. One local resident responded 'I saw this place being built . . . I never thought I'd be attending lectures myself.'

An enrolment survey ($n = 57$) of open lectures participants in 1986–7 showed that 65 per cent were female. As Tables 12.2 and 12.3 show, ages covered the full range (people aged over 50 years being the majority) and most participants were not employed and not seeking employment. It is also important to note, as Table 12.4 shows, that participants in university open lectures were normally educationally well-qualified people.

The Open College of the North-West

The Open College of the North-West, the first of the Open College Federations, started in 1975 and, therefore, long pre-dates the inception of the Extra-Mural

Table 12.4 *Highest Previous Educational Qualification of Participants in Open Lectures 1986–7 (per cent)*

Degree; teacher's certificate; other professional qualification	60
A-level; Open College Stage B and equivalent	14
O-level and equivalent	4
No qualifications	12
No response	11

Studies Office. However, although it has no formal role in administering the Open College, the Office has attempted to play a substantial role in its development through conducting a series of monitoring and evaluation studies and, on the basis of what is learned from these and from developments elsewhere, giving advice, raising issues and problems and making proposals.

The Open College of the North-West is (1987–8) a federation of seventeen adult and further education colleges and centres (in Lancashire and in four other local education authorities) and two institutions of higher education, the Lancashire Polytechnic and the University of Lancaster. Originally called the 'Alternatives to A Level Scheme' for adults, it claims to be 'a new approach to part-time learning for adults returning to study who want to take courses for:

- Interest
- Preparation for higher education
- Improvement of job prospects'.

The part-time courses are taught in the colleges and centres under LEA regulations and fee structures, but the syllabuses are agreed with, and validated by, the polytechnic and the university, at two levels. At Stage B level (the level prior to entry to higher education) coursework and examination assessments are also agreed with the institutions of higher education. Passes at Stage B with certain grades are recognised as achieving the general matriculation requirements by the polytechnic and the university and are increasingly recognised elsewhere in the country by institutions of higher education and professional bodies.

The Open College of the North-West has very large enrolments on its courses – 5,003 in 1986–7 and expected to show a 40 per cent increase in 1987–8. However, although seventy-seven different courses are potentially available at Stage A and Stage B, adults enrol in predictable clusters. At Stage A (1985–6 enrolment figures) 23 per cent were on social science courses, 22 per cent on computing and 17 per cent on study techniques and only 4.5 per cent on technology and 2 per cent on science. At Stage B (1985–6 enrolment figures) the largest of enrolments were 35 per cent in social sciences, 19 per cent in English and 13 per cent in languages and European studies. A September 1986 enrolment survey (Lucas 1987), with a response rate difficult to ascertain but probably about 60 per cent, showed that 55 per cent of Open College students were female, 74 per cent between the ages of 21 and 45 years, 47 per cent in full-time employment and 26 per cent registered unemployed, 2 per cent of ethnic black origin, 21 per cent reporting no educational qualifications and a further 35 per cent reporting educational qualifications no higher than GCE O level. Socioeconomic grouping of students was not attempted in this survey; a previous survey (Percy and Powell 1980) suggested that only 5 per cent of Open College students could be classified in Registrar-General's categories 4 and 5 (partly skilled and unskilled).

In October 1985 (and there is no automatic procedure for collecting such statistics) only 64 Open College students could be traced as entering higher education (35 into the University of Lancaster, 20 into the Lancashire Polytechnic and 9 elsewhere). The ratio between this figure and the total course enrolment (not individual student) figures for the Open College in September 1982 (three years before) is of the order of 1:23. What does this ratio indicate about the performance of the Open College? The range of monitoring and evaluation studies conducted over the years sheds some light. It is clear that the Open College has great success in attracting certain kinds of adult to return to study (Percy *et al.* 1980, pp. 465–6). It has a strong and clear image of being 'specially for adults'; it places emphasis on induction counselling and the provision of study techniques courses; and students can gain success at Stage A without taking formal examinations. Students report that their educational confidence is boosted by their experience of their first one or two Open College units (Percy *et al.* 1980, pp. 433–42). However, few students on Open College courses have deliberate and unequivocal notions of preparation for higher education, of moving through several Stage A and two Stage B units towards entry to higher education. Rather the pattern is for adults, once over the initial confidence hurdle, to do their own thing, to use Open College courses to fit their own intrinsic, and often short-term, study and life plans and, perhaps, to move on to other course provision or forms of study. Thus a follow-up enquiry into Open College students showed that, of a sample of 185 Open College students, 56 per cent had taken no more than two Stage A courses in a twenty-month period. Yet, at the time of the follow-up, 42 per cent of the total sample were engaged in forms of 'academic' study other than at the Open College (Percy *et al.* 1983b, pp. 553–5).

The Summer Programme

The Lancaster University Summer Programme of residential holiday courses for adults and their children, which was begun by the Extra-Mural Studies Office in 1981, can be characterised as a cuckoo in the nest in two senses. It has grown to be by far the largest provision organised by the Office, requiring large amounts of staff time throughout the year. And, of all the activities of the Office, it is the one with the greatest emphasis on income generation. Because it consumes university residential and catering services at a slack time of the year, the Summer Programme now makes a significant contribution to the University's finances.

The Summer Programme lasts for three weeks in late July and August and offers week-long courses in a wide range of subjects and activities, from the academic and in-service professional to sporting, craft, outdoor and hobby courses. There are no entry qualifications to courses but some require previous knowledge or skill. About 60 per cent of tutors are university members or have university connections. In 1987, there were about 1,100 participants over the three weeks, 70 per cent of these being fully resident in the university. Eighty per cent of the total were adults (the remainder being between the ages of five and seventeen years). The Summer Programme has a good student return rate. In 1987, 22.5 per cent were returning for the second time and a further 11 per cent for the third or further time.

Table 12.5 shows the age distribution of the adult students attending the

Table 12.5   *Age Distribution of Adults Participating in Summer Programme, 1985 (per cent)*

18–19	0.6
20–29	5.5
30–39	18.3
40–49	28.1
50–59	28.7
60 +	18.6

Summer Programme in 1985 on whom information was available ($n = 327$). This information on age, analysed by 'situation of client' (that is, whether they come to Lancaster on their own, with a spouse or partner, in a family group or in a group of friends) showed that students most likely to come alone were those in the thirty to thirty-nine age group (63 per cent) and the over-sixties (49 per cent). Students in the forty to forty-nine age group were most likely (58 per cent) to be in a family group; those in the fifty to fifty-nine age group were equally likely to be alone (38 per cent) or in a family group (38 per cent).

Table 12. 6 shows that there is no ambiguity about the socioeconomic groups from which residential Summer Programme students come (data were available on 385 from about 600 residential adult students in 1987). They are professional and middle-class people.

The Summer Programme is priced as a holiday and is not inexpensive for the students. Yet it is more than a holiday; most students spend thirty hours and more per week on their courses and coursework. Yet not all of them attend adult education classes at home. In a survey in 1984 (about 65 per cent of adult participants responded, $n = 243$), 22 per cent reported that they never attended classes at home (48 per cent attended 'sometimes' and 30 per cent 'often'). Why, then, do they do so at Lancaster? Students use words and phrases such as 'informality', 'friendliness', 'the tutors are experts here', 'facilities are purpose-built', and 'if you make a fool of yourself on the course, it doesn't matter: it's a holiday' to explain their participation. A blend of the atmosphere generated by the ambience of a holiday, the supportive and non-competitive nature of a student body living, eating and relaxing together and the quality associated, rightly or wrongly, with university teaching and facilities comes together to develop learning interests which, on students' reports, survive the journey home.

Table 12.6   *Summer Programme Students, 1987 (per cent)*

Upper middle (A)	3.6
Middle (B)	68.8
Lower middle (C1)	27.0
Skilled working (C2)	0.5
Semi-skilled and unskilled (D)	0
Lowest levels of subsistence (E)	0

Discussion

There is little justification for lengthy conclusions to this paper. In comparison with the volume of adult education provision in universities, colleges and centres throughout the country, the activities of the Extra-Mural Studies Office at Lancaster are small-scale. The core staffing of the Office is tiny; there are only eight years of work on which to reflect; there are obviously assumptions yet to test and expediencies to remove. There are no grounds for building an elaborate superstructure of theory or policy on this work.

It does seem, however, that the current rhetoric about access to higher education is concerned with securing adult students for institutions rather than adapting institutions to adult students. The emphasis is on institutional survival rather than upon the circumstances of adult learning. What seems to matter is to get students on to degree courses for the 1990s as the effects of the declining birth-rate of a decade and a half ago are felt; adults are one of the most obvious and welcome sources of such students.

There is nothing wrong with this rhetoric but it seems to follow from the evidence and argument of this paper that it is only a partial rhetoric. Pragmatically, the indicators of success and performance for universities in access provision will continue to relate to the increased admission of non-traditional students to degree courses and to their nurturing to a good degree performance. But the indicators ought also to measure a university's performance in being a community educational resource, in offering experimental and discontinuous educational opportunities to adults, in seeking to give access points to university learning expertise and facilities in a variety of ways and levels. The starting point has to be the adult learner, not the syllabus, the course or the institution. The model of the educationally unqualified adult, 'returning to study' and beginning a deliberate and hopefully unhindered educational march towards higher education entry is the one on which much university thinking about access is founded. This paper suggests that it is not a totally appropriate one. Nor is the model which has much currency in the adult education world of much validity – that of the unpredictable and capriciously participant adult student who needs to be ensnared, seduced or bought into enrolment by methods not yet discovered. We would prefer policy and practice based on the model (for which there is much evidence) of the learning and curious adult who will turn to educational providers when they make their offerings flexible and attractive enough to fit in with the adult's sometimes short-term and short-lived interests and goals.

That model is relevant to the general observation (to some, criticism) which can be made about the work to date of the Extra-Mural Studies Office at Lancaster. It has barely touched working-class and disadvantaged people. That is largely true, although one can cite individual exceptions and much depends on the definition of the amorphous notion of 'disadvantage'. Certainly, for example, elderly and retired people have taken significant interest in what the Office has been doing. The image of a university is, of course, a strong one which can act both as an incentive and as a deterrent. To some it is of a promised land, a purveyor of opportunity and status; to others it is of an incomprehensible, alien and remote world. Universities – particularly those situated on green hills in the country – do not appear to 'fit in' with the lifeworlds, the interests and goals, of many people. The burden of this paper, however, is that they can do. To do so, they will have to change and their image will have to change. The dialectic is theoretically possible. On the one side, the university is a unique assembly of intellectual resource and physical facilities; on the other side, adults in the community learn to live their lives using means which make sense to them. The two can come together.

References

Brookfield, S. (1980) 'Independent adult learning', unpublished PhD dissertation, University of Leicester.

Lucas, S. M. (1987) 'Open College students: September 1986. An analysis of their characteristics', University of Lancaster, unpublished report.

Percy, K. A. *et al.* (1980) *The Open College in the North West: A Research Report.* Coombe Lodge, The Further Education Staff College.

Percy, K. A. *et al.* (1983a) *Post-Initial Education in the North West of England: A Survey of Provision*, Leicester, Advisory Council for Adult and Continuing Education.

Percy, K. A. *et al.* (1983b) *Students in the Open College of the North West: A Follow-Up Study.* Coombe Lodge, The Further Education Staff College.

Percy, K. A. *et al.* (1988) *Learning Activity in Voluntary Organisations*, Leicester, Unit for Development of Adult Continuing Education.

Percy, K. A. and Powell, J. (1980) 'A first evaluation of the Open College' in K. A. Percy and S. M. Lucas (eds), *The Open College and Alternatives*, University of Lancaster, IPCE.

Percy, K. A. and Ramsden, P. (1980) *Independent Study: Two Examples from English Higher Education*, London, Society for Research into Higher Education.

Tough, A. (1979) *The Adult's Learning Projects: A Fresh Approach to Theory and Practice in Adult Learning* (2nd edn), Toronto, Ontario Institute for Studies in Education.

13

Opening Access to Higher Education by Recognising Capability

Edmund P. Clark

Expansion of higher education and selection policy

There seems to be broad agreement that the United Kingdom should increase the graduate proportion of the population. Currently the aim is to raise that proportion from 13 per cent to 18 per cent. The arguments for such an increase seem to be accepted both by higher education and by industry, and they relate primarily to the nation's industrial competitiveness in world markets.

This paper in no way dissents from the broad agreement about growth. It does, however, raise questions of *quality* and *equity*. It is calculated that if present entry standards were to be lowered by 2 A-level points overall about 10,000 more students would be eligible for higher education places. This would be one way of 'opening access', but not the best way. Those selected would tend to be less able young people from economically, socially and educationally more favoured backgrounds of the sort that keep young people in school and bring them through A-level courses, rather than brighter people from less advantaged circumstances and in a wider age-bracket. This approach would tend to depress standards overall, perpetuate an inequitable pattern of opportunities and fail to procure maximum national benefit from the investment made. It would also tend to inhibit the growth of alternatives to A levels as preparation for higher education and to weaken the impulse to provide more useful forms of learning in higher education which recognise and develop a wider range of capabilities in the students than it has traditionally done. This would be a pity, as such curriculum reform is now clearly on the agenda and it promises benefits to *all* students, not only mature and/or non-standard entry ones.

Academic and other models of learning

The traditional academic models of learning, by no means universal but still widely influential both in higher education and at A-level, are less and less considered to be the ideal model for developing crucial capabilities. Sooner or later those models are likely to be largely replaced or modified.

Polytechnics are generally more accustomed than universities to recruiting applicants with vocational qualifications and defined vocational aims. They have a better appreciation of the implications of recent curriculum developments in colleges and schools (BTEC, CPVE, etc.) They are more open to mature students: students with non-standard qualifications and those interested, out of preference or necessity, in modes of study other than grant-supported full-time attendance. For all these reasons they are in a better position to recognise 'capability' as a human value and as a relevant factor in selection for courses, and to develop 'capability' further in their provision. There are indications that some universities are now following the polytechnics' lead in curriculum and selection policy. High-level reviews of the content and method of university courses are in hand. Enterprise elements are to be introduced into all courses. Current proposals to broaden A levels need to be seen as part of the same trend of thinking.

Factors likely to widen access

Concomitant questions relating to access and opportunity management are also being debated. It is possible that higher education institutions will be discouraged from setting A-level point-score targets. Institutions that demonstrably respond best to learners' and employers' needs (that is, arguably, by prioritising 'capability' aims) may attract extra funding, both from the public and the private sector. Likewise there may be incentives for accepting higher quotas of mature learners and/or learners with non-A-level qualifications, and for offering more diverse modes of study to accommodate more part-time and evening students, more 'open' and distance-learning students, and more students wishing to use credit transfer, to switch modes and to accumulate credits on a stop-and-start basis. Some of these developments will prove more useful than others but the overall effect should be to open higher education access to more able and motivated people from a much wider range of circumstances and age groups, to make higher education learning more life-related and useful, and to achieve cost benefits.

The key to curriculum reform in higher education may be modularisation. This should facilitate a swing towards more task-based learning, which will suit the less academic sorts of learner and those who have developed, from their life experience as much as from their education, an appetite for solving problems and getting practical results and skills in working with others. This implies a redefinition of success and excellence, which will be increasingly reflected in the assessment arrangements and in the learning experiences offered by the courses.

If A-level studies are merely broadened, but continue in their present style, problems will remain. There will be a marked discontinuity between GCSE, which is increasingly task-based, and A-level studies, and from A levels to higher education where changes in learning style are already in evidence and can now be expected to accelerate. The National Council for Vocational

Qualifications (NCVQ) intends to improve the routes from vocational learning to higher education and it could come about that these routes will become more popular, and effective, than unreformed A levels.

Capability Audits

Higher education admissions tutors and gatekeepers are likely to find themselves confronted by more and more applicants whose qualifications are not comparable in the direct way that an A-level grade B is comparable with an A-level grade C. They will feel the need for *evidence of capability* as a key and common element among whatever other evidence of eligibility is offered. It will help them to pick the brightest applicants available and to be assured that the candidates they pick will be resourceful, well-motivated learners likely to rise to the challenges provided by the course they are entering.

Such evidence of capability does not at present exist in standard public form, but it would not be difficult to develop it. First, there seems to be agreement among vice chancellors and industrialists that more eighteen-year-olds should be encouraged to spend a year or more in a non-educational setting before entering higher education. It might be in 'industry' (in its broadest sense) or in community service at home or abroad. In any case it would need to be a *challenging* experience. The capability evidence to be drawn from it would include an account of the experience, written under tutorial advice, to demonstrate that the applicant can give an audit of what he/she has learned from this (and other relevant) experience; knows what the higher education selectors are looking for in terms of interests, experience and personal qualities (determination, intelligence, resourcefulness, social skills, initiative, etc.); and can relate evidence of his/her interests, experience and personal qualities to those course selection requirements.

Second, mature students who do not need to take a year out to acquire non-educational experience can carry out a similar capability audit, using experience in employment or business, in child-rearing, community activity, travel, cultural activity, etc., as well as educational experience, of course. The capability audit, one would hope, would be of use, in its own right, to applicants, in helping them to recognise their own capabilities, to clarify their aims and test their motivation and to relate many aspects of their abilities and personal qualities to the requirements and opportunities of higher education. They should become better self-advocates, and readier for higher education when they reach it. Capability audits will also help selectors by providing suitable reference material for the selection interview, which should help them to make better choices.

Five things to be done

Five things have to be achieved before this new kind of evidence can assume its proper place in the educational system.

1   Admissions tutors in higher education need to prepare statements of what they are looking for in terms of interests, experience and personal qualities, as well as knowledge and study skills. These statements will vary from course to course and will clearly be quite different from A-level grade requirements and terms of exemption.

2   General guidelines need to be worked out and agreed by a range of participants, especially in higher education, and circulated. They would include advice on the sorts of experience that might be relevant as a basis for qualification, on the distinction between evidence-and-argument as against anecdote-with-implication, on the format and length of applicants' submissions and on the format and contents of higher education course selection requirement statements.

3   For applicants who are not students tutorial advice on drawing up a capability audit needs to be readily available all over the country; it could be provided by higher education and further education staff in the form of individual advisory interviews. It might also be a substantial feature of further education access courses and indeed of a wide range of vocational and A-level courses for school and college students. Different applicants will need different amounts and kinds of advice.

4   Development work needs to be done on the formats and procedures, borrowing, as appropriate, from developments in accreditation of prior learning in further and adult education and from records of achievement in schools.

5   Development work also needs to be done on the two kinds of staff involved: the advisory tutors, who will need to display considerable skills in helping learners to assess and advocate themselves effectively; and the higher education admissions tutors and interviewers, who will need to be able to evaluate such evidence about applicants with confidence, and to give it due weight in their selection decisions.

The next step

We next have to set up a working group of interested parties, to draw up proposals for a pilot project. Enquiries welcome.

14

Marketing Courses to Overseas Students: A Case Study of Two Universities

Margaret Kinnell

Marketing higher education

The importance of marketing, as a management activity of particular relevance for institutions concerned with overseas student recruitment, has become something of a truism recently. The British Council has been particularly active in promoting the view that marketing activities, if properly organised, can improve both the initial recruiting drive and, equally importantly, consumer satisfaction. London University Institute of Education has recently completed a survey of the marketing strategies of British higher education institutions – evidence for the increased general awareness that marketing is about more than promoting courses. Universities and polytechnics have woken up to the need for a strategic approach to the serious business of competing in world markets for students. That said, co-ordinated marketing activities within British higher education are still relatively novel, although they are becoming of greater significance. The Overseas Student Trust (1986) survey found a distinct shift of emphasis towards a more clearly defined marketing approach, with those universities which had the most to gain financially the most active in developing recruitment strategies. Nevertheless, of the thirteen institutions studied in some depth, only six had well-developed policies. It is clear, from the Jarratt Report (Committee of Vice-Chancellors and Principals 1985) and other evidence, that tertiary institutions will increasingly be expected to relate their management functions to market forces, and that the overseas student question is one of the first instances of how this might operate in practice. CVCP (1985, p. 16) specifically stated that: 'Overseas students are welcomed by universities as an important contribution to the international character of the institutions. They are also a valuable source of income as they can often be educated at marginal cost to the universities.' Even here, however, despite the implicit recognition that marketing activities are of importance, there is little concrete offered by Jarratt suggesting ways in which these should be linked to other management functions.

The effective management of overseas student recruitment which, it is accepted, represents an important contribution to the intellectual and cultural life of universities as well as a source of revenue, is of obvious importance to institutions – although much more, it seems at present, on account of financial considerations than a desire to maximise cultural enrichment. Not least, it is important for institutions to 'get it right' as an indication of the extent to which they can make use of established business practices. Jarratt has laid a marker for future expectations of performance:

> a university which has not given corporate consideration to the questions of where it stands academically in relation to quality, spread and market performance, and where it wants to be in five years time, will have less chance of success and will be in danger of drifting (CVCP 1985, p. 21).

Competing in the world's market place for students exposes British higher education to very public scrutiny of its ability to meet the challenge of both recruiting in and retaining a share of the market.

To suggest that a wholesale adoption of business-related marketing techniques could solve universities' resource problems would, however, be to deny the complexity of both the institutions and the environment in which they operate.

Partly analytical, partly prescriptive, the learning and living experiences of students will be related to business and service organisation marketing. However, marketing is not offered as a panacea; although it will be argued in conclusion that marketing principles may usefully be applied by universities as a means of structuring their management of overseas student recruitment – an important aspect of universities' strategic planning.

Marketing principles and overseas student recruitment

It has been taken as axiomatic throughout the study that gave rise to this paper that 'marketing' should not be viewed simply as 'promoting' services to prospective students. On the contrary, marketing is about the whole range of those activities within institutions that result in consumer satisfaction, including: assessing the institution's strengths and weaknesses in relation to provision for overseas students; analysing environmental influences on overseas student recruitment; understanding the nature of relevant markets and publics; analysing overseas students' needs; defining organisational objectives in relation to overseas students; analysing the institution's services (and 'products') for overseas students; designing courses and research programmes to meet the needs of overseas students; determining fees, costs and designing the appropriate administrative structures to implement financial controls; deciding on effective support services and how they should be implemented; and promotion and publicity (Kotler 1975).

In summary, those aspects of marketing theory used for the present analysis were those which provided the means of relating the organisation of universities to students' needs. Marketing assumes a client orientation on the part of institutions, a point of view that lies at the heart of marketing philosophy. The following account of overseas student recruitment in two universities – Loughborough and Nottingham – was considered from this marketing viewpoint precisely because such a client orientation has been shown to be an effective means of both planning for and implementing service delivery in an educational setting, as indeed in other types of service organisation. Nevertheless, the caveat noted above must be reiterated – marketing alone cannot achieve results. As Cuthbert (1980) noted somewhat pessimistically in his study of public sector higher education marketing: 'The formal management structures completely fail to acknowledge the marketing function, and provide conclusive evidence of the product or the selling orientation which describes prevailing management attitudes.' Marketing principles can only achieve results where the prevailing management philosophy and, most importantly, organisational structures, acknowledge the primacy of societal marketing concepts in managing overseas student recruitment.

Marketing principles and problems: Marketing and overseas student recruitment in two universities

The analysis of marketing and overseas student recruitment in the two universities focuses on the following principles:

1 The importance of understanding environmental influences, external and internal. This will include an appraisal of relevant external factors, an understanding of the market and of competition, together with the nature of the internal environment.
2 The significance of clients' needs (clients here are defined as students), as the basis of a marketing orientation.
3 The need to analyse the institution's service provision, relating this to clients' expectations and the objectives of the organisation.

While not a comprehensive consideration of the 'marketing mix', which would also include analyses of fees policies, promotion and publicity, these factors form the basis for a marketing audit, setting out the institution's strengths and weaknesses in matching students' expectations with the university's 'products' (its courses and research programmes).

Environmental influences

The external environments in which universities are operating at present are both complex and dynamic. Pressures arising from continuing change are now endemic, and have to be accommodated in strategic planning by institutions. Demographic shifts, shrinking resources and the full-cost fees policy (which despite its amelioration by the Pym package is a continuing constraint on recruitment) are three of the salient factors that impinge on universities' policies on overseas student recruitment, influencing decisions on how many students to recruit and from where. There are several significant sets of actors who influence recruitment, including: the government, through its policies and resource allocation; foreign governments, through their sponsorship of students; a range of organisations, notably the British Council, through sponsoring students and offering advice to universities on recruitment, as well as practical facilities like the English Language Testing Service and promotional activities; and, importantly, the network of past graduates who spread the word amongst their compatriots.

All have considerable influence through a complex network of relationships, with each other as well as with the institution. While the significance of the external environment is well recognised and common to all institutions at present, the importance of the internal environment, what Handy characterises as the 'culture' of the organisation (Cuthbert 1980), is less easily captured and is, by its nature, specific to the university under scrutiny. In considering the cultures of Loughborough and Nottingham universities, in relation to overseas student recruitment, the researchers interviewed a range of staff across all functions, including vice chancellors and academic staff, administrative and domestic staff as well as those from welfare and support agencies on both campuses. A picture as complex as that painted by the external environment emerged from these discussions, with a range of attitudes and practices in dealing with overseas students very much in evidence. While there was general unanimity on the need for universities to recruit overseas students, some of the attitudes about how to manage interactions with students produced conflicting messages. To take what might appear a trivial example, but one which was not untypical: when a domestic supervisor responsible for a hall with a high proportion of overseas students was interviewed, it came as something of a surprise to her to be asked about the special needs of overseas students. Initially, she considered all students to have similar needs, until the questions set her thinking and she acknowledged that foreign students probably did have special requirements. It was apparent that her well-meaning policy of treating all students alike may have resulted in a lack of sensitivity to the needs of separate groups – especially within the misleadingly blanket term 'overseas students'. This attitude of 'treating all students alike' was manifested by other, more senior staff, both within residential management functions and other support services. While there was general acknowledgement of the need to recruit overseas students, for financial and educational reasons, there appeared to be a lack of understanding of their expectations and needs.

The more formal organisational structures were also crucial when considering the systems which managed recruitment. These systems were seen to be fragmented across the functions most relevant to overseas students. While some of the administration of recruitment was centrally organised on both campuses, much was also left to departments to organise. The autonomy of the academic departments and a lack of co-ordination between them was very much in evidence. There was an apparent lack of policy direction. The late Vice Chancellor of Loughborough was frank in stating that as far as he was aware there was no overall policy statement as such, although there was an

Inter-School Working Party on Recruitment. Nottingham has a similar, Senate Committee on Overseas Students Recruitment. Since the start of the research project both universities have begun to formalise policies: the need to produce academic plans in the wake of the Jarratt Report had considerable impact on this, as did the climate of opinion represented in the lobbying by the United Kingdom Council on Overseas Student Affairs (UKCOSA) and the Overseas Student Trust (OST). However, even with the development of policy-making now under way, the formal structures in both universities have changed little at present. There continues to be considerable fragmentation of those systems that deal with recruitment and support for overseas students. Academic departments, in both universities, still bear much of the responsibility, in addition to academic matters, for much of the administration in relation to overseas students and for students' welfare in general. While Loughborough and Nottingham are dissimilar institutions in many senses – the one being a relative newcomer and technologically orientated, the other having the atmosphere of a longer tradition than its forty-year-old Charter would suggest – there were remarkable similarities in the autonomy accorded to academic departments, within very broadly defined parameters. Such important considerations as entry requirements were very much matters for departmental discretion, within certain limits at the lowest level. Admissions tutors would take the different educational opportunities of overseas students into account, for example, in a way which they would not for British students. While, in talking to a senior policy-maker, it was made clear that standards were to be maintained overall – at the departmental level, with the pressure to recruit overseas students wherever possible, there appeared to be a flexible approach.

Student welfare was organised somewhat differently on both campuses; Nottingham having a designated Overseas Students Bureau, while at Loughborough the overstretched Student Counselling service spent much of its time on overseas student support of various kinds. Again, despite these different structures, there was a similarity in the needs expressed by staff for additional resources. Much of the support for students came from dedicated individuals and on one campus resentment was expressed by some at having worked unfunded and largely unrecognised for many years. The internal environment, it was expressed by several staff on both campuses, did not encourage academics to spend time and effort on the administrative and welfare aspects of managing overseas student support, in a climate where publications and research funding were the accepted criteria of staff performance.

The market and the competition posed by other institutions, here and abroad, appeared to be well understood. Market research undertaken by the British Council has enabled universities to concentrate their recruiting efforts in particular countries, those which it has singled out as especially favourable to British higher education – either through links stretching back over many years, or because recent changes in the economic and political climate have opened up the market (as is the case with China). Individual departments, on both campuses, had also developed their own links, some of long standing, with specific countries: for example, Nottingham's School of Education with Hong Kong, and Loughborough's Department of Civil Engineering with a range of developing countries which send students on a specialist water engineering course.

The external environment and the nature of the market were therefore given careful attention by both universities, in the setting up of committees to oversee and to foster recruitment. Monitoring the external environment was well developed, both through these formal university committees and by individual departments. Those responsible for admissions in departments appeared well versed in the competitors and market for their subject fields. There was little evidence, however, of a similar awareness of the nature and significance of the internal environment, nor indeed of the interaction between internal and external environmental pressures.

Students' needs and expectations

In order to relate the needs of students to the marketing activities of the universities, investigating students' perceptions was considered to be particularly important, as the literature on overseas student recruitment had largely overlooked the value of a phenomenological appraoch to clients' perceptions of their learning and living experiences in a British university. The methods used in the present study were to administer questionnaires, first, to all foreign students on both campuses completing their studies in 1986, and second, to groups of new students beginning their studies in the autumn of 1986 – those attending pre-sessional orientation courses. Follow-up interviews, one-to-one and in groups, were then conducted with those students volunteering their names on completed questionnaires.

As research students presented especially difficult problems of access (they had no set start or finish dates), they were also considered separately; a series of structured interviews was conducted with those students volunteering for this exercise.

Overseas students completing their studies in 1986

The emphasis in analysing students' needs and expectations lay with this component of the data; this first survey (questionnaires and interviews) supplied the majority of the information, which was later supported by findings from the interviews with research students and the 'expectations' survey. In 1986, there were 713 overseas students at Loughborough, of whom the majority were postgraduates, and 619 at Nottingham, most of whom were undergraduates. Those leaving, and making up the sample, were 354 and 204 respectively (see Table 14.1).

The initial questionnaire was designed to identify students' feelings about their experiences at Loughborough and Nottingham, concerning: receipt of prior information; level of fees; teaching and tutoring approaches; language issues; study methods; sources of academic and personal guidance;

Table 14.1 *Sample and Response of Overseas Students Completing their Studies 1986, by Home Country Groupings:*

Country groups	Loughborough University of Technology		Nottingham University	
	Sample	Completed questionnaires	Sample	Completed questionnaires
Far East and Antipodes	120	20(17%)	101	58(57%)
Europe	38	7(18%)	35	10(29%)
Americas	12	2(17%)	31	9(29%)
Africa	94	21(22%)	20	15(75%)
Middle East and Arab countries	88	10(11%)	17	5(29%)
Not known	2	1(50%)	–	–
Total	354	61(17%)	204	97(48%)

accommodation; orientation issues and contacts with British students. The major findings are given in summary:

1 Pre-arrival communications to students in their home countries were seen as a vital prerequisite to a proper understanding of, first, British culture and higher education in general, and second, the specific institution, its expectations, academic programmes and facilities. This information did not always reach students, because of postal delays and often erratic communication services in their home countries. There was a need for clear, appropriate and well-timed pre-arrival information, giving accurate factual detail to alleviate students' anxieties.

2 On arrival, it was considered important that suitable permanent accommodation should be available as soon as students reached the university. Spending a large part of the first term in temporary accommodation caused considerable stress in students. First impressions stayed with students.

3 Appropriate information, advice and help on arrival were important to help create favourable first impressions and to prevent the student's experiences becoming problem-centred. A pre-sessional orientation course was a worthwhile means of easing culture and language difficulties and helping adjustment to living as a student in the United Kingdom. Those students who did not attend such a course could not easily find such in-depth help towards adjustment subsequently.

4 Students approved the relatively informal lecturing styles adopted in both universities; however, the perception that this was an 'undirected' means of teaching, as contrasted with their earlier educational experiences, created difficulties for some.

5 Early contacts with academic tutors seemed to be crucial; students wanted their teachers to take the initiative in making these contacts. The need for structure and support from sympathetic faculty tutors was expressed – those

tutors responsible for students' general academic development throughout their course. A clear system giving regular, adequate access to such support, with plentiful opportunities for consultation and discussion, was seen as particularly important by research students.

6   The organisation of accommodation did not seem to take sufficiently into account the vacation needs of overseas students, nor their special dietary requirements. The needs of mature students with family commitments, especially women, were noted in particular.

7   Students generally appreciated the good quality of courses. They found them relevant on the whole, although an international dimension was considered to be missing in some. It was felt that dividing students into home and overseas classes in some teaching situations could give rise to resentment.

8   Many students were concerned with their inadequate English and/or study skills and would have liked there to be more emphasis on these, especially in the early weeks.

9   The opportunity to meet and befriend British people, especially other students, was seen as important, but this could be an unfulfilled expectation where the initial welcome to an institution dissipated and students retreated into their own national groups. Contact with home students was a particular problem for mature postgraduates. Both universities, it was felt, were organised primarily around undergraduates' needs while postgraduates considered that they too were often not coping and suffered from similar problems of adjusting to a new situation. Assumptions about their ability to handle this were sometimes ill-founded.

Expectations on arrival at university: Overseas students beginning their studies in 1986

When new students were sampled on their expectations of life in a British university many of these points re-emerged. A general desire to make the most of a unique opportunity to study in the UK and to gain vocational qualifications were, unsurprisingly, the concerns most often mentioned. Significantly though, and in line with the findings of the first survey of existing students on both campuses, they were also aware of the likely problems they would encounter in a strange environment:

> I am used to living as part of the majority. Being in the minority will require adjustments. I look forward to it because so far a good number of people seem friendly. Some people however give me uncomfortable looks.

Emphasis on the broadening of personal as well as educational experience was very strong; students were eager to meet with people from other cultures and exchange experiences. Being a student at university gave important status; it also entailed the responsibility of succeeding, which created great pressures for some. The cost of coming to study in England heightened these expectations and pressures:

As an overseas student in England I think I have paid tremendously. Therefore in return I am expecting quite a lot from it.

Content analysis of students' writing on their expectations revealed that, in both institutions, the achievement of a qualification, strongly related to vocational needs, figured prominently. The predictable fears (already identified in the first survey) about coping with academic work were exacerbated by communication worries and the fear of failure. The sense of reverence in which they held their tutors was a further complicating factor:

> I am also interested in knowing how the lecturers and tutors study deeply in their own areas. The ways, the approaches and the spirits they own and behave may stimulate me . . . I think not only their methodology and their academic achievements are significant to me but more valuable may be their attitude of learning, and their ways of thinking are striking to me (*sic*).

Students recognised the need to adjust personally to English culture; food was most often mentioned. The climate also caused worries, as did the English attitude to foreigners. Two Americans summarised the twin aspects of the problem:

> [I need to] overcome stereotypes concerning the English culture. As an American I have to overcome the stereotypes about my own country.

In the two student surveys, the needs of clients were clearly stated. To summarise: they expected to acquire an educational qualification, of vocational use to them; they wished to gain, academically and in personal terms, from their own and their sponsors' considerable investment in money and time. While these expectations differ little in some respects from those of home students, they appear to be much more keenly felt and to be overlain at all points by the fears, as well as the hopes, of cultural exchanges. Major areas for concern were information, accommodation and pastoral support.

Provision for overseas students

The data on which the analysis of the universities' provision for overseas students is based were largely taken from interviews across the various functions, academic, administrative and welfare, on both campuses. Specifically, staff were interviewed who had involvement in recruitment; pre-arrival administration; arrival procedures; academic and departmental provision; language provision; academic support; non-academic and welfare support; and social provision. To equate with the student side of the picture, the *perceptions* of staff were the principle means of gauging how students were dealt with.

As noted above, recruitment was a major focus for senior staff. Both universities had formal committees that were responsible for co-ordinating recruitment activities across departments and both offered financial incentives to departments who were particularly successful in this. There had also been serious attempts at public relations, with videos, glossy brochures and missions to various countries – Hong Kong and Malaysia, for example – partly in response to British Council promotional initiatives.

On both campuses there were reservations expressed by interviewees about the 'hype' surrounding these approaches, although senior policy makers were quick to insist that academic standards would not be sacrificed. However, departmental autonomy, discussed earlier, was a significant feature of the cultures of both universities: recruitment has traditionally been regarded as a departmental matter and incentives appeared to encourage this. There was confusion, therefore, between centralised policy and decentralised implementation. The point was made, in both universities, that admissions tutors receive little, if any, advice and guidance on their crucial role in the universities' recruitment of students. One professor felt that 'British personnel for recruiting need *training*'. While a staff-training programme was offered to admissions tutors on one campus, not all attended, and some, a senior administrator commented, exercised departmental autonomy in any event.

Publicity material, as staff on one campus noted, emphasised selling, rather than informing. Relevance, truthfulness and factual information on basic living requirements were seen to be important, especially before arrival.

On one campus there was the ironic situation that the 'post room', which handles all the university's mail, unless specifically asked, would try to save the university money by sending out all overseas mail surface, rather than air. This, as one academic commented, 'could lose the university thousands of pounds' worth of business'. While only a relatively minor administrative anomaly, this serves as an example of a lack of co-ordination that was noted by staff.

The handling of accommodation, a topic that recurred again and again in interviews with students, was a further case in point. Students expected this basic service to be offered to them as a package when they registered for courses, despite the universities' publicity indicating otherwise. However, there appeared to be a problem of co-ordinating offers of accommodation with offers of places on courses. Additionally, new overseas postgraduates were treated the same as other postgraduates, despite their needing, in many cases, as much support over finding accommodation as new undergraduates. Neither of the universities gave preference to overseas students, and on one campus it was explicitly stated that all students were treated alike. Both universities generally only made accommodation available during termtime, and overseas students had to be moved, either to another hall, or to other rooms within their own hall.

Academic support for overseas students particularly centred on language teaching: one of the commonest observations by staff was the greater time commitment needed for both teaching and supervising overseas students. English language support and pre-sessional orientation courses were offered on both campuses, but academic staff nevertheless were concerned at the poor English of some students. However, once again there appeared to be a problem of co-ordinating a policy on language qualifications required from students. Both universities had a minimum requirement but, as one member of staff wryly noted, 'If departments are insisting on university requirements, why is anyone turning up with inadequate language?' One reason may have lain in the uncertainty as to whether English was indeed the students' first language, and on one campus there was no specific language competency required for research students.

Despite the language problems, it was found that, when examining success and failure rates for overseas students in the previous three years, there was little difference between home and overseas students, so that the most important need of students was being met. This accounted for the general satisfaction expressed by students with the courses they were taking; teaching had been generally well received by all the students surveyed. The cost to the university, in terms of staff time, of this general academic success, could only be guessed at. No costing of the extra demands on resources, especially staff time, was undertaken by departments on either campus. If one added to this the cost of central support services – counselling, medical and academic support – the overall cost to the institution could be considerable. The goodwill of individuals in coping with the additional demands made on them by overseas students was observed in both universities, but there was a telling comment on the presumption that this was universal: 'Departments are rewarded for recruiting overseas students. Individuals in departments are not rewarded for teaching them!'

The 'marketing' of courses to overseas students appeared only to involve the planning of recruitment policies. As we have seen, however, the implementation of even these policies was beset by the problems of fragmented systems. Communication flows between the student and the university before arrival appeared sometimes to founder because of this lack of coherence. On one campus it was acknowledged that mechanisms for answering students' enquiries before arrival were in need of improvement. There were examples, departmentally, on both campuses of excellent and well-considered marketing programmes, which included all the elements of accepted marketing principles: clearly targeted initial publicity and recruitment; course design to meet specific needs; pastoral support from an experienced and skilled tutor. However, there was little evidence that this good practice had influenced the development of systems across the universities.

Conclusion

There are significant conclusions to be drawn from this evident mismatch between marketing principles and what is actually happening in the marketing of courses to overseas students. First, there appears to be no ongoing strategic planning of the institution's response to its complex external environment. Universities, like all organisations, have a need constantly to redefine their strengths and weaknesses as the demands on them change. Monitoring the outside world was well developed; relating this intelligence to internal structures appeared to be less clearly considered.

Second, the needs of overseas students were not always reflected in services. Academic and living needs were perceived as a package by students, but not by the universities. Defining organisational objectives in terms of these needs, rather than institutionally orientated needs, would seem to be a priority.

Third, evaluating an overseas student recruitment policy in terms of overall costs and benefits is a further priority. Much of the work on recruitment has tended to shirk this question. A marketing approach would ensure that, from the outset, when considering how universities should respond to threats from the environment, alternative courses of action would be generated. At present, overseas student recruitment is perceived as a major solution to resource problems. However, there is little, if any, evidence that this will prove to be the case in the long term. Some institutions have indeed perceived the converse to be true and are no longer actively recruiting in the overseas market. Accounting for the intangible benefits to universities, and to the country, has been abandoned by these institutions. In the current climate, it is easy to see why.

Further investigation is needed, particularly into cost measures that truly reflect the complex variables in the marketing of courses to overseas students. Only when marketing loses its image as an activity wholly bound up with publicity and recruitment practices and is seen as a co-ordinated management function is it likely that this complexity will be fully acknowledged and acted upon.

References

Committee of Vice-Chancellors and Principals (1985) *Report of the Steering Committee for Efficiency Studies in Universities* (the Jarratt Report), London, CVCP.

Cuthbert, R. (1980) 'The marketing function in education management', *Coombe Lodge Report*, 12(12) 521–34.

Kotler, P. (1975) *Marketing for Non-profit Organisations*, Englewood Cliffs, NJ, Prentice-Hall.

Overseas Student Trust (1986) *Overseas Students and their Place of Study: Report of a Survey*. London, Overseas Student Trust.

15

Management and Leadership Development in Universities: What's Happening and Where Are We Going?

Robin Middlehurst

Introduction

This paper is related to a two-year research project funded by the Department of Education and Science (DES) and entitled 'Leadership Development in Universities'. The contract is due for completion in December 1988. The objectives of the project are as follows:

(a) to evaluate the practical application of the current programme of leadership courses for senior university staff mounted for all universities by the University of Surrey under the direction of Professor John Adair;

(b) to undertake comparative research regarding leadership/management development in universities and other organisations which would enable the content of the course to be developed;

(c) to evaluate new course initiatives in related areas (such as finance/resource allocation, marketing, managing staff development and appraisal).

Since the start of the project in November 1986, a fourth objective has been added:

(d) to consider future requirements which might lead to a national strategy for leadership development in universities.

It is this fourth objective which provides the main focus for this paper. Mention will also be made of some of the findings relevant to objectives (a) and (c) where appropriate. However, the Interim Report of the project covers these in greater detail. It was submitted to the DES in September 1987.

Definitions and context

Throughout the life of this project two factors have proved a major headache: definitions and context. I shall deal with each in turn as they affect the whole position of management/leadership development in universities.

Definitions

There is no agreement about the terms 'management' and 'leadership' as they relate to the academic enterprise. As Atkins (1986) illustrated in a lecture at this conference last year, both words have 'high' and 'low' connotations. The values attached to the words will also affect the way in which the roles are performed: some heads of department see their position as academic 'leaders' while others regard themselves primarily as 'managers' of the department. Vice chancellors may see themselves as both managers and leaders.

Since both terms are drawn originally from sectors other than education, there is considerable disagreement as to whether either is appropriate in relation to academe. In deciding whether or not either *is* appropriate, the task of academic management or leadership must itself be defined. As Davies and Lockwood (1985) have indicated, this is an extremely complex process. The pluralistic nature of the university, its different functional forms, the various levels at which power and authority are exercised within it, all contribute to this complexity. It is unlikely that one definition of academic management or leadership will be appropriate to all levels. The task will include different skills, knowledge, attitudes and styles at different points in the enterprise. As a consequence, defining management or leadership development in universities is extremely problematic.

It is comforting to note from a recent study (Constable and McCormick 1987, p. 45) which reviewed management development in industry, that similar difficulties were encountered in that context:

(a) the terms education, training and development of managers meant different things in different organisations;
(b) to articulate the skills, abilities and competencies required of managers produces different answers, not only between companies but *within* companies;
(c) the term 'management' does not have a commonly shared meaning, some favouring the term and concept of leadership to that of management.

In order to avoid getting lost in the debate over terms, it is more appropriate to consider what it is that academic managers or leaders need to *do* and what they need to *know* in order to carry out their task effectively. It is these areas which will be focused upon here. The debate as to the nature, boundaries and conceptual framework of the task is best undertaken as part of the development process. Providers of programmes should make explicit the terms they adopt and negotiate with participants as to their validity and relevance.

Context

The context in which the research project is taking place is important in a variety of ways. In the first place, the context is that of universities in the United Kingdom – where the concept of management and leadership training for academics is relatively novel. There is thus no tradition of a training 'culture' in this field. Indeed, the organisational culture of universities as a whole has until recently been antipathetic to the notion of such training – in many quarters this tradition continues.

Second, the emergence of management/leadership development in universities is associated with unprecedented external 'assaults' on the system. The economic and political climate in which the task of university management is undertaken contributes formidable difficulties to this task and continues to change its character. It is a considerable challenge to design programmes which take account of both current and future directions when the ground is constantly shifting. This challenge is extended further by having to fund this new initiative from ever-decreasing resources.

Third, the need to provide management or leadership training at all for academics is viewed as representative of the assault on universities' traditional values. For some, it is seen as contributing to the imposition of an inappropriate model of management on universities. The source of this model, the Jarratt Report (CVCP 1985), is of considerable importance in relation to the 'Leadership Project'. Its recommendations and implications for training will be considered next.

The Jarratt Report

The Jarratt Report aims to encourage the streamlining of managerial systems in universities. It is intended that they become tighter, clearer and more explicit, quicker to respond to outside stimuli, incorporating greater internal and external accountability. Its emphasis is on altering university structures and procedures. Although the brief did not extend to a consideration of academic matters, emphasis on management immediately affects the functioning of the academic enterprise. The task of academic management is sketched, including outlines of some of the skills, responsibilities and accountabilities involved. The Report is therefore a prime source for identifyng training needs.

As universities already know, the Jarratt Report has considerable implications for senior academics and their role within the management of their institution. Heads of department are the most severely affected. They must still be eminent academics but should also be 'good managers'. In other words: they are to be budget-holders, capable of managing and budgeting resources, in accordance wth an agreed academic and financial plan and with responsibility for the plan's outcomes. They are to undertake major personnel functions, including staff management, appraisal and selection. They are, in addition, to continue their traditional roles representing the department internally and externally, promoting discipline, teaching and research as well as shouldering their share of committee responsibilities on behalf of the university.

In some recognition of the fact that these 'super dons' may not be able to maintain the pace indefinitely, they are encouraged only to serve in office for three to five years. This has implications for planned management succession and relevant training earlier in an academic career. It also has implications for who might be suited to the task and want to undertake it – when the task is stressful, time-consuming, poorly rewarded and likely to have detrimental effects on research and teaching. The former is still in practice the main criterion for promotion and status in universities.

At this point it may be worth looking at some views of the role of a head of department. The list of tasks and activities (Table 15.1) was compiled by a group of about twenty academic heads of department participating in a leadership course at Farnham Castle in Surrey. They also listed the skills they thought necessary to perform the task (Table 15.2). No doubt the lists could be added to, but even as they stand they comprise a considerable range of activities and responsibilities. Effectiveness in all areas demands ability, agility and excellent time management. It is not a role that should be undertaken without formal preparation.

In the Jarratt Report, the role of the dean is expected to continue to involve the provision of academic leadership within the faculty combined with responsibility for implementing university policy towards departments. Deans may also have control over budgets and resource allocation and be involved in appraisal of staff. Clearly, deans are required to be politically astute, competent negotiators and conciliators as well as effective resource managers in some cases. As one dean (not responsible for resources) has put it:

Table 15.1   *Tasks and Activities Undertaken in the Role of Academic Head of Department*

Monitoring teaching
Monitoring research
Effective and efficient leadership of the department
Communication with staff
Discipline: carrot and stick
Policy and planning: the department's direction
Resource development: finding the money
Academic leadership: professional commitments
Personnel management
Financial management
Representation of the department: internal adversarial role
Selection of staff
Link between central management and the department
Stimulating research activity
Attending committees
Teaching
Researching

Source: Compiled by participants in a course on leadership for heads of university departments, held at Farnham Castle in January 1987.

Table 15.2 *Skills Required for Academic Leadership and Management*

Communication	Listening
Presentation	Coaching
Negotiation	Decision-making
Committee work	Delegating
Judging/assessing	Political
Interpersonal	Research/scholarship
Planning/objective-setting	Catalyst in motivating
Controlling	Public relations
Financial	Teaching
Counselling	Holding a group together
Setting an example	

Source: as Table 15.1.

> Being Dean is an intensely political position . . . it is excellent practice in
> self-awareness, and by times exhilarating and very wearing. I can negoti-
> ate, reconcile, persuade and object (and am taken seriously), but have no
> authority to *decide*, unless a specific task is delegated to me by the VC.

With increased pressures on heads of department, the position of deans may be
formalised as a new level of management in the reporting structure.

Pro-vice chancellors at present have a variety of roles, ranging from executive
action with delegated responsibility through policy-making and co-ordination
to 'trouble shooting'. They should possess, therefore, a variety of skills: those of
politicians and negotiators, planners, initiators and co-ordinators of policy,
with a detailed understanding of university structures, constraints and procedures. As a recent course for new pro-vice chancellors and vice chancellors at
Windsor Castle indicated, they must be prepared to be flexible, to be figure-
heads and stand-ins where necessary; they must be efficient chairpersons and
good 'servants' – of the vice chancellor and the university. As questionnaire data
indicate, their roles vary widely between institutions. In many cases, responsibilities are ill-defined and often *ad hoc*. Like heads of department, they are trying
to be both managers and academics – protecting the latter interest to return to
on completion of their term.

In the Jarratt Report, the position of the vice chancellor (rector or principal)
as both academic leader and 'chief executive' responsible for the effective
management of the institution is given formal recognition. The postholder is
required to be a skilful negotiator and politician both internally and externally,
to be able to initiate, promote and gain consensus for strategic academic and
financial plans, to make and implement hard decisions – like closing the Classics
department while taking dignified account of the future of the staff within it – to
maintain morale and to consult, inform and communicate as widely as possible.
As one new vice chancellor described his role: 'the VC must be in the mould of a
super-head of department'. Professor Sizer argues that today's vice chancellor
should be a 'high quality manager of change of appropriate academic standing,
capable of overcoming institutional inertia' (Sizer 1987, p. 42). The Jarratt
Report recommends that all staff likely to have management responsibility

should receive appropriate training. This is reiterated in Sizer (1987). Some of Sizer's findings and recommendations will be considered next. This will provide some interesting examples of development programmes.

The Sizer Report

The Sizer Report (1987) illustrates the response of nine universities to the 1981 cuts, and in a sense puts flesh on the Jarratt bones. It illustrates changes that were made in internal structures and processes in order to respond quickly to conditions of financial stringency, contraction and changing needs. These changes were undertaken, in the main, before publication of the Jarratt Report. Out of the analysis of the nine universities' responses, twenty 'Managerial Guidelines for Vice-Chancellors and Principals' are identified. Many of the guidelines are concerned with the development of structures and procedures. However, others have strong implications for management/leadership development. I have chosen three of these at random.

The first discusses public relations:

(13.) Make positive efforts, and involve all staff, to continually promote the external image of the university and to secure additional income . . . . Develop and implement a planned and co-ordinated Public Relations programme directed at communicating to appropriate audiences the institutions' distinctive characteristics, strengths and appeal (Sizer 1987, p. 43).

An example of such a programme comes from the University of North Carolina. Here a training and development programme has been undertaken involving non-teaching support staff in a range of activities. Workshop titles include 'Communication and Relationship Maintenance' and 'Creative Leadership Development'; these have reportedly resulted in

an increased level of employee knowledge concerning the university's mission and goals, improved employee morale witnessed in a decrease of employee grievances and a better image of the university being projected by its staff (University of North Carolina 1987, p. 1).

The second discusses the external environment:

(2.) Recognise the importance of being aware of the external environment, in particular:
    (a) being aware of external factors and influences at work and being able to interpret these authoritatively within the institution;
    (b) being able to relate to and work effectively with external bodies; and
    (c) keeping a finger on the pulse of the local business and wider community (Sizer 1987, p. 42).

Two organisations include the development of competencies in this field in their management development programmes:

(i) the Civil Service Senior Management Programme under the heading 'Knowledge/Understanding of the Context of Your Work'. Seminar topics under this heading include: 'Government and Industry Study Group', 'Developments in the EEC', 'European Briefings', 'Current Social Issues' (Cabinet Office 1987).

Such topics might be of equal relevance to vice chancellors and their senior colleagues.

(ii) the Local Government Training Board runs a programme entitled 'Partnership at the Top'. This aims to link management theory, practice, project and consultancy work for trios of senior participants from local government, central government departments and the private sector. One of the main purposes of the programme is to encourage continuing working relationships amongst the trios when back in the community (Local Government Training Board 1987).

A programme of this kind could be valuable in universities at a time when links with industry and government (or grant agencies) are being actively sought.
    The third is concerned with communication:

(20.) Communicate with all departments, staff and student unions regarding progress in implementing the university's academic plan to maintain a shared commitment to its successful implementation (Sizer 1987, p. 45).

(This is intended to follow earlier consultation and communication with these groups in relation to the philosophy, planning process, timetable and monitoring of the plan.)
    Carrying out such an exercise would provide a major and effective example of management development in practice. It would also offer the associated benefits of raising morale and motivation throughout the institution. Effective communication is not something which is always practised either within or between institutions and their constituent parts, as Table 15.4 will illustrate later.
    In summary, both Jarratt and Sizer make recommendations about the staff who would benefit immediately from leadership and management training. They also indicate areas of knowledge, skills and attitudes which might be included in training and development programmes. Both reports imply that the purpose behind all such programmes is the need for the university and its staff to view themselves as a corporate enterprise with appropriate responsibilities and accountabilities (CVCP 1985, para. 3.41, p. 22).
    Although the implementation of the Reports' recommendations make management and leadership training essential in universities, they do not provide the only motive for such provision. A comprehensive strategy for individual and institutional development in this area *will* serve the purpose of providing knowledge and skills relevant to academic management in universities. It should also raise awareness of the issues and possibilities involved in such

management: alternative styles, approaches, structures and procedures. The provision of opportunities for management and leadership development are certainly necessary for the full implementation of Jarratt's recommendations. But equally, if the structural recommendations are *not* regarded as appropriate or useful, development opportunities will offer a forum for discussing and shaping viable alternatives to the Jarratt proposals. At present there is no such forum which can act on an informed basis to consider the implications and influence the direction of changes in the academic management of universities.

Definitions and delivery

Management 'education', 'training' and 'development' can be viewed at several levels. Constable and McCormick (1987, p. 9) differentiates between the three, defining *management education* as 'that process which results in formal qualifications up to and including post-graduate degrees'; *management training* is taken to be 'the formal learning activities which may or may not lead to qualifications and which may be received at any time in a working career'; *management development* is still broader and 'job experience and learning from other managers are integral parts of the development process'.

Delivery of programmes can also be varied. In large companies planned job rotation and secondments, in-company and external training courses, workshops and seminars, coaching, delegation, project work, assessment centres and regular appraisals will all form part of management development programmes. The whole 'package' will be part of a 'human resources' policy conceived in conjunction with the corporate plan and approved at the level of the board of directors. In smaller organisations, management development may be largely reactive – specific skills training related to particular needs (for example, computer literacy). If universities are to take seriously the development of their human resources, then a broad and coherent management development policy is essential. It is likely to include all staff at particular levels and involve a variety of opportunities. It should be linked to academic and financial plans and anticipate desired outcomes. As with appraisal and staff development in general, it is the only way to ensure coherence in matching the individual and institutional benefits of the process.

The current scene in universities

It is clear from UGC (1987), which outlines the *Universities Responses to the Jarratt Report* (as well as from my own investigations), that some institutions have established or are planning internal management development programmes. Some of these, for example at the Universities of Sheffield and Liverpool, have been conceived with the intention of improving managerial skills and awareness, as well as developing 'corporate spirit' within the institution. The advantage of such internal courses is that they can be linked to a range of optional topics and can provide detailed information on local procedures.

Feedback and support can be built in. As experience at the University of Exeter is beginning to show, such programmes can also have a very positive impact on inter-departmental communication and collaboration.

Other universities are employing outside consultants to organise programmes for them. The Scottish universities are approaching Henley, The Management College to contribute to a regional programme, while the Industrial Society is used by others. The field of education consultancy is mushrooming – management development programmes, appraisal schemes, new curricula, and departmental reviews can be bought and tailor-made to universities' requirements.

Where universities are not running their own programmes, or are seeking ideas with the intention of doing so, the University of Surrey's national leadership course for heads of academic departments has provided a training opportunity. This takes the form of a two-day introduction to leadership theory, practice and techniques. The Industrial Society also offers an 'off-the-shelf' course of this kind.

Experience of the Surrey courses and seminars for more senior staff indicates that the major reported benefits (at the level of immediate reaction) are: awareness raising in relation to leadership role and responsibilities; techniques for effective management (time-management, delegation, planning, and so on); and the sharing of common experiences and problems amongst peers. It is likely that these benefits will be mirrored in the reports of other universities' courses. Apart from criticisms of the course which are specific to it, the major problems to have emerged in relation to the national course are:

1   Its limited scope: the subsequent training needs identified by heads of department far exceed the capacity of a two-day course – as Table 15.3 indicates.
2   Lack of follow-up support: this project has attempted to provide some, but it is quite inadequate.
3   Its isolation from a co-ordinated institutional and national strategy for management/leadership development which relates course outcomes to individual and institutional benefits. Both need to be developed.
4   The lack of a 'management training culture' in universities makes it difficult for participants to implement changes emerging from the course.

Table 15.4 illustrates some of the difficulties reported by heads of department when trying to implement changes arising from the leadership course; some are personal, some departmental or institutional.

The northern universities are planning to launch a regional programme which may solve some of these problems. A ten-day programme is to be offered in modules over a year interspersed with action-learning projects. Individual commitment to the programme is to be matched with institutional commitment. Follow-up and support are to be provided by course members and tutors as well as seminars in the home institution. The programme has senior management support with costs to be spread among contributing universities. It is modelled to some extent on the Conference of University Administrators (CUA) management modules offered to administrators and has been developed

Table 15.3   *Training Needs Identified by Heads of Department* (1984–7)

Financial management
  Spreadsheets
  Human/team implications of FM
  Handling budgets
Office management
  Secretarial services (electronic, mail, WPs)
  Ways of organising record systems, filing systems, address lists, office technology
Personnel management
  Staff selection (individual)
  Appraisal
  Staff development
  Interviewing
  Counselling
  Delegation
  Selecting teams
  Judging and assessing
  Motivation
  Task allocation
  Keeping up morale
Administration/management (general)
  Conduct of meetings
  Committees: structuring and function related to objectives (advisory, executive,
    brainstorming, consultative)
  Reviewing the department
  Psychology of committees
Interpersonal
  Listening skills
  Communication
  Changing attitudes within groups
  Resolution of conflict: individuals/groups
  Effective interaction
  Negotiating effectively
Managing self
  Time management
  Self-assessment skills and methods
  Improving writing/reading skills
  Assertiveness: how to make things happen
  Dealing with stress
  Managing conflicting roles
  Presentation of self
  Work planning
  Decision-making
  Problem-solving
Leadership
  Power and rights of leader
  Authority
  Developing 'climate' (how to)
  Managing change: practicalities
  Styles
  Building teams

Application of leadership techniques/functions/roles
Universities and university management in relation to other organisations
  'Cultural' comparisons
  'Management' comparisons
  International comparisons
  Academic/administrative collaboration
  Knowing how to operate 'the system'
  University politics
  Heads of department in contexts: roles within the department, university and
    externally
Teaching
  Presentational, organisational issues
  Restructuring lectures
  New methods for running tutorials
  Encouraging student participation
  Using student feedback
Research
  Research grant applications
  Use of computers
  Presenting papers
  Locating and acquiring research funds and tapping

---

out of experience gained through mounting local management development courses. Original 'students' of the courses have become tutors and course advisers – a powerful development process for those involved.

This programme has been described at some length because in its conception, it has incorporated many of the necessary ingredients for success: relevance to clients' needs, both individual and institutional; integration with the management task in order to avoid 'transferability' and 're-entry' problems of the sort mentioned in Table 15.4; responsiveness to university culture; continued consultancy support through colleagues and course tutors; and visible senior management support. There are two remaining unknowns which will also affect its success: the quality of the learning activities provided and the problem of persuading senior academics to commit their time and energy to the programme.

Organisational and cultural changes

Many authors (Lockwood 1987; Taylor 1987; and the earlier Leverhulme Studies 1983) have documented the external pressures on universities and the changes that are emerging. Table 15.5 lists some of these in the present and in the future.

These external pressures are forcing changes within institutions which are in the main reactive. As Taylor (1987) has argued, they illustrate narrow conceptions of university priorities – survivalism, short-term market response – which are endangering the kind of educational leadership required of universities in relation to society. They have serious implications for the academic profession, endangering quality, responsiveness, morale and conditions of service.

The responsibility for turning this tide, for taking advantage of the creative potential of such strategic change, does not lie only with academics but also with administrators and policy-makers. However, academics have a vested interest, a prime professional responsibility to shape the nature of the university and to share in defining its educational role. Should not management and leadership, therefore, be as much a part of professional academic development as training in teaching and research? 'Training' must be conceived here in its broadest sense;

Table 15.4   *Difficulties Reported by Heads of Department in Trying to Implement Changes Arising from Attendance at the Farnham Castle Leadership Course*

Personal/general difficulties
1. It needs effort not to dissociate the course from everyday life.
2. Resistance to change on the part of staff.
3. It is very difficult to delegate if you lack the right senior staff.
4. Academic staff are generally old and resistant to change.
5. Academics in general are not interested in management unless they have grumbles.
6. Difficulties arise because of special circumstances in universities.
7. I found it quite hard to eliminate some of my inefficient work practices.
8. Time and other pressures.
9. Short-term pressures make longer-term planning and development difficult.
10. Very heavy load of routine administration and meetings.

Institutional/departmental difficulties
1. The institution's personnel procedures hinder structural changes.
2. Central administration would hinder in its hierarchical, autocratic approaches if allowed to.
3. There is very little interaction between institutions and departmental management.
4. The management ethos of the institution hinders by stifling middle-management participation in decision-making.
5. Optimistic and responsive university leadership.
6. The management ethos in our institution resists change from any source except the supreme leader. In that respect having attended the course heightens my frustration.
7. The management ethos of my department was to muddle through without leadership. The university ethos was more helpful.
8. My university has no discernible management ethos.
9. The university ethos is hostile to active management.
10. The real difficulty lies with the academics for whom administration is often no more than a nuisance.
11. The problem is that people who are running the universities may not be looking for leadership within the department.
12. Hindered because university management ethos is unclear and there is little backing or discussion with higher levels of administration.
13. The management ethos of our institution could script a series of John Cleese mismanagement films.
14. Hindered by vagueness of objectives, endless talking and few discussions; not helped by recent pressures of financial cuts.
15. They never listen and they never answer.

Table 15.5 *Pressures on Universities*

Present

Increased competition between institutions.

Requirement to live with external uncertainty.

Application of greater selectivity in the allocation of public moneys.

More direct political 'guidance' towards universities.

Shifts in the traditional markets (towards science and technology, continuing and professional education, disadvantaged groups).

A reduction in university influence on methods of assessment in the secondary schools.

Bridge-building across the binary line.

Pressures to adhere to common standards through demands for increased efficiency, value for money, public accountability.

Future

Pressure for the external validation of university curricula and awards.

The national employment of university staff (in order to achieve rationalisation through staff mobility).

The closure of some universities; ranking between others.

The transformation of the basic core curriculum into distance-learning packs to reduce the labour-intensity of university teaching, etc.

Source: Lockwood (1987, p. 95)

it should begin early and form an integral part of an academic career plan. Its benefits will be both personal, through increased competence and confidence, and institutional, through greater efficiency, more open communication and collaboration among the parts of university management, an informed view related to management and leadership issues, and the projection of a more positive image of university management both internally and externally.

Acknowledgements

Grateful thanks are extended to Mr D. Warren-Piper, of the London University Institute of Education, and Mr P. Helm, of the University of Liverpool, for comments and advice in relation to this paper.

References

Atkins, M. (1986) 'Management and the Academics: Concepts Models and Muddles', paper presented to the SRHE Conference, December.

Cabinet Office (1987) *Internal Training Opportunities Guide for Civil Service Senior Management Programme*, London Cabinet Office.

Committee of Vice Chancellors and Principals (1985) *Report of the Steering Committee for Efficiency Studies in Universities* (Jarratt Report), London, CVCP.

Constable, J. and McCormick, R. (1987) *The Making of British Managers*, BIM/CBI, London.

CVCP (1987) *Code of Practice on Academic Staff Training, April 1987*.

Davies, J. and Lockwood, G. (1985) *Universities: The Management Challenge*, Windsor, SRHE/NFER Nelson.

Leverhulme Studies (1983) *The Pursuit of Excellence: Research into Higher Education Monographs*, Guildford, SRHE.

Local Government Training Board (1987) *Partnership at the Top*, Luton, Local Government Training Board.

Lockwood, G. (1987) 'The management of universities', in Becher, T. (ed). *British Higher Education*, pp. 87–107.

Middlehurst, R. (1987) *Interim Report to the DES: Leadership Development in Universities Project* (unpublished).

Sizer, J. (1987) *Institutional Responses to Financial Reductions in The University Sector*, London, DES.

Taylor, W. (1987) *Universities Under Scrutiny*, Paris, OECD.

University Grants Committee (1987) *Report to the Secretary of State on Universities' Responses to the Jarratt Report*, July 1987.

University of North Carolina (1987) *Staff Development Program*, University of North Carolina.

16

The Great Appraisal Debate: Some Perspectives for Research

John Elliott

Who listens to research and why?

Increasing state intervention in the control and distribution of resources in schools and higher education institutions has placed teacher appraisal high on the agenda of educational debate. How is research being used in this context? Research results are from time to time selectively employed to support or undermine arguments being propounded, depending on their relevance to the issues which frame the discourse. In this context, as I hope to illustrate, one of the major uses of research is to facilitate a negotiated consensus between apparently inconsistent points of view.

In the current debate within the United Kingdon one of the few attempts systematically to review relevant research was made by a team of non-researchers in the Suffolk Education Department (1985). Their report was commissioned and funded by the Department of Education and Science (DES) following the publication of its White Paper, *Teaching Quality* (DES 1983). The review of the literature focuses on studies of implementation issues, particularly in the United States. The report was intended to apply to the appraisal of schoolteachers. But since it has also been referred to in the debate about appraisal in universities (see Waton 1987), where the issues raised have been very similar, I shall analyse it in some detail. Fourteen principles governing the implementation of successful appraisal schemes were culled from the review of research (Suffolk 1985, p. 26):

- There must be commitment, enthusiasm and support from the top – school and LEA – for the process;
- The appraisal scheme must have a clearly defined purpose and not a series of conflicting objectives;
- The appraisal process should take account of the differing contexts in which teachers work, and of the variables which can condition performance;
- The process should be evolutionary;

- Great care should be taken to ensure that all staff involved fully understand the system;
- All staff in the organisation (school and LEA) should be appraised;
- There should be a mutually agreed and up-dated job description;
- The process should start with self-appraisal; there should be a high degree of appraisal participation; and problems inhibiting performance should be discussed;
- Classroom observation is a central part of the process;
- The appraisal dialogue should concentrate on performance in the defined job and not on personality;
- There should be open, frank and immediate feed-back to the appraisal;
- There should be a mutually agreed set of goals (targets) for the succeeding years and an interim interview should be arranged for three or six months after the appraisal dialogue;
- Significant skills, interviewing and observational, are required of appraisers and, therefore, thorough training is necessary;
- The formal appraisal process is only one event in what is, and should be, a continuous process.

This summary of the 'research' literature indicates that the literature has been selected and scrutinised from a particular practical perspective, namely, whether appraisal can be made credible and acceptable to appraisees (teachers). Three of the six members of the Suffolk team were headteachers, two were senior LEA administrators, and the sixth member a senior adviser.

Headteachers in the relatively recent past knew that changes in schools could only be brought about if they could be accommodated within the culture of teacher professionalism. As Grace (1985) points out in an interesting historical account of the social and political context of teacher evaluation, the relaxation in the late 1920s of statutory controls over the curriculum, and criteria and methods for assessing teachers, laid the foundations for the growth of a professional culture. He accepts White's (1975) account of the political motivation behind this gift of autonomy. The Conservative government at the time feared the use a socialist government would make of their statutory powers to control and monitor teachers' practices in schools. White argues that the Conservatives had everything to gain and nothing to lose by taking control out of the hands of politicians so long as a form of non-statutory control could be devised. According to Grace, control was exercised by an ideology which publicly legitimated the relative autonomy of teachers from state control. Central to this ideology was the idea of the non-political teacher. Other elements included expert knowledge and skills, and white-collar status and security. Between the 1930s and 1970s this culture, described by Grace as 'legitimated professionalism', grew and received a considerable boost from the Houghton pay awards in 1974. Grace (1985) points out that the relaxation of statutory controls over teacher performance effectively devolved responsibility for evaluating teachers to headteachers.

Headteachers had become the agents of a process now made much more difficult by the existence of the ethic of legitimated professionalism and, in the 1960s and early 1970s, by the existence of a strong sense of freedom and of bargaining power amongst teachers. In the face of teachers confident in their market situation, headteachers were in an awkward position as agents of assessment and evaluation.

It is against this sort of historical background that one needs to understand the concern of the Suffolk team with the 'acceptability' of appraisal schemes in reviewing the research literature. They assume that the credibility and accept-ability of appraisal within the professional culture of teachers constitutes a problem. But does it? Let me offer a possible political perspective on appraisal at the present time. It is that the best way to respond to the resistance of the professional culture is not accommodate it but to defeat it. Professional confidence and morale are pretty low at the present time. The contraction in the supply and training of teachers brought about by falling rolls and the need to reduce public expenditure has weakened the position of schoolteachers in the marketplace and their bargaining power. The decline of any effective socialist opposition in the national Parliament and the widespread popularity of the Government's economic policies has made the original political legitimation of teacher professionalism redundant. The political and social context of teachers' work no longer produces a supply of legitimation from government, local communities and parents, for the kind of professional culture which developed in the mid-twentieth century in this country. Teachers are increasingly socially and politically isolated. They are undergoing a legitimation crisis of enormous proportion.

In such circumstances the state is in a good position effectively to impose whatever appraisal scheme it pleases, regardless of whether teachers find it acceptable. Holding this point of view, politicians could simply ignore research which focuses on teachers' views of what form of appraisal is professionally acceptable. In some social and political contexts acceptability may be a condition of effective implementation. But no research findings are context-free. Reviews of research carried out in a particular social and political climate may not be generalisable to the UK in 1987 or match political estimations of what is now achievable. Ten years ago the state would have had to make considerable accommodations to the professional culture in implementing appraisal schemes. But does it today? Politicians may dismiss such presentations of research as those contained in the Suffolk Report as simply biased support for the professional consensus lined up against them.

What the Suffolk principles specify is a distillation of the compromises and 'trade-offs' that have been negotiated in particular contexts. Neither their feasibility nor desirability in the present social and political context of university teaching should be presumed. I feel very dubious about the desirability of some in any context and will try to explain why.

The costs of compromise

The suggestion that there should be a mutually agreed and updated job description constitutes a compromise between the existing professional culture of teachers and something rather alien to it. The job description is an externally imposed device of management to regulate the activities of teachers. The 'mutually agreed' job description constitutes a partial accommodation to a degree of professional self-regulation. But the latter is still somewhat restricted. The danger of such a restriction is that it provides less opportunities for professional practitioners to create their own roles in the light of their evaluations of the work situation.

Similarly, the suggestion that 'there should be a mutually agreed set of goals (targets)' represents a compromise between a technique of management control and the professional self-determination of worthwhile aims. The setting of tangible targets restricts autonomy to means rather than ends. Mutually agreed targets between management and teachers represents a compromise between the managerial regulation of the teaching–learning process and a professional culture which gives teachers the right to codetermine means and ends.

Other principles express an even more protectionist perspective. The view that appraisal schemes should have a single clearly defined purpose and not a series of conflicting objectives effectively rules out the use of appraisal data by management except for the single purpose of professional development, that is, the enhancement of teachers' professional expertise. What might be interpreted, from the standpoint of the professional culture, as punitive objectives are ruled out – for example, managerial control over the placement, advancement and dismissal of teachers. The view that the appraisal process should take the differing contexts of teachers' work into account is clearly aimed at safeguarding professionalism, since claims to expert knowledge and rights to exercise discretionary judgement rest on the perception of the context-dependent nature of teachers' work.

What appears in the Suffolk Report is a tacitly negotiated settlement of issues between rather different perspectives on teacher appraisal: namely, the manager's concern with 'control' over the work-force and the practitioner's concern to protect and maintain those rights of self-determination which are central features of the professional culture. The Suffolk principles are about establishing a framework for practice which accommodates both 'managerialism' and 'professionalism' at a mutually acceptable level.

Consensus-seeking practical discourse cannot simply be represented as a series of 'trade-offs'. The principles listed by the Suffolk team do not all indicate either compromises or safeguards. In responding to the perceived threat of alien managerialism the professional culture may spawn creative responses, acknowledging the problems and issues raised by the oppositional culture, but rejecting or modifying the proposed solutions in favour of others which appear to be more consistent with its own values. One of the Suffolk principles is that appraisal should begin with self-appraisal and there should be a high degree of appraisee participation throughout the process. Formal or even conscious self-appraisal is not a significant feature of the traditional professional culture of teachers. It is only embraced by 'innovatory' teachers in their attempts to move away from a transmission pedagogy. The majority of teachers have clung to a craft notion of teaching, in which self-evaluation is largely informal and intuitive rather than a formal and conscious process of self-reflection. The

Suffolk principle of self-appraisal reflects research findings which are picking up a potential development in the professional culture – from a 'craft' to a 'reflective' conception of teaching – in response to external pressures for formal appraisal.

Another example of cultural transformation is the view that 'classroom observation is a central part of the process'. The Suffolk Report acknowledges that this is a very threatening aspect for teachers. It is seen to carry a threat of managerial regulation over the teaching–learning process, and therefore as an intrusion into the very heart of a professional culture which holds individual teachers' rights of autonomy in their own classrooms virtually sacrosanct. At the same time the Report acknowledges the potential value of classroom observation as a context for helping teachers reflectively to improve their performance. What the Report offers is a 'trade-off' which opens up the possibility of both managerial access to classroom performance and the development of the professional culture from an intuitive craft to a reflective practice. This trade-off is mediated by a set of conditions aimed at safeguarding a high degree of individual autonomy in the classroom: namely, an element of self-appraisal by the teacher, acknowledgement of the importance of taking the context of classroom practice into account, the collection of low-inference as opposed to high-inference observational data aimed at assessing personal qualities, agreement with teachers about criteria for observation, and the sharing of the data.

It is important that we do not see the 'consensus-seeking' function of practical discourse as necessarily stifling the creative development of professional cultures. The threat of political/administrative control brings not only accommodation but a challenge. External threat may well be a necessary condition of cultural transformation. However, the process of negotiating consensus also involves imposing boundaries on what constitutes relevant issues to be resolved. In the context of teacher appraisal, items ruled 'off the agenda' are likely to signify high potential for conflict. However, the tacit refusal to confront such issues may impose severe limits and constraints on the capacity of the discourse to generate creative developments in the professional culture. For example, one Suffolk principle argues that the appraisal dialogue should concentrate on performance in the defined job and not on the person doing it. This effectively rules out any appraisal of personal qualities. Research may well have discovered that the degree of threat aroused by this form of appraisal stimulates a great deal of resistance and obstructionism from teachers, and therefore constitutes a considerable obstacle to effective implementation. The reasons for this are not hard to discern. Accounts of personal characteristics embody implicit evaluations of the person as opposed to the surface performance. Such evaluations can therefore be used to determine an individual's future career prospects in a way in which appraisals of surface characteristics cannot. The latter are bound to a particular task context while the former are used to predict performance in a variety of contexts.

Sidestepping such problems is not necessarily the best response to teachers' anxieties and fears. Another would be to find ways of minimising the degree of threat by changing the context of appraisal. The threat is posed by infrequent and direct hierarchical surveillance of performance. It would be considerably reduced if data were collected from a variety of people who constantly interact with, and are trusted by, the appraisee at the work-place. The manager would have only indirect access to the appraisee's performance because the data would be collected and processed at a different level.

The Suffolk team argue that the primary purpose of appraisal should be the professional development of teachers. If such development is viewed largely in terms of the improvement of specific performance skills implicit in teaching tasks then the appraisal of the teacher's personal qualities will appear somewhat irrelevant. Such a view fits the dominant political view that poor standards in education are caused by deficiencies in teacher performance. What is masked by this apparent politico-professional consensus is a very different view of the nature of teaching. From the political point of view the skills of teaching are technical in character – standardised means of producing standardised ends. From the professional point of view teaching involves context-bound judgements and skills based on either an intuitive feel for the situation of conscious reflection in context.

However, the view that professional development is about improving performance skills rules out other conceptions of teaching. On its very first page the Suffolk Report lists four quite distinct concepts of teaching, the first two – 'teaching as labour' and 'teaching as craft' – being the same as those depicted above. The third view, 'teaching as a professional activity', is very close to what I have called 'reflective practice' based on conscious self-monitoring of situation and self. The fourth view is 'teaching as an art'. Suffolk (1985, pp. 1–2) describes this view as follows:

> teaching techniques may be unconventional, improvisatory, highly personal . . . . The teacher makes use not only of a body of professional knowledge and skill but also of personal resources which are possibly unique and almost certainly uniquely expressed according to the teacher's personality and the interactions between him and individual pupils or whole classes.

The Suffolk team quote approvingly from Wise *et al.* (1984) who argue that:

> Teaching competence may be conceived as a continuum. The further one moves along the continuum from minimal competence to excellence, the more wide-ranging and inferential the source of data and the less uniform, and generalisable the specific indicators . . . . The demands of evaluation differ along this continuum.

The implication of all this is that the four concepts of teaching they identify constitute stages of professional development from minimally acceptable levels of competence to excellence. One might have some reservations about this. 'Teaching as labour' might not be considered as a professional view of teaching at all since its essential dependence on externally imposed standards of practice and evaluation negates the autonomy which is a central element in any professional culture. It is in fact the view of teaching which the relaxation of statutory controls in 1926 emancipated teachers from, and enabled the professional culture to emerge in a legitimate form.

However, one can make out a case for a developmental continuum from 'craft teaching' to 'teaching as an art' via 'teaching as a reflective practice'. At each stage of the transformation in practice there is nevertheless a retention of continuity with the previous stage(s). Reflective practice focuses on problematic areas while leaving the unproblematic to the tacit craft knowledge of the teacher. Teaching as art depends on a whole range of personal qualities but does not totally negate the reflective and craft aspects of teaching. The Suffolk team do not point out the inconsistency between the view of teaching competence they describe in the first section of their Report and the way they later rule out the appraisal of personal qualities. They fail to recognise that the form of appraisal they recommend 'screens out' any acknowledgement of teaching competence at the highest level of its development. In fact Dow (1984) argues that the use of the term 'competence' to refer to low-level performance skills at all is a departure from customary usage: 'Competence refers essentially to a state of being or to a capacity . . . performance is the outward and public manifestation of underlying and internal powers.'

I would argue that the different levels of competence suggested by the Suffolk team reflect different kinds of power and capacity. At the level of externally standardised and controlled performance it is the capacity to follow and apply correctly a programme of rules and procedures which is the source of competence. At the level of craft skills the source of competence resides in the capacity for processing contextual and situational information as a basis for performance. For 'reflective practice' competence resides in a teacher's capacity to control his/her performance through self-monitoring. This capacity is at the basis of performances which are regulated by conscious decisions and action-plans. But its exercise reveals that decisions and plans do not always take effect as the teacher wants and intends. Performance is affected by emotional and motivational states, of which the teacher may be unaware, and whose manifestations in action make him or her powerless to effect decisions and plans. In this context competence involves the development of emotional and motivational states which are appropriate to the teaching task. Hence personal qualities can justifiably be viewed as a fundamental source of teaching competence.

One reason which might be used to justify the exclusion of any evaluation of personal qualities from a process of teacher appraisal aimed at professional development is that the motivational and emotional tendencies of individuals cannot be easily improved. Appraisal for professional development should focus only on improvable performance. Such a focus must assume that one is dealing with individuals whose background motivational and emotional tendencies are appropriate for the job. The appraisal of personal qualities should be a quite separate process operating at the point of entry (selection) into the job.

The assumption that motivational and emotional tendencies cannot be improved is one of the legacies of an individualistic trait psychology, which posited them as elements in relatively fixed and unchangeable structures. As Harré (1983, pp. 199–200) points out, for example, Eysenck explained dispositions and tendencies as properties grounded in physiological structures. But

Harré argues that emotional and motivational tendencies are grounded in systems of belief developed about oneself and others which are acquired in the social process of personal development. If this is correct then emotional and motivational tendencies can be improved by modifying and changing the beliefs which underpin them.

But how might such changes in belief be accomplished? Do individuals possess the capacities to develop themselves into the sort of person they want to become? Harré makes a rough distinction between 'powers to do' and 'powers to be'. The former are the capacities individuals acquire to perform their tasks and roles. So we can ask what personal qualities teachers need to acquire to teach well. In my view this question is central to any consideration of what constitutes teaching quality in education. The quality of teaching cannot be assessed in terms of performance-referenced criteria but only in terms of the personal qualities displayed in the performance.

'Powers to be' are the *reflexive capacities* individuals acquire in relation to the emotional and motivational core of their personal being. The object on which they are exercised is not 'performance' but 'the self'. Harré lists such powers as those of *self-knowledge* and *self-control*. His distinction points up an ambiguous use of the concept of the self-monitoring teacher. In one sense it can simply refer to the self, consciously monitoring its performance. It refers to a non-reflexive power. But in another sense the concept is used to refer to the self, consciously monitoring the quality of being manifested in performance. It refers here to a reflexive power; to the power to develop the self's knowledge of itself.

This analysis of competence illuminates what professional development involves. First, it involves the acquisition of capacities necessary for the successful completion of a set of professional tasks – for example, recording student progress, bringing about learning, planning the curriculum. Such capacities refer to information-processing skills, ability to make decisions, formulate plans, and self-monitor performance. Second, it involves the acquisition of appropriate emotions and motivations and the theories about human nature and conduct which underpin them. These capacities cannot be derived from an analysis of tasks since what are defined as tasks in the first place are determined by the exercise of such powers. For example, one cannot identify the abilities involved in bringing learning about unless one has an understanding of the nature of learning. What counts as learning will depend on a set of beliefs about human nature and the attitudes it is appropriate to adopt towards students on the basis of such beliefs. Inasmuch as the acquisition of attitudes constitutes a source of competent practice, in addition to performance skills, then professional development implies personal development – the acquisition of emotional and motivational tendencies which constitute the core of personal being.

However, personal development itself, at least in our culture, involves self-development, that is, a process in which individuals accept responsibility for changing the personal core of attitudes and motivations manifested in their performances. This process involves the development of powers of self-determination – for example, reflexive self-monitoring and self-control. The higher levels of professional competence will draw on these powers as an important resource. In summary, then, the development of professional competence involves the acquisition of skills and abilities which are implied by performance tasks; appropriate beliefs and attitudes; and reflexive powers.

The appraisal proposals of the Suffolk team define professional development as the acquisition of capacities which can be directly derived from an analysis of performance tasks (job descriptions). I would claim that even the development of relatively low-level cognitive capacities will depend upon and be shaped by the exercise of a teacher's reflexive powers. As the teacher becomes reflexively aware of the attitudes and motivations manifested in his/her performance and renders problematic the structures of belief which underpin them, he/she is able to control the sort of person he or she wants to become in the teaching role. The changes effected in this way result in new conceptions of teaching tasks and the skills required to perform them well. An exclusive focus on improving professional performance skills is ultimately self-defeating as a process of professional development. Such an approach tacitly transfers control over performance from the teacher's self to others. It enables management, for example, to exercise control over performance by preventing teachers from reflexively developing new understandings of the nature of teaching and learning tasks.

The process of developing professional competence, as I have outlined it, involves self-appraisal. Appraisal by others is often contrasted with self-appraisal. The distinction is made in the Suffolk Report. In DES (1983) self-appraisal is dismissed with faint praise in favour of appraisal by others. The assumption underlying this contrast is that self-appraisal is a private activity conducted in solitude and isolation from other people. I want to argue that this is not necessarily so. I will begin by trying to explain how this contrast between two kinds of appraisal is drawn.

Self-appraisal, or reflexive self-monitoring, is a central feature of the process of personal development. This process is basically social in nature. According to Harré (1983, pp. 259–61) public conversations play a fundamental role in this process. Personal or private conversations with oneself are also a feature. What we need to understand are the relationships between the private and public conversations in the development of persons. Harré *et al.* (1985) attempt to explain these relationships in terms of a four-quadrant model based on two axes; one axis he calls *display* and the other *location*. The display dimension marks the distinction between public and private space. In public space individuals manifest or provide accounts of their psychological states. In private space they keep these states to themselves.

If we look at the Suffolk appraisal proposals in this light we can see that they impose restrictions on the assessment of psychological states manifested in a teacher's performance. The focus of observation and the appraisal interview is on low-inference performance data rather than psychological data.

The location dimension marks a difference in the way psychological states and processes are realised. Is it realised in a collective of individuals or the individual? Harré *et al.* question the assumption that cognitions, emotions, and motivations are exclusively the property of individuals. Collectives can reason or think, express emotion, and so on. He makes much of the idea of 'psychological symbiosis' in which the psychological states of individuals are dependent upon their interactions with each other – for example, a husband believes certain things but these beliefs are taken over from his wife rather than developed by him. Harré *et al.* illustrate 'psychological symbiosis' by reference to the analysis by Martin Richards of tape-recordings of conversations between mothers and their children. The analysis revealed that most mothers address their infants 'as if the infants had well-developed psychological repertoires of intentions, wants, feelings and powers of reason from the moment of birth'. The infants develop as persons by acquiring psychological states supplied by the mother.

It is only when individuals begin to take responsibility for their own development by exercising reflexive powers of self-monitoring and self-mastery that we can talk about the individual as the location of psychological states and the processes of realising them. According to Harré *et al.* (see Fig. 16.1) human beings rarely appear as psychological individuals but are usually in a situation of psychological symbiosis in which each supplements the psychological defects of another or others.

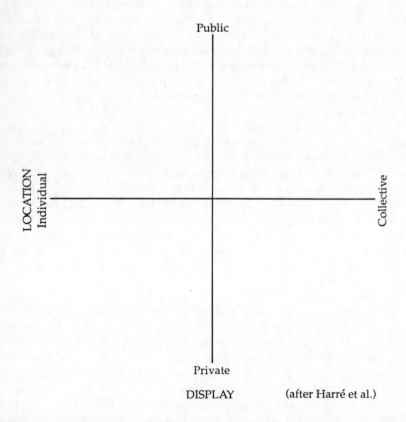

Figure 16.1   Model of personal development

From the two axes of display and location Harré derives a four-quadrant model of personal development. Quadrant 1 constitutes the *public-collective* space, which marks out the process of 'psychological symbiosis'. Quadrant 2 constitutes the *private-collective* space, which marks out a process in which the individual develops a sense of personal identity by appropriating beliefs, emotions, and motivations operating in the collective as his or her own. Quadrant 3 constitutes the *private-individual* space, the realm of the personal in which the individual privately converses with him or herself. Reflexive self-monitoring appears to fall into this quadrant. The individual creates a private space in which to reflect about his or her psychological states in terms of their origins, their location, and their relationship to the sort of person he/she wants to become. Quadrant 4 constitutes the *individual-public* space, the domain in which the individual publicly manifests the 'self' in action, or accounts for the 'self' so manifested. The accountability process constitutes a form of reflexive practical discourse because it presupposes that the individuals involved exercise a capacity for reflexive self-monitoring. It is a form of self-assessment which operates in a context of public dialogue.

For Harré *et al.* personal development involves a series of transitions across these quadrants in the direction of quadrants 1 and 4. But this does not imply that individuals as totalities can be unambiguously located in a particular quadrant at different points in their life history. In accomplishing a transition the individual does not necessarily leave one dimension of psychological space behind. For example, in moving from private self-reflection to an involvement in reflexive public discourse the individual may continue to create future private space for self-reflection. Discourse in the public domain, however, constitutes an important resource for developing powers of self-knowledge and self-control.

Let us now look at the Suffolk proposals in the light of this model of personal development. A naive view of the appraisal process would be that it ought to facilitate a transition from a situation of symbiotic dependence on others as a source of psychological support for personal deficiencies, to one of psychological independence in which the appraisee has appropriated certain beliefs, attitudes and motivations as aspects of his personal identity. This would involve appraisers providing appraisees with feedback in the form of moral assessments of their personal qualities. Rather than being viewed as the helpful and beneficial process of fostering psychological independence in teachers, so that they can perform their professional roles more effectively, the process is often seen as a primitive and harmful one aimed at destroying the appraisee's sense of personal identity and creating a form of psychological symbiosis.

What is really at stake here, I believe, is not the value of external appraisals of personal qualities, but the quality of the organisational climate in which they are made. In contexts where relationships are characterised by lack of respect for persons, competitive individualism, and mistrust, external moral assessments of psychological states are highly threatening to individuals. In contexts where relationships are governed by respect for persons, co-operation in pursuit of common goals, and mutual trust, external appraisals are likely to be perceived as supportive rather than destructive of personal identity.

The rule 'out of court' by the Suffolk Report of a form of appraisal which would facilitate personal development from quadrants 1–2 is a sad reflection on the prevailing climate in the educational climate today. It suggests that the major problem of enhancing teaching quality in such institutions lies not so much in the psychological deficiencies of individuals as in the moral climate which prevails in the wider collectivities of educational institutions and systems. The Suffolk Report, and indeed the whole subsequent debate about teacher appraisal, suggests that priority should be given to the improvement of organisational and policy-making structures within the educational system.

The Suffolk Report appears to make provision for personal development construed as a transition between quadrants 3 and 4. It proposes that teachers produce self-assessments on the basis of solitary and private reflection and then make them available to the appraiser prior to the external appraisal. The espoused aspiration is to create a dialogue. Does this indicate an awareness of public discourse as a medium of self-appraisal? Perhaps, but it is a distorted awareness. The focus should be, it is argued, on low-inference performance data rather than personal data. Self-assessment and external assessment are both understood as appraisals of observable performance rather than the states they manifest. As such they can contribute little to the personal development of teachers.

We must, therefore, conclude that the Suffolk proposals, if implemented, will do little to foster the development of personal qualities in teachers, and therefore little to raise teaching quality to reflect the highest levels of professional competence. By screening personal development out of the appraisal process, the proposals construct a dangerous contrast between the professional and personal. In the context of the large-scale ill-health they presume to exist in the educational system, the proposals may be interpreted as a justifiable means of safeguarding the personal identities of teachers from destructive manifestations of managerial and bureaucratic intent. But they can also be interpreted as a means of legitimating the use of a power-coercive strategy for establishing bureaucratic control over the performance of teachers. Such an appraisal process would not only discount teachers as persons but foster a process which segregated their professional from their personal identities. The professional identity simply becomes a social identity – a 'being-for-others' from which the core of the personal self has disengaged.

Perhaps the most significant political manifestation of mistrust of teachers was the publication of Sir Keith Joseph's White Paper on *Teaching Quality* (DES 1983). In this document the DES blamed individual teachers for deficiencies in the quality of educational provision. It proposed appraisal as the means of rectifying them. Within the White Paper the purposes of appraisal are starkly and clearly pinpointed in terms of the training, deployment, and dismissal of individual teachers. Moreover, all these purposes are viewed as management functions.

> The Government believe that those responsible for managing the school teacher force have a clear responsibility to establish, in consultation with their teachers, a policy for staff deployment and training based on a systematic assessment of every teacher's performance and related to their policy for the school curriculum.

Concern for quality demands that in the small minority of cases where, despite in-service training arrangements, teachers fail to maintain a satisfactory standard of performance, employers must, in the interests of pupils, be ready to use procedures for dismissal . . . unsatisfactory performance can be sufficient reason for dismissal.

The overriding model of 'management' which emerges in the White Paper is a power-coercive one. This is not because appraisal is seen as serving management functions but because of the form of appraisal envisaged. The White Paper dismisses self-assessment with faint praise in a single sentence: 'The Government welcome recent moves towards self-assessment by schools and teachers, and believe these should help to improve school standards and curricula. But . . .'.

The same paragraph then proceeds to legitimate hierarchical control over the collection, analysis, and release of data about each teacher's performance:

employers can manage their teacher force effectively only if they have accurate knowledge of each teacher's performance. The Government believe that for this purpose formal assessment of teacher performance is necessary and should be based on classroom visiting by the teacher's head or head of department; and an appraisal of both pupils' work and of the teacher's contribution to the life of the school.

The assumption here is of a hierarchy of credibility in which the appraisals of managers are presumed to be more accurate than those of the appraisee, professional peers, and his/her students. If this assumption is a questionable one, as I believe it to be, then there is no necessary reason why management decisions could not be based on the assessments of the appraisee, professional peers, and students. Decisions about training, placement, and dismissal do not have to be based on a form of hierarchical surveillance which effectively empowers managers to exercise control over the details of performance.

The Suffolk Project was established by the DES to develop proposals for appraisal within the framework set out in the White Paper. The focus on classroom performance, and the acceptance of appraisal as a tool of management, which emerged in the Suffolk Report are fully in line with the White Paper's statements of intent. But it builds into its proposals a measure of protection for individuals against the intrusion of bureaucratic control into the personal domain. It attempts a formal linkage between self-assessment and formal appraisal, rules out 'personal qualities' as criteria of assessment, and claims standards cannot be defined in terms of a set of generic skills (since skills are context-bound). Instead of coming up with criteria or standards as part of its brief the project team defined 'areas of teacher action' which contribute to effective performance: climate, planning, management, subject knowledge, the act of teaching, and interpersonal relationships. These provide the major categories in which low-inference performance data are to be collected and skills-in-context assessed.

In claiming that multi-purpose appraisal did not work and that professional development, focused on improving classroom performance, should be the primary overriding purpose, the Suffolk team also built in further protections against bureaucratic intrusion into the realm of the personal. It did not rule out 'placement' and 'grounds of dismissal' as purposes, but made them subordinate by restricting the data base to a form which limits the extent to which it can be used for making judgements about 'placement' and 'dismissal'. It is difficult to see how one could dismiss individuals entirely on the basis of low-inference performance data. Deficiencies in performance require explanation before they constitute relevant grounds for dismissal. Faulty training, inadequate development opportunities, and external constraints on the exercise of acquired skills, could all be cited as reasons for non-dismissal. Grounds for dismissal normally have to refer to undesirable character traits, personal attitudes, and motivations. Placement decisions about individuals are normally based on predictions of successful and non-successful performance on tasks other than those they are currently performing. Data about performance skills in relation to specific tasks and contexts are hardly likely to be very relevant to placing and developing individuals on other tasks in other contexts. What is relevant is data about personal qualities, which, although manifested in current performance, are deemed relevant to task performance in other contexts.

I have recently completed a study of the personal qualities competent police constables display in their handling of incidents on the streets (Elliott 1987). In the course of cross-checking my analysis of behavioural event interview data with the formal appraisals of the officers interviewed I discovered that supervisors' assessments largely referred to 'personal qualities' as opposed to specific performance skills. A separate analysis of the appraisals of officers who were either dismissed or 'forced' to resign revealed that negative assessments referred also to deficiencies in 'personal qualities'. The appraisal files of patrol constables did not indicate any intrinsic conflict about the purposes for which the data could be used. The same information appeared to be relevant to decisions about training, placement, and dismissal. Personal qualities were not seen as fixed traits incapable of development through training. Looking at the regular appraisals of individuals over time, it was clear that perceived improvements were acknowledged and judgements modified. Dismissal was indeed only contemplated after a period of time in which improvements could reasonably be expected.

I would argue that appraisal can serve a variety of purposes when it takes the form of an assessment of personal qualities. This kind of qualitative data is relevant to decisions about training, placement and dismissal. Intrinsic conflict only arises when the data about performance are confined to low-inference data about tasks-specific skills. This renders it unusable for purposes of placement and dismissal. One can therefore conclude that the Suffolk proposals produce a conflict of purposes in order to legitimate a policy of excluding the assessment of personal qualities from the appraisal process.

The appraisal of personal qualities in police organisations

Some would no doubt argue that police organisations are quasi-military institutions in which the performance of constables is controlled through the rank structure. The appraisal of personal qualities is simply a means of shaping the individual psychologically into a form which guarantees compliant performance. But all this ignores the nature of police work. Patrol constables are expected to be capable of working alone on the streets, without close supervision. The nature of their work calls for high levels of skill. Observational studies of patrol practice suggest that the following abilities are generic to good policing:

   (i) sensitive observation and a capacity to impute motive on the basis of deep local knowledge;
  (ii) the ability to convey power in a tangible but generally understated manner; and
 (iii) a refined capacity for negotiation (Fielding 1984).

The 'personal qualities' extracted from police appraisal files are highly congruent with these broad clusters of abilities. They constitute the psychological characteristics individuals need to possess in order to exercise such abilities. Moreover, they are the converse of the 'dependent qualities', which would enable the organisation to control the details of performance. Observational research by Fielding and others portrays the police 'as massively competent social actors'. They are not simply reproducing in performance sets of formal rules whose application is rigidly controlled and monitored by supervisors. The formal rules are continuously interpreted in the light of the requirements of action within the working environment. Fielding (1984) argues that 'the apparently rigid hierarchy of authority was notional in the face of its circumvention by members who were granted various degrees of discretion'. He contrasts the formal rules of the organisation with the occupational culture which emerges as a response to the everyday working situation, and suggests that one of the major competencies required in officers is the ability to offer satisfactory accounts of practice within the organisation in those areas of discretion and licence it permits. This requires 'a thorough knowledge of the justifications available to ensure an account is honoured'. Fielding claims that unlike other occupations enjoying professional licence, 'officers are continuously obliged to account for (or disclaim) their action or inaction and must do so variously in relation to peers and supervisors'.

Management appraisals of police constables are not based on direct observation of patrol work. In describing the form they take I shall draw largely on the 'notes of guidance' produced by a particular Force. But I have no reason to believe the process it describes is in any way untypical.

Part 1 of the appraisal report consists of a pen picture report of the officer's work in the context of his/her life beyond it. The notes of guidance state: 'It would be quite unfair to judge performance at work without taking into account other pressures.' The report also consists of gradings against a lot of personal qualities 'which are felt to be of basic importance in all people'. These are 'appearance', 'professional ability', 'report writing', 'ability to work alone', 'initiative', 'judgement'. The report is completed by the constable's senior work supervisor – the unit or shift inspector. Its focus is on the constable's work over the past 12 months, but includes 'any recommendations for employment, training and suitability for any expressed job preference'.

Although the inspector is expected to have a detailed knowledge of each constable's work this is not based so much on close surveillance of his/her patrol practice as on the written and verbal accounts he/she produces back at the station. The supervisor's appraisals constitute 'audits' of self-appraisals, perhaps cross-checked against appraisals provided by peers and members of the public. In considering various justifications for action or non-action, a supervisor not only takes into account the forms of licence permitted by the organisation, but also the motives, attitudes, and beliefs cited as reasons and explanations. As Fielding (1984) again points out, in the frequent absence of tangible results, the quality of police action is assessed in terms of the attitudes manifested in action rather than the action itself. The notes of guidance claim that: 'It is of more importance in any assessment of character, of motivation or vitality, not so much to know what a person did but rather why and under what circumstances.' This explains why data about life beyond work are considered relevant:

> It is not unknown for an indifferent performer on duty to be a bundle of energy and full of resourcefulness when pursuing off-duty interests. We might ask ourselves if we can harness these assets during duty time and so reap the benefit of much that is good in the officer.

In addition to the reasonableness of the justifications provided by an officer during the course of his/her work, the supervisor will want to assess the authenticity or credibility of the officer's account in the light of his/her knowledge of the person. In this informal 'accounting' context the constable has opportunities to disagree with the views of the supervisor and to convince him/her of the merits of the course of action in question. The work supervisor's formal report must be viewed against the background of this continuous accountability process. It is read and signed by the constable: 'By seeing the report a person can correct any misstatements of fact and give views on any aspect of behaviour that may have been misunderstood.' It is then used as the basis for Part 2 of the process: the appraisal interview with a senior officer (chief inspector or superintendent), and a further report.

The main purpose of the interview is to assess 'the officer's needs and to see that the best use is made of personnel'. Whereas the supervisor's primary task is to assess the personal qualities manifested in performance, the senior officer's primary task is to discuss this assessment with the constable in order to identify his/her needs and potential within the organisation, and to make recommendations about future placement and training. The constable is expected to make a major contribution to the discussion.

Many police appraisals appear to adopt the form of a two-tier model. The first tier, at the level of the supervisor, is the outcome of an 'accountability' discourse about practical incidents, between patrol constables and their supervisors at work. At this level the appraisal process is not managerially controlled, and it calls for the display of considerable competence by the appraisee in reflectively self-monitoring practice in the light of organisational goals and norms. It is the supervisor's responsibility to mediate these goals and norms through calling his/her constables to account for their actions.

The second-tier appraisal process at the level of management is grounded in the outcome of the first-tier process. But its purposes are different. The supervisor has the role of ensuring high-quality patrol practice. The senior officer's management role involves placing individuals in positions where their personal qualities benefit the organisation and make it more effective.

I have made much of appraisal in police organisations because their hier- archical nature is frequently presumed to imply the suppression of individu- ality. What I have tried to show is that hierarchical appraisal systems in police organisations are not necessarily power-coercive. The two-tier model I have outlined, if implemented properly, can foster the development of dynamic and reflexive qualites in appraisees.

This integration is made possible by structural features of police organisa- tions which do in fact limit and restrict the operation of power-coercive control over police practice. The nature of the constable's work places the supervision function in an accountability rather than surveillance context. And within the hierarchy the supervisory function is differentiated by roles from management functions. The two-tier model of appraisal which obtains in the police reflects these organisational characteristics. The result is an appraisal system which leaves little room for the development of observational systems of hierarchical surveillance – that major device of power-coercive control – and quite a lot of room for self-appraisal as a central feature of the process.

The appraisal of individual constables in police organisations by managers is grounded in data that emerge from interactions in what Harré *et al.* call 'the individual-public space' (quadrant 4). It consists of assessments of the psycho- logical states manifested by officers in publicly accounting for their actions to supervisors and peers within the organisation. The appraisal interview with a senior officer (manager) need not simply be a mechanism which makes the individual accountable to the organisation. It can also enable the organisation to be responsive to the individual. Such responsiveness would indicate a direction of influence from 'individual-public' (quadrant 4) to 'public- collective' (quadrant 1) space. The personal development of individuals can, in principle if not practice, influence the organisational development through the manner in which the management responds to the accounts of individual prac- titioners during quadrant 4 interactions at both levels of the appraisal process.

The hierarchical appraisal of individuals in police organisations is certainly concerned with promoting the acquisition and maintenance of desired psycho- logical states. But, as I argued earlier, such appraisal is a feature of the process by which personal identities are developed generally. One must make a clear distinction between the fact that personal identities are socially acquired and the kinds of identity so acquired. It is not the exercise of hierarchical influence over identity formation which can reasonably be objected to, but the manner of such influence and its ideological content. One can object to a form which prevents the individual from having a say in the appraisal process, since this would stifle those reflexive powers and capacities upon which the higher levels of personal development depend. One can also object to the promotion of psychological states which are inconsistent with the values embodied in our concept of personhood – for example, passive qualities as opposed to the dynamic qualities which characterise human agency.

Toward a two-tier model of teacher appraisal

From my study of police appraisal I would conclude that hierarchical appraisals of teachers by managers in the educational system need not be incompatible with the development of dynamic personal qualities within the professional role. The belief that they are stems from the style of management teachers read into the appraisal proposals and the ideological content embedded in them: a power-coercive style which entails the acquisition of passive and dependent psychological states as opposed to personally empowering dynamic qualities. I think there is little doubt that schoolteachers were correct to interpret the White Paper (DES 1983) in terms of a passive and dependent view of their role (see Elliott 1985 for a critique of the theory of teaching implicit in the White Paper). But this does not necessarily entail that the three management functions of appraisal, as outlined in the White Paper, cannot support a process whereby the professional practices of teachers are empowered with personal qualities. It is not the government's view of the functions of management which lies at the heart of the problem but its power-coercive model of how those functions are to be carried out.

During the teachers' dispute with the government over conditions of service, and following the publication of the Suffolk Report, the ACAS Independent Panel negotiated an agreed set of principles for appraisal between the teachers' unions, the government, and local authority employers. I shall now examine those principles with a view to comparing them with the proposals in the White Paper (see also Elliott 1987) and the Suffolk Report.

The ACAS document outlines six functions of appraisal, covering the identification of training and professional development needs, the assessment of potential for career development, the selection of staff for new posts, and the 'recognition of teachers experiencing performance difficulty'. They do not differ in many respects from the purposes stated in the White Paper, though they are rather more specific. They might be seen merely as clarifications of the latter, as 'negotiated' shifts of emphasis, or as obscurations of real intent. For example, 'deployment' was used in the White Paper to refer to the involuntary relocation of teachers to different schools. In the ACAS document the term is used in a general statement about the functions of appraisal, but when these are put in specific terms there is no clear implication of involuntary relocation. The only functions which appear to cover the term are those of identifying potential for career development, and staff appointments. But do these rule out involuntary relocation? The National Union of Teachers (NUT) raised this point in their comments on the ACAS document's use of the phrase 'deployment of teachers':

> Whilst the words can fit, quite precisely, one aspect of successful and acceptable career development, for most teachers and LEA's it will bring to mind the process of redeployment . . . it remains for most people a

disagreeable and threatening process. One must seriously question the
necessity for retaining the words, if one believes that successful Teacher
Appraisal will have its own beneficial effect on the more sensitive placement of teachers.

This is just one example of an attempt to get sufficient precision of language to
rule out power-coercive uses of appraisal by management.

The White Paper clearly saw dismissal as a possible disciplinary action
following from appraisal. The ACAS document argues that disciplinary procedures would remain quite separate from appraisal, emphasising constructive
purposes in relation to defective performances. However, having said this, it
then proceeds to connect the two processes by stating that disciplinary action
may 'need to draw on relevant information from the appraisal records'. If
appraisal is used as such a basis for disciplinary action then surely this is one of
its functions. Again an apparent shift of emphasis may turn out to be a more
glossing over of intent. The NUT was aware of this as well, although one might
doubt if appraisal is necessarily power-coercive because it is linked with
discipline procedures. As the union admits, 'appraisal could work to the
advantage of a teacher faced with disciplinary procedures'. It goes on to argue
that there should be no connection between appraisal and discipline in order to
maximise the acceptability of the former. This sounds like quite unwarranted
professional protectionism. The individual can come to see the reasonableness
of the sanctions brought against him/her, and surely appraisal can be an
important means of demonstrating this. The real issue is the fairness of the
appraisal process and not its connection to disciplinary procedures.

The ACAS document addresses this issue by outlining a number of procedural principles:

- everybody in the system should be appraised at all levels of the hierarchy;
- each appraisal should benefit from a 'second opinion';
- the appraisal should, where possible, be agreed with the appraisee and any
  remaining points of disagreement reported;
- appraisal reports would have a limited life-span on file, be kept by head and
  appraisee, and made available to the appraisee and others authorised by the
  Chief Education Officer;
- all those involved – appraisers and appraisees – should be trained.

The NUT expressed reservations about the possibility of unspecified but wide
access to records which it felt the ACAS document allowed. The union stated its
view that appraisal records

should be confidential to the appraiser and appraisee; that it should have
an agreed 'life' to better inform the subsequent appraisal processes
between the appraiser and appraisee; that its use for any other purpose
was entirely a matter for the appraisee; that for the purpose of school-
based management decisions (e.g. INSET planning; school organisation)
an *appropriate separate extract* be made available to the Head Teacher.

The ACAS document develops the proposals in the White Paper in a form
which appears to eliminate much of the power-coercive intent evident in the

latter document. The outcome was no doubt influenced by the arguments and views vehemently expressed by teachers and their associations in response to the government's original proposals.

I have argued elsewhere that as it stands the ACAS framework can be interpreted as open to a form of appraisal which empowers rather than diminishes teachers as professionals (Elliott 1987). But I also argued that it is open to a rather different interpretation – as enabling direct hierarchical control over teacher performance. The document lacks the precision necessary completely to reassure teachers that the proposed framework describes a real shift of intent, rather than a glossing over of very real issues about the use of power. Certainly the ACAS document is far less protectionist towards teachers than the Suffolk Report. Like the White Paper the ACAS document makes classroom observation by appraisers an essential feature of teacher appraisal. I believe that hierarchical surveillance of classroom performance is a pretty good indicator of power-coercive intent. The ACAS document introduces an ambiguous element by specifying the appraiser as either a headteacher *or* an experienced teacher appointed by him or her. What is implied by 'experienced' is left open to interpretation. Does it imply someone in a middle management position or simply an experienced peer? The ambiguity perhaps represents an attempt to tone down the hierarchical surveillance of performance clearly proposed in the White Paper. However, the connection with this form of observation remains. The appointment of the appraiser is to be hierarchically determined.

The Suffolk Report deals with the power-coercive implications of hierarchical surveillance in a different way. It accepts it but limits its focus to low-inference measures of performance, thus screening off the person as an object of scrutiny. This protection offered to the person could, as we have seen, create very negative effects by alienating the person from his or her performance. The ACAS document makes no stipulation about the nature of the data to be collected. The framework as it stands is quite open to the appraisal of personal qualities. Combine such openness with the possibility it allows for hierarchical surveillance through classroom observation, and we must conclude that, while in many respects offering a better framework for promoting teacher development than the Suffolk Report, it leaves too many loopholes for the exercise of power-coercive control.

In my view the NUT's suggestions that the appraisal process be separated into two quite distinct but connected processes with different functions offers a possibility for the constructive development of the ACAS framework. One process involving appraiser and appraisee would be aimed at fostering the self-development of the teacher. The records would remain confidential to both parties. Another process of appraisal, for the purpose of making management decisions, would be based on extracts selected by the appraiser of the first process and his or her appraisee, in terms of their relevance to the particular decision-making domain. This suggestion separates the classroom observation role of the appraiser at the first level from a necessary location in the formal hierarchy, and even if the appraiser is a member of management he/she is prevented from utilising observational data for management purposes. Management is given indirect access to practice through the accounts of practitioner and observer, selected and agreed by both parties in the light of the legitimate functions of management – for example, training, selection and placement.

This model, which has much in common with the police appraisal system described above, is also remarkably similar to more detailed proposals developed in 1985 at an International Seminar on Education Evaluation (see Bridges *et al.* 1985). The report of the seminar outlines a non power-coercive appraisal system which can genuinely foster the personal development of teachers by promoting a reflexive discourse about their practices with peer observers and students. The accounts of practice generated from this discourse can be drawn upon by the practitioner when compiling a further account for the purposes of appraisal by management. Appraisal by management should not simply be concerned to fit the person to the organisation, but to discover how the organisation might utilise and develop further the personal qualities evidenced in the appraisal data. Subsequent management decisions about training requirements, placement in the organisation, and career potential can serve the purposes of both organisational and personal development. Moreover, in the accountability context of this second level of appraisal the teacher can draw on the accounts produced at the first level to argue for certain training, placement and career opportunities. The fact that there are ultimately management decisions in no way implies he/she has no right to influence them. And it is the reflective production of accounts at the first level which empowers the teacher to take this responsibility for his/her own development.

What has been sketched above is a variant of the two-tier model of appraisal which supports the self-development of the individual in his/her professional roles, and the development of the organisation by those responsible for its management. It respects both the professional discretion of the teacher at the work-place and the organisational functions of management. And it reconciles the professional licence or discretion of the practitioner with the right of the management to call him or her to account.

At the policy level we still wait to see such a model of schoolteacher appraisal developed. Perhaps it will emerge from the national pilot projects which are currently attempting to implement and evaluate schemes in the light of the ACAS framework. Or it could emerge as a model for teachers in universities where the appraisal debate has also emerged. It is to this area of debate that I shall now turn.

The debate in the universities

The 'debate' about appraisal in universities has, in a sense, been a more private one. In general 'the crisis of schooling' has received greater publicity in the media than 'the crisis in universities'. Structural features have also ensured that the number of parties actively involved in the debate were fewer. At the national and local levels of the universities, for example, the debate has been between a single union, the Association of University Teachers (AUT), and the vice chancellors. As Waton (1987) pointed out, conditions of service for university staff have been negotiated between university managements and local associations of the union, the central committees confining their deliberations to general policy objectives. In contrast to the debate about teacher appraisal in schools – where it was tied to central negotiations about conditions of service between government, local authorities, and a number of staff associations – the appraisal debate in universities has been far more localised. The trend however has been towards greater centralisation. In a recent article Waton (1987), an AUT executive member, argued that: 'Experience has shown that, within such a system [of local negotiation] only a minority of Local Associations can deliver conditions as good as, or better than, those set by national policy.'

Within universities the movement towards formal appraisal was stimulated by the Jarratt Report (CVCP 1987) recommendation that consideration should be given to policies for staff development, appraisal and accountability. Working parties were spawned as a result and local associations of the AUT began to formulate position statements on the issues.

The focus of the debates has tended to revolve around the professional autonomy versus managerial control issue. In the University of East Anglia the AUT at one time drew a strong contrast between 'professional' and 'managerial' appraisal, accepting the former and rejecting the latter. The former embraced the aim of improving performance through self- and peer appraisal and rejected any linkage between the appraisal process and management decisions about promotion and salaries. As with schoolteachers, appraisal by management tended to be viewed as a threat to professional autonomy, and an agent of power-coercive intent. But this particular response by university teachers displayed a greater disdain towards appraisal by management.

It could be argued that university teachers inherit a stronger tradition of professional independence from regulation by management and administration than schoolteachers. The tendency for the latter to give in to the growth of managerialism in education is therefore much greater. The professional status of teachers in schools, compared with university teachers, doctors and lawyers, has historically been less well established, and over the last sixty years subordinated to an administrative hierarchy. Schoolteachers, therefore, were not in a strong position to resist the transformation of administration into management, and the penetration of the latter into all aspects of schooling over the last decade and a half. The transformation began in the early 1970s as central government began to put the squeeze on local authority spending. Headteachers were pressurised to become line managers, rather than professional leaders, of their teaching staff, and were required to deploy and utilise resources (inputs) in the light of articulated aims and objectives (outputs). Although 'management' penetrated into many aspects of schooling – such as the organisation of the curriculum, pupil groups, discipline and pastoral care – it stopped short at the classroom door until Sir Keith Joseph's White Paper of 1983 introduced performance appraisal. But by this time teachers were accustomed to operating in a managed environment.

The transformation of universities from administrative to management systems is a more recent phenomenon. Restructuring has been a rapid rather than gradual process in response to external pressures for greater accountability from central government, in a context where the university teacher had historically enjoyed greater professional autonomy from administrative regulation. Within this process it has been difficult to evolve non-threatening models of management. Universities are full of inexperienced 'man-managers' seeking to accommodate political pressure, and doing so in a manner which academic staff, accustomed to considerable independence, may well perceive as power-coercive and unfair. It is therefore hardly surprising that many university teachers view 'management' as an alien and malign concept.

Such a concept is very much in evidence in Waton (1987) and it no doubt accurately reflects how management is currently operating in many universities:

> It became very clear from early responses to Jarratt that many vice-chancellors and university management either believed in the vision of the hierarchical university or were willing to implement such structures in the belief that it might mitigate future treatment by Government. Believers or fellow-travellers, the end result would be the same, i.e. more rigid hierarchies, greater managerial control of staff, with appraisal as a key element in achieving these goals.

The hierarchical university appears to Waton as an essentially power-coercive institution. This is reflected in the form of appraisal he believes it entails:

> It consists simply of a 'superior' measuring the performance of a more junior member of staff to discover those areas in which performance is satisfactory and those where improvement can be made. Those who consistently perform well are to be considered suitable candidates for promotion.

He claims, rather dubiously, that such a model has long been discredited in education and industry. What he finds objectionable about it is the linkage between appraisal of performance and promotion, and cites the Suffolk report in support of this point:

> Those having torches . . . , use national and international examples to demonstrate that where systems of staff appraisal are linked formally to the award of privileges (merit awards, promotion) or punishments (sacking, disciplinary action) they become bureaucratic procedures governed not by the scheme's objective (to improve performance) but by its latent consequences, i.e. to use the formal rules of the system to make performance look as good as possible, leading to individual enhancement or avoidance of disciplinary measures. In such situations, beneath a veneer of efficiency, little is done to enhance the system as a whole, which is no whit improved.

He accepts the Suffolk team's proposal of detaching appraisal from 'advancement' and 'discipline' and harnessing it to the single purpose of professional development.

> Under such a model teachers are encouraged, in the context of a formally structured system, to identify those aspects of their job in which development is possible and desirable, and to identify those resources needed to make improvements.

Any link to promotion and the recognition of merit is indirect but, as the individual is motivated to improve performance and to develop talents, it is nonetheless real. As the individual improves, so do prospects of advancement, but since advancement of the individual is not the primary goal, the system as a whole improves.

It is undoubtedly true that within the single-tier system of hierarchical appraisal he envisages, promotion is likely to be the overriding purpose. The identification of professional development and training needs and ways of providing for them will take a subordinate position. What both Waton and the Suffolk team fail to realize is any conception of a system which identifies the professional development and training needs independently of any surveillance by management, and then uses this data as a basis for a management appraisal of how those needs can be best provided, e.g. through a formal training programme, the allocation of new assignments, or promotion. In this two-tier process the agenda for hierarchical appraisal is established non-hierarchically.

What is required in both schools and universities are the appointment of people to professional team leadership roles which are detached from management functions. These leaders would have a major responsibility for helping teachers to improve their practices reflectively, and to identify their development needs. They would be responsible for negotiating public accounts of individuals' performances and needs as the basis of the appraisal interview with a member of management.

The ACAS-assisted agreement between the CVCP and AUT emerged in November 1987. Like the ACAS agreement about teacher appraisal in schools, this agreement did not accept the Suffolk Report's proposal for a single-purpose appraisal system confined to improving performance. In the end the AUT appears to have accepted that one of the major purposes of appraisal is to 'identify and develop potential for promotion'. The statement of objectives is in many respects similar to the ACAS framework for schoolteachers. But the university agreement is stronger in emphasising the need for reciprocity between managers and teachers in the appraisal process. Two of the stated objectives oblige managers to identify changes in the organisation or operation of the institution which would enable individuals to improve their performance; and improve the efficiency with which the institution is managed. These are obviously built-in safeguards against any tendencies to project blame away from the management onto teachers through the appraisal process. They appear to constitute what the vice chancellors were prepared to 'trade off' in return for an AUT acceptance of 'identifying potential for promotion' as a major function of appraisal.

The procedural criteria specified in the agreement also emphasise reciprocity between appraiser and appraisee. Although it is proposed that the formal appraisal should operate on an annual or biennial basis it is portrayed as a continuous process which encourages 'staff to reflect on their own performance, and to take steps to improve it', and involves 'an appropriate mixture of self-assessment, informal interviewing and counselling'. The document defines appraisal as a 'joint professional task shared between appraiser and appraisee, with the latter involved at all stages'. From this continuous process of discussion agreed records should be compiled. In cases of disagreement the dissent of the appraisee should be recorded. In cases of severe disagreement the system should provide for a second opinion.

There are obvious continuities between these criteria and both the Suffolk principles and the ACAS framework for schoolteachers. However, in my opinion they provide a much sharper description of the sort of appraisal process intended – one which supports the development of the reflexive capacities of both teachers and appraisers. The procedural criteria clearly delineate the kind of process I specified as the first level of my two-tier model.

The CVCP–AUT document also goes to 'the brink' of the two-tier model itself. In this respect it is a marked improvement on the Suffolk Report and less ambiguous than the ACAS framework for schoolteachers. Like the latter, it suggests that appraisers should be 'experienced and responsible members of staff who have been formally recognised by the institution as such and have been properly trained for, and have sufficient time to devote to their appraisal duties'. But, unlike the schoolteachers' document, it does not leave open the possibility that such a member of staff could always be a manager. The document states that the head of department in a university (or equivalent) 'will have a significant role to play in the appraisal of staff in their department, but this will not exclude the designation of other staff as recognised appraisers'. What this significant role is, when others are operating as recognised appraisers within the continuous, reflective, and dialogical process described, is far from clear. This is a matter for future development within the guidelines provided. But in my opinion it leaves few options for universities to develop towards anything but a two-tier model.

It is far from clear how an experienced peer could effectively realise a further procedural criterion outlined in the document, that is, 'provide for effective follow-up action in relation to staff development needs, weaknesses in organ-isation, provision of resources or other matters identified at the appraisal interview'. This is the only statement which actually refers to a formal interview as integral to the appraisal process.

Reading 'between the lines', a two-tier system appears to be implicit in the way the document establishes the parameters for future development. It is a system which gives the head of department the responsibility for the manage-ment functions of appraisal, executed through the formal interview on the basis of records compiled from an independent first-level process aimed at fostering reflective practice. I would argue that the strong united resistance of university teachers to managerialism has resulted in a better and clearer framework for development than the schoolteachers achieved. They may also have benefited from lessons learned from the earlier negotiations with schoolteachers.

There is one proposal in the university teachers' framework which I find disquieting: 'Appraisal should focus on present and future performance in the job, not on an individual's personal characteristics.' The proposal appears to be derived from the Suffolk Report. In this paper I have tried to indicate how it is ultimately inconsistent with any system of appraisal which genuinely fosters the development of high-quality professional practices. As an initial strategy for overcoming fear and mistrust it has short-term pragmatic value. As a geneal rule it distorts the nature of professional competence and the conditions of its development.

One of the issues that needs to be resolved is that of the kind of criteria to be employed in the appraisal of university teachers. A crude system has already evolved in many universities of assessing staff against quantifiable indicators of research performance. In the light of UGC proposals that resources for research should be distributed according to the profile of the university there is a current pressure from 'management' to assess staff in terms of the quantity of refereed papers they have published and the amount of research money they have attracted.

These crude performance indicators presume quality is evidence by the fact that the publications are refereed, or the fact that the research is sponsored by a prestigious funding agency. We know that neither is a very reliable indicator of high-quality research. In my own field, education journals have proliferated to capitalise on the increased demand for more outlets for publication. Every editor has to fill each volume from the best of the material submitted. But I know from my editorial experience that the best need not be particularly high in quality. Many editors are on the receiving end of numerous papers which have simply been written to maximise an individual's prospects of advancement in academia, and not because he/she has anything very original or creative to contribute to the field. One knows that a rejection slip will activate the dispatch of the same work to another journal. In the field of educational studies at least, we are witnessing an increase in the quantity of publications without any commensurate increase in the quality of educational theorising and research.

Similarly, success in securing research money in the educational field may be more related to the sponsor's perceptions of the chances of securing the desired results and of the researcher's willingness to compromise academic freedom in order to secure the contract, than to the quality of thinking manifested in the research proposal. Will developments in staff appraisal simply generate more valid indicators of quality?

A better indicator of the quality of an academic's research would be the qualities of mind he/she displays, not only in the products of the research but also in the way it is executed. Quality cannot be judged from afar on the basis of numerical data. It can only be judged by those who are in a position to judge – the researcher's supervisor and/or collaborators, and others working in the same field of inquiry. This would entail, within any formal appraisal system, a two-tier model in which recommendations for training, placement, and promotion were based on appraisals generated quite independently from the 'work-face'.

There is the further question of whether research performance should have priority over 'teaching' in making decisions about promotion and advancement. Universities have a reputation for neglecting teaching in favour of research, a state of affairs perpetuated by the crude system of appraisal currently evolving in response to government pressures for greater accountability. The priority given to research stems from the universities' traditional understanding of their primary function to generate public knowledge. But this function was not always insulated from that of disseminating knowledge through teaching. The great university teachers – such as Peter Abelard and Wittgenstein – used teaching as the medium for developing their ideas, and used their research as the basis of their teaching. This integrated view of teaching and research treated ideas as continuously problematic.

Wittgenstein published little in his lifetime. Would the *Tractatus* have been sufficient to secure him a senior lectureship in one of our provincial universities today? Probably not. His posthumous publications are simply edited collections of notes and reflections generated and developed in the context of his teaching. What he transmitted to his students was, not so much a set of inert ideas, as a set of attitudes and dispositions towards the treatment of philosophical problems. It was the qualities of mind manifested in his thinking which he conveyed in his teaching. Because generating and disseminating ideas were a single and unified enterprise the qualities manifested in his thinking were also manifested in his teaching. The great teacher was necessarily a great thinker.

It is often said that 'good minds' do not necessarily make good teachers. Teaching is a matter of communicating ideas. This is true. But this does not imply the reverse; namely, that good teachers do not necessarily have to possess those qualities which are constitutive of the good mind. Many skilful communicators of inert ideas have long been forgotten by their students. Communication skills are only a necessary condition of good teaching. They are not generic to good as opposed to minimally acceptable performances. What differentiates good teaching are the qualities of mind communicated. Hence we return to the inconsistency in the Suffolk Report between its account of teaching at the highest level of competence and its insistence that personal qualities are screened out of performance.

There is a considerable overlap between the personal competencies which are generic to good research and good teaching. We need better descriptions, grounded in systematic investigation, of what these qualities are. We will then have a common criterial framework for appraising university teachers as both teachers and researchers, and a basis for staff development programmes which develop the qualities essential to both. In this way appraisal could enhance both the quality of teaching and of research in universities. But there are grounds for pessimism.

The growth of sponsored projects as opposed to personal research in the context of increased staff–student ratios has created a boundary between 'teachers' and 'researchers'. The University Grants Committee's proposals for differential research funding to universities threatens to remove personal research time from the vast majority of university teachers and to increase their teaching loads further. They will have less opportunity or incentive to engage in research as a basis for their teaching.

On this scenario the emphasis in the appraisal of most university teachers will shift from research to teaching. But one should not be deceived into thinking that this will significantly improve the quality of teaching in universities. Torn adrift from its traditional roots in personal research, university teaching will be transformed from 'art' to 'labour'. The focus of appraisal will be on low-inference, observable performance skills, whose acquisition and maintenance can be hierarchically monitored and controlled. External regulation can be 'glossed' by talk of discussion between appraiser and appraisee, of providing training and opportunities for advancement. But all this is framed by a conception of teaching which separates the task from the person engaged in it. As it stands, the ACAS-assisted framework for university teachers embodies this conception. It could, therefore, degenerate into a single-tier form of managerialism. Such a single-tier appraisal system would be similar to that proposed for schools in the Suffolk Report. It would reflect the growth of bureaucratic structures in educational institutions generally, and the subsequent deprofessionalisation of university teachers.

The two-tier model I have proposed acknowledges the professionals' rights of self-determination but renders them accountable for the way these rights are exercised. It also acknowledges the rights of managers to take decisions which enhance the quality of their organisation's overall performance. The hierarchical university is not necessarily a bureaucratic one. It will try to resist a sharp segregation of teaching and research functions in its organisational restructuring, and establish a two-tier form of appraisal which focuses on the development and deployment of those personal competences which constitute excellence in both teaching and research.

This raises the question of the kinds of qualities managers in universities need to possess. Throughout the field of management research there is a new focus on the manager as a person rather than a functionary. Which personal qualities are generic to good management generally is a question research will be increasingly addressing. Whatever qualities might be generalised across organisational contexts, there will be context-specific qualities the good manager will need. Good managers in universities should possess the demonstrable qualities of good teachers and researchers. Without a developed self-awareness of the personal qualities in which good teaching and research are rooted, managers will unwittingly reproduce organisational and ideological structures which alienate the primary practices of universities from their sources of excellence.

Research and appraisal

The appraisal of teachers represents just one strategy in the structural transformation of power relations in the educational system. In this paper I have tried to show that the outcomes are rarely predictable. The intentions which underpin the original proposals are modified and changed in a series of 'trade-offs' and compromises negotiated in the course of debate. Research is utilised selectively if it justifies the position of one of the parties in the dispute, or can be used by one party to undermine the position of the other. Research which falls outside the parameters of the issues as they are defined in the dispute is simply ignored.

As issues are settled the established consensus will frame future agendas for the utilisation and conduct of research. For example, an agreement to focus on observable performance leads to a search for 'performance indicators'. These are either derived from psychological theories of teaching and learning – for example, Skinner's theory of reinforcement – or from research which discovers the task components of teaching and then analyses each task into the specific skills it involves.

Evaluation research has had little opportunity to affect the terms of debate. Evaluations are usually commissioned by the most powerful policy-maker, and then only to provide him/her with feedback about the extent to which his/her policies are being effectively implemented in the system. The criteria of evaluation are framed by the policy. The policy-maker does not expect the evaluators to question the policy framework, although they may be audacious enough to do so. But there are ways of suppressing data which throw the framework into doubt. One is to formulate the evaluation contract in terms which give the sponsor ownership of the evaluation data and control over their release. Evaluations sponsored by policy-makers are expected to recommend 'fine tunings' rather than fundamental critiques.

As far as I know, no evaluation studies of teacher appraisal have been commissioned in the UK which focus on the policy-making process. With respect to teacher appraisal in schools, the DES commissioned the Cambridge Institute of Education to evaluate national pilot schemes developed within the ACAS framework. It was conceived as an implementation study. The Suffolk team carried out a review of largely American evaluation studies, which again focused on implementation issues.

The reasons for the absence of evaluation research on the policy-making process are not hard to find. The policy-making agency usually commands the financial resources necessary to establish such research. The other agencies involved in negotiating the policy are normally less able to sponsor research. The commissioning of a study of policy-making by the policy-makers would imply a considerable openness to critique, and a willingness significantly to shift their understanding of problems and solutions. Such shifts of understanding may undermine the reasons and arguments they have employed to justify their policy proposals, and unmask the power-coercive intentions they conceal. An evaluation study would also provide the parties with whom the policy-makers are in dispute with fresh understandings of problems and solutions. In short, an evaluation of policy-making will undermine the capacity of the policy-makers to control the agenda and boundaries of the discourse.

Evaluation studies of the negotiation of appraisal policies at national and local levels could have played a critical role in helping the parties in dispute to clarify the issues at stake between them, and to reflect about their stances and positions in the light of data which are continuously collected and fed into the debate. Such studies might have prevented premature closure on issues, which achieves consensus through compromise and 'trade-offs' rather than authentic resolution. In the context of such evaluation studies the appraisal debates and negotiations could have exposed the relevance of research areas which were very much neglected.

It is interesting that evaluation researchers have so much defined the study of change in terms of implementation that they have tended to neglect the political process which shapes the change policies. Power over access to sites is one explanation for this. Independent funding agencies are not often tapped for evaluation research. They have no power to secure entry to the system. Policy-makers want implementation studies and have the power to facilitate access to the system they govern. They do not want policy-making studies and would block access. So the focus of evaluation studies is essentially defined by the power relations which exist between policy-makers and researchers.

In my view the sponsors for evaluation studies of educational change should be those who represent the targets of change – the staff associations and unions. They have the problems of sorting out what to let go of, what to hang on to, and what to take on board when debating the negotiating change. These are precisely the problem areas which an evaluation study could illuminate.

It occurs to me that one of the things the unions have almost let go of in the negotiations over a framework for appraisal is the view that the source of a teacher's professionalism lies in the personal qualities he/she manifests in his/her practice. It is often argued that agreement on such qualities is impossible. People will pick out different attributes on the basis of their own personal prejudices. And so one searches for more objective 'criteria' derived from either theory or task analysis. The problem with both these approaches is one of the validity of the criteria rather than their reliability as measures of performance. What is attractive about both is their instrumental value in facilitating external regulation over performance. If one can derive specific performance rules from behaviourist, or even humanist psychology, then one prescribes the details of performance externally and monitors the extent to which it conforms to these prescriptions. Similarly if a job can be broken down into performance tasks, and the specific skills involved in each specified, then one can control externally the performance through assessing the range of skills performed, and identifying deficiencies to be remedied through structured training programmes.

However, as Spencer (1979) points out, detailed lists of job tasks are of little use 'without supplementary information about the competencies a superior job incumbent uses' to accomplish the tasks successfully. And, with respect to theory-based approaches, he points out that they 'lack supporting empirical data to show that the knowledge or skill characteristics they posit are in fact related to on-the-job performance'. Spencer argues that there are also problems with respect to the validity of intuitive and commonsense theories about the personal qualities manifested in good practice. He argues that they tend to reflect idealised images of professional identities derived from the folklore of the occupational culture.

So where do we go in search of valid criteria of performance appraisal? McBer & Company in the USA have pioneered empirical research aimed at discovering the personal competencies which are generic to 'good' as opposed to 'marginally acceptable' performances in a variety of professions. The method of sampling is to select a group of practitioners which a range of people, in a close working relationship with them, agree to be superior performers. This group is then compared with a group of practitioners who receive an agreed average rating from peers, clients and immediate supervisors. The main research method is the behavioural event interview. Each practitioner is asked to describe in narrative detail how he/she handled one or more difficult and complex work situations. The interviewer does not pre-structure his/her questions, but probes the interviewee's handling of the incident responsively, in a search for explanations of various aspects of the performance. The interview data is then analysed, with a view to extracting those competencies which characterise the superior performers and differentiate them from average ones. The analysis can be validated by cross-checking against a further sample, and follow-up observations of the performance of members from each sub-sample.

To my knowledge no such study has been carried out on either teachers in schools or teachers in further and higher education. Most of this kind of research has been carried out in the USA by McBer & Company, who have now identified competencies which appear to be generic to good practice in a variety of occupations (see Klemp 1977).

I have recently completed a study which identifies four fundamental competencies which are generic to good patrol police officers: competence in 'assessing the total situation', 'self-monitoring one's own conduct', 'empathising accurately with the concerns of others', and 'exercising power and authority in a manner consistent with organisational goals and the professional ethics'. Moreover, the analysis identified a number of criteria for assessing the extent to which these competencies are evidenced in behaviour (see Elliott and Shadforth 1987). The analysis was consistent with the cross-professional findings reported by Klemp, but a number of more job-specific qualities were identified as generic to good policing. The latter did, however, presuppose one or more of the four more generalisable competencies. These appeared to constitute 'the deep structure' of professional competence, upon which the other job-specific qualities depended. Research into generic competencies offers to provide a basis for making objective and valid assessments of the quality of professional practices. Such assessment avoids the tendency to reduce judgements of competence to measures of performance, and thereby protects professionals from forms of assessment which foster external regulation and control. It also avoids the atomisation of competence into checklists of dozens, or even hundreds, of specific skills. Generic competencies consist of broad clusters of abilities which are conceptually linked. Research suggests that they are relatively few in number compared with the results of atomistic task analyses.

An assessment system based on generic competencies would also avoid the fears which accompany intuitive assessment of personal qualities. While such a system acknowledges the significance of personal qualities for competent practice, it minimises the element of personal prejudice which often operates in impressionistic and intuitive selections of criteria.

The major problems with this form of assessment are methodological, and connected with gathering a sufficient qualitative data base on which to make fair and valid inferences. Since it is based on high-inference data, procedures for involving more than one person in the appraisal are necessary. Inferences made by one assessor will need to be cross-checked and challenged by others, including the appraisee. Moreover, the data base can only be generated by those who work closely with the appraisee over prolonged periods – work-face supervisors, peers and clients. This form of competency-based assessment has to originate from those involved at the work-face. As a basis for appraisal by management it has to operate as a two-tier system.

'Generic competency' research on teachers, at all levels of the educational system, could mark a significant breakthrough in the development of a valid professional model of staff appraisal. Research projects can be carried out on the basis of very small samples fairly inexpensively. Two of us (a police officer and I) interviewed 22 constables operating in a variety of policing environments, and then cross-validated our analysis against the cross-professional findings reported by Klemp, observational studies of policy competence reported by Fielding, and the provisional results of research in progress on a much larger sample. I concluded that one could make valid generalisations using the behavioural event interview method with a small sample. The experimental piloting of appraisal schemes in universities, which will now follow the agreement between the CVCP and AUT, provides an opportunity for research into generic competencies as a basis on which to develop a system for profiling professional development.

References

Bridges, D., Elliott, J. and Klass, C. (1985) 'Performance appraisal as naturalistic inquiry', *Cambridge Journal of Education*, 16 (3).

Committee of Vice-Chancellors and Principals/Association of University Teachers (1987) *Career Development and Staff Appraisal Procedures for Academic Related Staff*, London, CVCP.

Department of Education and Science (1983) *Teaching Quality*, Cmnd 8836, London, HMSO.

Dow, W. E. (1984) 'Developing competence' in E. C. Short (ed.), *Competence*, University Press of America.

Elliott, J. (1985) 'Evaluating teaching quality' in Review Symposium on the White Paper *Teaching Quality*, *British Journal of Sociology of Education*, 6(1).

Elliott, J. (1987) 'Knowledge, power and appraisal', paper delivered to the Annual Conference of the British Educational Research Association. Centre for Applied Research in Education, School of Education, University of East Anglia, mimeo.

Elliott, J. and Shadforth, R. (1987) 'Qualities of the good patrol constable: A report for discussion', Centre for Applied Research in Education, School of Education, University of East Anglia, mimeo.

Fielding, N. (1984) 'Police socialization and police competence', *British Journal of Sociology*, December.

Grace, G. (1985) 'Judging teachers: the social and political contexts of teacher evaluation', *British Journal of Sociology of Education*, 6(1).

Harré, R. (1983) *Personal Being: A Theory for Individual Psychology*, Oxford, Basil Blackwell.

Harré, R., Clarke, D. and de Carlo, N. (1985) *Motives and Mechanisms: An Introduction to the Psychology of Action*, London and New York, Methuen.

Klemp, G. O. (1977) *Three Factors of Success in the World of Work: Implications for Curriculum in Higher Education*, Boston, MA, McBer & Co.

Spencer, L. M. (1979) *Soft Skill Competencies*, Oxford, Oxford University Press.

Suffolk Education Department (1985) *Those Having Torches . . . Teacher Appraisal: A Study* (funded by the Department of Education and Science). Ipswich, Suffolk Education Committee.

Waton, A. (1987) 'The politics of appraisal', *AUT Bulletin*, September.

White, J. (1975) 'The end of the compulsory curriculum' in *The Curriculum; the Doris Lee Lectures*, London, University of London Institute of Education.

Wise, A. E., Darling-Hammond, L., McLaughlin, M. and Bernstein, H. (1984) *Teacher Evaluation – a Study of Effective Practice*, The Rand Corporation for the National Institute of Education, June.

17

Rethinking the Aims of Higher Education

Peter W. G. Wright

British higher education is at present going through a period of transformation which involves not simply its restructuring but also a re-evaluation of its aims and social worth. There are several reasons for believing that this transform-ation will be more fundamental and have more far-reaching repercussions than the changes which occurred in the period of rapid expansion in the 1960s and early 1970s.

To begin with, the ideological standing of the academy is now being challenged; neither its basic assumptions nor its definitions of educational needs and how they should be met are any longer unquestioningly accepted by the wider society (Barnett 1985). Thirty years ago, in contrast, there was general consensus that the aims and nature of higher education were matters best decided by higher education itself – which at that time meant, in practice, the universities (Carswell 1985). Now, however, the view is increasingly gaining ground that higher education needs to be made far more accountable to the public – along with education as a whole and, indeed, many other branches of the public service and the professions – and ought to serve ends laid down by groups external to it, especially the state.

Relatedly, there is a mounting suspicion (on which Mrs Thatcher's govern-ment has skilfully drawn) that professional groups, including academics – however high-sounding and disinterested their public pronouncements may be – if left to themselves, allow their own convenience and self-interest to predominate in the management of their affairs (Haskell 1984).

Manifestations of this attitude can be traced in many of the forces currently impinging on higher education: in the pursuit of 'value for money'; in pressures towards a greater degree of managerialism; in the encouragement of a closer relationship between industry and higher education; but also, if less obviously, in changes in curriculum and pedagogy such as the General Certificate of Secondary Education (GCSE), the Technical Vocational Education Initiative (TVEI), Credit Accumulation and Transfer and the Manpower Services Commission's Enterprise in Higher Education initiative. All of these begin to define the educational experience and its assessment in relation to ends which come from outside the educational system – preparation for employment, personal competence, career advancement, and so on; all are at some degree of variance with the dominant assumptions of the British academic tradition (Wright, forthcoming).

Second, changes in the clientele of higher education also seem likely to reinforce these pressures since they bring into the system a greater proportion of students not already socialised into the culture of the academic world.

In the Robbins period the students recruited to fuel the expansion came from backgrounds not greatly dissimilar to those of the students of the previous generation: like their predecessors they were eighteen-year-olds who had been through a specialised academic schooling in which traditional forms of teaching were the rule; if they differed, it was only in that they came from somewhat less privileged backgrounds than previously (Halsey 1977), and were, perhaps, more inclined to question explicitly some aspects of the university ethos. None the less, even when the students of the 1960s were at odds with the system of higher education in which they found themselves they nevertheless shared a substantial number of its ground-rules and possessed academic qualities which it valued: they had, after all, come into it through, and succeeded in, a school system finely tuned, not simply to the formal requirements of the academic world, but also its tacit assumptions.

Today, things are different. Not only does demographic change force higher education to recruit a larger proportion of older students – many of whom are unlikely to have had a conventional academic schooling and may well find the traditional ethos uncongenial – changes occurring in the schools and colleges will mean increasingly that even eighteen-year-old entrants will come into higher education with a less-specialised subject knowledge and will bring with them experience of new approaches to learning which have so far been little practised in degree teaching.

These developments, I believe, create a growing tension between, on the one hand, the social expectations placed on higher education and, on the other, the values and interpretative frameworks which those working within the sector use to frame and make sense of their own experiences.

It seems inescapable that the factors described above will lead to major changes within higher education itself, some of which can already be discerned in a more developed form in other countries. The first of these is a shift away from the high level of subject specialisation which is so characteristic of English degree courses. The dominance of specialisation is being undermined from many directions but, especially, by the movement in schooling from forms of teaching and assessment based on the accumulation of specialist subject knowledge towards others based on the goal of independent learning and the acquisition of general competencies.

The second is the tendency to stress preparation for employment. In times of rapid economic and technological change highly specialised courses – even if explicitly vocational – come to appear as a poor basis for subsequent flexibility and possible career change. What is more, disciplinary specialisation, by its very nature, stresses the esoteric face of knowledge: by emphasising disciplinary boundaries, specificity of subject matter, internal intellectual coherence and the specialist culture of the disciplinary group, it distances itself from the practical problems of everyday life which are typically multifarious, touch many different disciplines, and require interpretation from several different standpoints. Thus, a higher education organised around tight disciplinary concentration is inherently unsuited to wider access because this demands the lessening of the barriers between education and the outside world. Extreme specialisation is best suited to forms of higher education which are essentially exclusionary. In these, quality tends to be regarded as proportional to the degree to which the mass of the population are absent from the system: places where, as the opponents of British higher education used to put it: 'More means worse.' Thus, it is natural that such systems should tend to lay great weight on the value of the discipline as the template for shaping experience in higher education. It is surely no coincidence that for most of the last hundred years English higher education has both been one of the most exclusionary systems in the developed world as well one of the most highly specialised (Jarausch 1983).

The third change which is likely to take place is that an increasing proportion of teaching in higher education will be structured according to externally-given ends, such as the needs of employment or the career demands of individual students, rather than in terms of how the academic community has traditionally interpreted internal principles such as intellectual progression, disciplinary coherence and so on.

Fourth, changes in the context and clientele of higher education will encourage a tendency to define both the elements of courses, and courses themselves, in relation to explicit and precise learning objectives – even competencies. At present, most courses tend to be presented in terms of disciplinary content, supplemented by passing reference to certain general educational values. Seldom is there much attempt to link the two. It appears to be taken for granted that there is little need to specify exactly how a degree course in a discipline such as physics or history meets general educational objectives. Possibly it is assumed that the connection is either self-evident or purely contingent. At all events, there is relatively little pressure for explicitness, apparently because the activity of higher education still draws – or purports to draw – on a set of shared presuppositions about its purpose. Thus, the airy references to intellectual curiosity, independence, imagination, or whatever, which are frequently to be found in statements about the aims of higher education need to be read as celebratory and rhetorical conceits: they are so vague as to be incapable of measurement; for their plausibility they rely on no more than a general and unquestioned consensus over aims. But this apparent plausibility is likely to dissolve as institutions come to broaden their audience and find it necessary to respond to a wider range of external demands.

This is well illustrated by the development of credit accumulation and transfer schemes. The accreditation of prior learning (whether certificated or not) only becomes practicable if there is something fairly precise and concrete against which to measure it. It therefore exerts pressure on all elements in courses embraced by such schemes to define themselves in terms of specific learning objectives in order to facilitate decisions about their equivalence, or otherwise, to other elements or to learning achieved through practical experience.

If developments such as these are, indeed, to take place within at least some parts of British higher education there are obvious implications for the culture of academic life. Clearly, there will be considerable tension and disorientation unless values develop within the academic community which are in sympathy with such changes. Basil Bernstein's (1971; 1975) concepts of 'classification' and 'framing' may be a fruitful way of exploring the nature of these changes.

Bernstein suggested that any educational system can be considered as embodying a particular code of educational knowledge – a set of implicit, underlying, structural principles that are manifested through three 'message systems', as he terms them: curriculum, pedagogy and evaluation. Each, he contends, plays a part in transmitting the general principles on which the educational system is based; which, in turn, is shaped by its social circumstances – in particular, by relationships of power and mechanisms of social control. One of the ways in which codes differ, he suggests, is in the relative strength of 'classification' or 'framing'.

Classification, refers to 'the degree of boundary maintenance between [the] contents' (Bernstein 1971, p. 49) of a curriculum. That is to say, a curriculum is highly classified to the extent to which it is divided into units, such as disciplines, which are strongly insulated from one another. Although it is quite possible for a broad curriculum to be of high or low classification (for example, a large collection of discrete subjects, or an integrated range of subjects between which relationships are deliberately encouraged), a highly specialised curriculum is also, typically, highly classified because specialisation is almost invariably defined in terms of bounded disciplines.

Framing, for Bernstein, refers to the 'degree of control teacher and pupil possess over the selection, organization and pacing of the knowledge transmitted and received in the pedagogical relationship' (Bernstein 1971, p. 50). Teaching is thus highly framed if its content is strictly circumscribed – if there is, that is to say, a sharp boundary between what may and may not be taught.

When these categories are applied to the educational systems of various countries a variety of combinations of classification and framing become apparent. Bernstein, for example, suggests that in continental Europe secondary education involves strong classification and exceptionally strong framing: that is, he believes that both curricula and pedagogy are tightly and explicitly defined and permit neither innovative flexibility in teaching nor integration between different subjects.

Secondary education in the United Kingdom he regards as characterised by exceptionally strong classification but having relatively weaker framing than on the Continent. There is, he argues, a high degree of insulation between subjects which is associated with high specialisation but coupled with more freedom for the teacher and pupil to negotiate the nature of the pedagogical relationship, particularly in the teaching of those pupils considered to be the less able. Interestingly, he notes that the universities exert a high degree of control over secondary schooling, especially through the examination system (Bernstein 1971, p. 50).

By contrast, he sees the system in the United States as one where both classification and framing are weak with the result that students are able to exert a great deal of choice in determining the content of their programmes of study, and there is relatively little insulation between educational knowledge and everyday community knowledge (Bernstein 1971, p. 53).

For Bernstein there is a close relationship between the form of an educational knowledge code, on the one hand, and, on the other, the structures of power and authority with which it is associated, and the values held by those who work within the system.

The changes in British higher education towards something closer to the American model, which I have argued are now taking place (more general programmes of study structured to an increasing extent around needs external to the academic world) would amount, in Bernstein's terms, to a substantial reduction in both classification and framing. This, in turn, according to his analysis, would have substantial consequences for the organisation, authority structure, and values of higher education. It would, for instance, tend to erode the power of the discipline to act as the central principle of organisation and major source of identity for both students and staff. For students, this might not be particularly important as other sources of identity such as course- or cohort-membership might be easily acceptable alternatives. For academics, however, the problems would be much greater; typically staff derive their own professional identities from the discipline in which they have qualified, probably occupy posts defined in disciplinary terms, and generally see their own research and career advancement in a disciplinary framework.

Indeed, in higher education the very concepts of quality and standards are hard to disentangle from disciplinary assumptions; disciplines tend to form the grid through which all such questions are viewed. Thus, for example, the 1985–6 University Grants Committee (UGC) research evaluation was organised in terms of discipline, as is the validation system of the Council for National Academic Awards (CNAA). The issues which, in the future, seem likely to become increasingly important in higher education – responding to the needs of students, developing new strategies for learning, fostering personal transferable skills, preparing for employment – are not simply overlooked in the present discipline-based structure, although that does often happen; more important than that, they tend to become by being fragmented into a set of secondary issues ancillary to the main focus of attention – the transmission of the discipline. Their marginality means that they are the main business of almost no one, other, perhaps, than a few careers advisers and specialists in educational development. Teaching staff who take such questions seriously tend to be regarded by their peers as neglecting the 'main business' of academic life – their discipline.

However, Bernstein also points out that, although the discipline is constrictive from some points of view, it also has great merit as an organising principle. In particular, it provides a secure, easily understood identity and a ready-made cognitive framework strong enough to maintain the structure of the educational experience even when the standard of teaching is indifferent.

The development of courses based on other principles is a hazardous enterprise precisely because these other principles are less familiar and generally more open to interpretation than is the notion of discipline. Not surprisingly, Bernstein reminds us that an integrated curriculum depends for its success on its teaching staff having both a high level of understanding of its intended aims and a high degree of consensus about how to achieve them. On such courses it is not possible to impose structure in an authoritarian manner, as it may be in discipline-based teaching, because work with low classification and little framing is, by definition, dependent upon such factors as individual initiative and a flow of critical discussion about the process of teaching: things which cannot be enforced externally.

This absence of conventional given structure in courses characterised by low classification also, in Bernstein's view, changes the nature of the curriculum in several significant ways: in particular, it focuses attention on the deep, methodological structure of the subject taught; it emphasises modes of learning over states of knowledge; and it calls into question conventional notions about level of difficulty and the criteria for progression in a particular field.

If higher education is to change in the ways in which I have argued it is being pressed to do, there is an urgent need for it to develop new forms of organisation to prepare for the growth of integrated courses which aim to address externally-given ends. To do so, it must, I believe, adopt new values in order to avoid fundamental conflict between the forms of activity expected of it and its own internal culture. In particular, organising principles and forms of identity have to be developed other than those deriving from the concept of discipline.

These cannot simply be any one, or even an aggregate of all, the expectations held by those who place demands on higher education, whether government, industry, potential students, or whatever. To adopt those externally-given values, even if possible, would be calamitous since it would destroy the very characteristics which make higher education distinctive and desirable. Any attempt to model an academic institution on a firm, or a local community, or a government department, is inherently self-defeating since it removes the difference, the necessary tension, with the outside world. Higher education is attractive to that world, when it is, precisely because it differs from it and because its special characteristics enable it to do things which those other groups either cannot do or cannot do as well, such as cultivating new knowledge, fostering a dispassionate critical awareness and maintaining ethical independence.

What British higher education now appears to me to need are publicly proclaimed principles which both reflect its own general purpose and are accessible to the outside world without simply being reducible to the preoccupations of the various groups in that world. The concept of discipline, though valuable and important, is not sufficient for this purpose and seems likely to become progressively less relevant in the future when higher education will be working with a larger, more heterogeneous clientele than at present. In other words, the academy needs to have distinctive values which are capable of mediating the relationship and research – which has generally been formed within disciplines or in even smaller specialities.

These principles, it seems to me, must be general educational values; they must be couched in terms of intellectual qualities and practical capabilities of a far more general nature than the arcane skills traditionally prized within particular disciplinary cultures. Perhaps the present emphasis in policy statements on personal transferable skills suggests one way in which these might take shape (Bradshaw 1985).

Values, however, neither come into being, nor persist, in a social vacuum; they take root and are propagated in particular institutional practices. If new values are to develop and flourish in higher education new organisational forms and associated practices will be needed to make this possible. It will be necessary, for instance, to give more emphasis to patterns of organisation based on principles other than the academic discipline and to devise promotion criteria and career paths related to the furtherance of the new educational values rather than, simply, on advancement within a disciplinary field.

References

Barnett, R. A. (1985) 'Higher education: legitimation crisis', *Studies in Higher Education*, 10(3), 241–55.

Bernstein, B. (1971) 'On the classification and framing of educational knowledge' in M. F. D. Young (ed.), *Knowledge and Control: New Directions in the Sociology of Education*, London, Collier-Macmillan.

Bernstein, B. (1975) *Class and Pedagogies: Visible and Invisible*, Paris, OECD.

Bradshaw, D. (1985) 'Transferable intellectual and personal skills', *Oxford Review of Education*, 11(2), 201–216.

Carswell, J. (1985) *Government and the Universities in Britain: Programme and Performance, 1960–80*, Cambridge, Cambridge University Press.

Halsey, A. H. (1977) 'Towards meritocracy? The case of Britain' in J. Karabel and A. H. Halsey (eds), *Power and Knowledge in Education*, New York, Oxford University Press.

Haskell, T. L. (ed.) (1984) *The Authority of Experts*, Bloomington, Indiana University Press.

Jarausch, K. H. (ed.) (1983) *The Transformation of Higher Learning: The Expansion and Diversification of Higher Learning and Professionalization in England, Germany, Russia and the USA 1860–1930*, Chicago, University of Chicago Press.

Wright, P. W. G. (forthcoming) 'Access or exclusion? Some comments on the history and future prospects of continuing education in England', *Studies in Higher Education*.

The Society for Research Into Higher Education

The Society exists both to encourage and to co-ordinate research and development into all aspects of higher education, including academic, organisational and policy issues; and also to provide a forum for debate, verbal and printed. Through its activities, it draws attention to the significance of research into, and development in, higher education and to the needs of scholars in this field. (It is not concerned with research generally, except, for instance, as a subject of study or in its relation to teaching.)

The Society's income is derived from its subscriptions, book sales, conferences and specific grants. It is wholly independent. Its corporate members are universities, polytechnics, institutes of higher education, research institutions and professional and governmental bodies. Its individual members include teachers and researchers, administrators and students. Members are found in all parts of the world and the Society regards its international work as among its most important activities.

The Society discusses and comments on policy, organises conferences and encourages research. Under the imprint SRHE & OPEN UNIVERSITY PRESS it is a specialist publisher of research, having some 40 titles in print. It also publishes *Studies in Higher Education* (three times a year), which is mainly concerned with academic issues, *Higher Education Quarterly* (formerly *Universities Quarterly*) which will be mainly concerned with policy issues, *Research into Higher Education Abstracts* (three times a year), and a *Bulletin* (six times a year).

The Society's committees, study groups and branches are run by members (with help from a small staff at Guildford), and aim to provide a form for discussion. The groups at present include a Teacher Education Study Group, a Staff Development Group, a Women in Higher Education Group and a Continuing Education Group which may have had their own organisation, subscriptions or publications; (e.g. the *Staff Development Newsletter*). The Governing Council, elected by members, comments on current issues; and discusses policies with leading figures, notably at its evening Forums. The Society organises seminars on current research for officials of DES and other ministries, an Anglo-American series on standards, and is in touch with bodies in the UK such as the NAB, CVCP, UGC, CNAA and the British Council, and with sister-bodies overseas. Its current research projects include one on the relationship between entry qualifications and degree results, directed by Prof. W. D. Furneaux (Brunel) and one on questions of quality directed by Prof. G. C. Moodie (York). A project on the evaluation of the research standing of university departments is in preparation. The Society's conferences are often held jointly. Annual Conferences have considered 'Professional Education' (1984), 'Continuing Education' (1985, with Goldsmiths' College) 'Standards and Criteria in Higher Education' (1986, with Bulmershe CHE), 'Restructuring' (1987, with the City of Birmingham Polytechnic) and 'Academic Freedom' (1988, the University of Surrey). Other conferences have considered the DES 'Green Paper' (1985, with the

Times Higher Education Supplement), and 'The First-Year Experience' (1986, with the University of South Carolina and Newcastle Polytechnic). For some of the Society's conferences, special studies are commissioned in advance, as 'Precedings'.

Members receive free of charge the Society's *Abstracts*, annual conference Proceedings (or 'Precedings'), *Bulletin and International Newsletter* and may buy SRHE & OPEN UNIVERSITY PRESS books at booksellers' discount. Corporate members also receive the Society's journal *Studies in Higher Education* free (individuals at a heavy discount). They may also obtain *Evaluation Newsletter* and certain other journals at a discount, including the NFER *Register of Educational Research*. There is a substantial discount to members, and to staff of corporate members, on annual and some other conference fees.